In His Exciting Service

ART MITCHELL

To Bob & Jean

Art

You have had a big part in this story

Ps 40:5

IN HIS EXCITING SERVICE. Copyright © 2016 by Art Mitchell. All rights reserved. The author asserts the moral right under the Copyright, Designs and Patent Act 1988 to be identified as the author of this work. No part of this material may be reproduced or transmitted in any form or stored in a retrieval system without the prior written permission of the author, except by a reviewer who may quote brief passages in a review to be printed by a newspaper, magazine or journal.

I have tried to recreate events, locales and conversations from my memories of them. In order to maintain their anonymity in some instances I have changed the names of individuals and places, I may have changed some identifying characteristics and details such as physical properties, occupations and places of residence.

Cover Design by Amy Virgin

Photography by Art Mitchell

First Edition: November 2016

ISBN: 1537720694
ISBN-13: 978-1537720692

APPRECIATION

Without the encouragement from my wife, Willie, who even though she knows me better than anyone, still calls me her hero, this book would likely not even have started. My "baby" daughter Amy was the main one to keep pushing me. Having written and published her own books, she guided me through the process for many long hours, at times assisted by Alain, her very helpful husband. Hope, my firstborn, was responsible for including and removing punctuation so that it became much more readable. All three of them spent many hours going over this text. Thank you, ladies.

There are many heroes and role models in my past, most of whom you will meet in these pages. My thanks to each one, for the courage and integrity you demonstrated so faithfully. Above all I thank God for calling and using me ***in His exciting service.***

TABLE OF CONTENTS

APPRECIATION ....
FORWARD..1
THE RECORDING OF A LIFE 2
WHY WRITE THIS STORY? 3
HERE WE GO ……..4
EARLY CHILDHOOD 7
ROUGE HILL 16
HAGERSVILLE 21
BACK TO TORONTO 27
ROUGE HILL AGAIN 29
CHERRYWOOD 34
FAIRPORT BEACH 39
AJAX HIGH 49
EVERYTHING CHANGED 54
ROYAL CANADIAN NAVY 56
THE LADIES 67
FROM RCN TO NBTC 71
NORTHWEST BAPTIST THEOLOGICAL COLLEGE 74
SUMMER JOBS 81
WILLIE 90
IN HIS EXCITING SERVICE 102
SWITZERLAND 107
AFRICA 112
PHOTOS..121
FILL'ER UP 149
WHAT NEXT? 155
CRASH COURSE IN AVIATION 158
IT'S A BOY! 165
MISSION AVIATION FELLOWSHIP 169

THE SHANTYMEN AND JOE OTTOM 173
TRINITY WESTERN 178
BACK TO WHERE? WITH WHOM? 181
BACK 'HOME' 185
BUKAVU 189
PRIDE COMETH BEFORE A FALL 220
TANZANIA 231
GOODBYE AFRICA 236
ESPERANZA 239
BACK TO MAF 247
FLYPASS LTD. 250
FLYPASS' CONNECTION WITH THE MOON 255
FLYPASS GROWS..258
HALF-TON 100 MPH AIRBORN PICKUP 263
VENEZUELA ADVENTURES 273
BRESLAU COUNTRY MANOR 280
BACK TO MAF (AGAIN) 282
MAPLE HILL BAPTIST CHURCH 288
WRAPPING UP 293
A SPECIAL REWARD FOR THOSE WHO HAVE READ THIS WHOLE BOOK 296
ATTACK OF THE KILLER BEES 296
TALES FROM THE BELLY OF LAZARUS 305
APPENDIX 326
ABOUT THE AUTHOR 328

ART MITCHELL

FORWARD

By Michael Dawson

"What a ride!" While I was scouring through my memories of my childhood experiences for writing down my adventures with the Yanomamö, I had thought I had lived a pretty exciting, dangerous, daunting life. After reading Art's book, I feel like I led a more sedate life than I had imagined. I have known Art since 1998 where I met him at the EAA Airventure in Oshkosh, Wisconsin where he was showing his new CH801. I had gone to Oshkosh with only a vague idea of what we needed as a STOL airplane to help in our ministry of planting churches among the Yanomamö. I stood at the back of a crowd of men listening to Art explain the different features of this new plane, and it was everything *plus* what we needed. I was hooked! Since that time, Art has been a mentor and friend.

Reading this book, I am in awe of all Art and Willie went through, the depths and the heights in their service to HIM. So many people quit and never have the blessing of learning the lessons God was teaching. But a lesson Art mentions learning early in life stands out and it carried him through the tough, lonely, discouraging times. This lesson can be summed up in one sentence from his book and describes Art's attitude, personality and determination. "…It was the feeling of 'I can't possibly make another step, but I can't possibly quit'. And somehow, you take another step…and then another."

Yes, reading his book, I can see why he would always end his prayer letters with "In His Exciting Service, Art & Willie Mitchell."

THE RECORDING OF A LIFE

How much of what we 'remember' do we really remember? Some of my earliest memories are clouded with stories that I heard about my childhood, told to me by my parents and others. I am told that my first word was "happy". Apparently, it meant "hungry". I was also told that I consumed several ounces of "hospitalized brandy" from a bottle, left open by my father, and I slept for most of three days. I certainly don't remember that. Of course, if I had done that as an adult, I may have had a good reason to not remember.

As time passes, memories can take on details that may not be true. Other details that are real get lost. Can anyone tell exactly what happened even moments ago? I am aware that, as I write, there may or may not be details added, subtracted or altered. More than that, the things that happened are frequently interpreted differently. Perception is always so limited. God alone knows all the details of any event.

As I have heard others describe, from their perspective, a story from my own life, it seems quite strange and even unfamiliar at times. "Remember the time we..." Well, I may remember something about it, but often what they remember is quite different from what I remember. Certainly, the tendency is for me to remember it in a way that makes me more of the 'good guy' than the 'bad guy'.

After writing all that, I want to say, it is my desire to record the events of my life as truthfully as I can. If the reader knows details that contradict what I share, please inform me – graciously.

WHY WRITE THIS STORY?

I suppose one reason for writing this is that I can hardly believe it myself. As I have shared parts of my life story, which is really the story of what God has done and permitted in my life, it all seems quite unreal. As a child and as I was growing up I was a proficient liar. I was good at it. I lied to make people believe that I was more and could do more than was true. It's funny now, as I look back over these 70+ years, reality has turned out to be a much more fantastic tale than anything that I could have made up back then. So it is helpful for me to recount all that God has permitted me to experience.

I have to be very careful when listening to someone share events that they have experienced. My tendency is to come up with some story from my own past that matches what they have done, where they have been, or what they know. Often, and recently more frequently, people have said, "You should write a book." I don't know if this will become a book but there has been enough encouragement for me to begin to take it seriously.

But probably the main reasons for writing this story are Isaac, Keirsten, Aaron and Vesper, my precious grandchildren. God has taken me through much, although I know He has more to take me through. He has taught me much, although I know so little. My story is His-story. It is the story of His faithfulness, love, mercy, grace, enabling, provision and long-suffering. It is a heritage that I want to leave for those with whom God has richly blessed me.

CHAPTER 1

HERE WE GO

July 2, 1942. I don't remember a thing about it but according to the records filed somewhere, I was born to Charlie and Edna Mitchell. At that time, they (we) lived at the corner of Pape Avenue and Queen Street in Toronto, Ontario, Canada. Shortly after I appeared we moved to 6 Blong Avenue just two blocks north. I must have made a pretty good impression on my parents because they decided to have another baby, and fifteen months later my brother Tom was born. Of course I have no memory of that, but I do remember that about three years later Florance was born. No, I did not misspell my own sister's name. My grandmother, my aunt, my sister and my daughter all spell their name with an 'a'. Everyone else is wrong!

My arrival was right in the middle of World War II, and that's how I got my name. Well, sort of. Let's do a quick rundown of my dad's family. His siblings in order were Myrtle, Florance (with an 'a'), Phyllis, Charlie (actually Thomas Charles), George, John (Jack), Arthur and Katharine. Jack and Art fought in France and Germany. George was also in the military but I don't know any details. I am told that when it was learned that Mom was expecting me, letters from Art continually inquired about "little Art". He was killed in action on August 11, 1944, over two years after I was born. I don't know if he ever saw me but somehow I got his name. There is no name I would rather have.

I am the oldest son of the oldest son of the oldest son…. I don't really know how far back that goes, but I suspect that there is a castle in Scotland that I could claim as mine if I searched hard enough. I hear that there was an argument from my aunts that I should be called Thomas Charles after my dad. My brother got to carry the name along and pass it on to his son, who has passed it on to his son. Isn't this exciting? Well, I could have written that Thomas begat Thomas, who begat Thomas, who begat John who begat Thomas, who begat Art... That's the way it was written in the world's best-selling Book you know!

    I don't remember anything at all about my paternal grandfather. I am told that he was a plumber and steam fitter. I do remember my grandmother, but I never heard her voice. In my earliest recollection of her, I picture her in a bed upstairs in the home of my Aunt Phyllis. She had had a stroke and could only hoarsely whisper. At times, if people had the time to help her, she could shuffle along behind a chair, very slowly. I suppose today she would have had a walker, but they didn't exist then. We had her at our house sometimes, and she seemed to enjoy that. There was the time that my sister was showing Granny how she could walk backwards and ended up falling into a crock of chokecherry wine that my parents had made. That got Granny Mitchell laughing, the only time I can remember her laughing.

    On my mother's side, we know very little. She was born Doris Audrey McGuire, on September 7, 1924, in Kingston, Ontario. We don't know if the name "McGuire" was her father's or mother's name, but it seems that it was not both. Her mother, and therefore my maternal grandmother, was apparently a young woman who "got in the family way out of wedlock" as they used to say. From what we are told, Mom was adopted at birth, and her name was changed to Edna May Homeniuk. And that was just the beginning of a list of family names that she acquired. It seems that Alex Homeniuk died, and her adopted mother, Mary, married Jack Thompson. He died, and was replaced by Peter Colisneck. Then Mom became a Mitchell when she married my dad. Dad died, and Mom lived with a Peter Kolinski. He died, and she reverted back to Mitchell. Do you have all of that straight? There will be a test at the end of the chapter. As a result of all of this, we have very little history to trace on my mother's side. And please don't ask me what my mother's maiden name was.

At the time of this writing, Dad, and all of his siblings but one, have died. Uncle Jack is 90 and still living in Toronto [Uncle Jack died in 2014]. Dad died of lung and colon cancer in 1971 at the age of 53. Mom lives in Newmarket and is now 88. [Since writing this Mom moved to a nursing home near our home and died on May 5, 2015 at the age of 90.]

CHAPTER 2

EARLY CHILDHOOD

    You may need a good strong coffee to stay awake during this but here goes. From today's perspective, I consider that I had a pretty good childhood. Of course, my parents would have been jailed for the way they raised us. They did not have the advantage of all of the books written by the many 'experts' today. They did foolish things like sending us out to play in the sunshine without lathering us with sun block. We had to walk to school two miles – yes in the snow, and there were no crossing guards. Would you believe that I walked across the 401 highway, now the busiest highway in Canada, each day on the way to grades seven and eight? True!

    We were made to drink water, right out of the tap and not from a plastic bottle. But that was only when we had taps. Some places where we lived we had to bring in water from the well or the spring by bucket. Everyone drank from the dipper that hung on the old pump, and nobody got cooties. Can you believe that our parents allowed us to ride our bikes without helmets? Seems the only helmets I can remember were worn by soldiers, other than those leather helmets that the football players wore. I can't remember ever hearing of anyone having a head injury from riding their bicycle.

    On weekends and in the summer when we weren't working, we would be gone from sunup till sundown, and our parents rarely asked or knew where we had been. We would swim (unsupervised!) in the rivers, lakes and farm ponds. I don't remember owning or wearing a life jacket until I joined the Navy. We built tree forts and snow forts to keep the 'enemy' (the girls) away. Yes, most of the memories of my childhood are good. But it seems that, as time goes by, the "funner" things linger and the not-so-fun things dry up and blow away.

My earliest memories go back to 6 Blong Avenue. You can still see the house if you Google the address and it still looks almost exactly like it did back in the early 1940s. My parents had the opportunity to buy that house for under $6,000 but couldn't afford it. Today it would sell for at least $600,000. One of the reasons they could not afford it was because of the tobacco and beer. Dad worked very hard to take care of us, and Mom could make a bag of potatoes and a bone into a week's suppers. In the early days I never thought of ourselves as poor. I thought everybody was like us.

Dad was a trucker. At one time I think he had four trucks of his own. I thought we were actually rich because he had business cards that said, "C. Mitchell, Salvage, Scrap Iron & metals, Gerard- 0148." (That was our phone number.) I suppose the bank actually owned the trucks, but Dad had his name on them. In the garage, out back of the house on Blong, I would watch him rebuilding an engine or change a pickup truck into a flatbed. He could take some old piece of junk and make it into something that was useful. One story I heard is that he bought his first car, a Model "T" Ford, for $10 that had rolled into the lake. After he fished it out, he turned it into a little truck and started doing deliveries. He always wore one of those train engineer style striped denim hats. And it was rare that he didn't have a cigarette hanging out of the left side of his mouth and an open bottle of beer on the workbench. In those days, 'everybody' smoked and drank beer – well, everybody we knew.

The garage out at the end of our yard was the last unit in a long building that ran along the back of the houses next to us. The doors would hardly open, because it was a cheap, flat-roofed, wooden frame building that leaned. I think that it is still there today. I would climb the rose trellis and run along the top of the building – great fun for a four-year-old.

The back yard was probably no more than 30 feet by 30 feet but I can remember riding my "kiddy-car" around the world in that yard. Actually, I preferred to turn it upside-down, sit on it and turn the front pedals with my hands. I don't remember many toys although I'm sure I had some. I liked to make things out of scrap wood that was left around from Dad's projects. For some reason, I recall a piece of 2 by 6 that I was able to saw a point on and nail some bits of plaster lath to create a 'ship' that could sail the seven seas.

There were huge, high wood-board fences (over 5 feet!) on both sides of the yard. On the east side there was a dog named Sandy that didn't like being teased. Ask me how I know. He seemed to get really upset if I tried to walk along the top of the fence. I can't remember what was on the west side, but everybody knew everybody, and if they had a dog, it probably wasn't as much fun to tease.

We had some pets. Brownie was our Cocker Spaniel. She taught the three of us kids to walk. We would grab on to her fur and pull ourselves up. She would walk along supporting us and probably losing fists full of fur in the process. Brownie lived to a very old age for a dog. I can't remember how old, but the Toronto Star newspaper came by and did a little story about her. Whenever we would get a spanking, which I can hardly believe we ever deserved, Brownie would go behind the big chair in the living room and "cry".

Donny was our duck. We didn't have him long. When we were out camping on the river at Cherrywood, Donny got in trouble for chasing a lady. It seems that he liked to run his beak up the back of the leg of anyone wearing silk stockings. I don't remember seeing it, but I am told that as Donny was chasing the lady around her lawn, the husband was chasing Donny with a lawn-mower. Too bad there were no iPhones and Facebook around in those days.

Mickey was our skunk. We found him as a baby one summer and brought him home to Toronto. He never was 'de-skunked' but he didn't seem to know that he had the ability to 'alter the environment'. He followed my mom around everywhere, even when she didn't know it. That made for some interesting times on the streets of Toronto. Mickey loved to hide in the dirty laundry beside the old wringer washing machine when Mom was working. I have heard stories of how he often ended up in the wash and had to get fished out. One time he didn't get noticed. Poor Mickey!

Can you handle more stories of Blong Ave? We had this huge furnace that burned wood or coal. Dad was a "coal man" in the winters. More of that later. The coal would come in bags of 77 lbs. and would be dumped through the cellar window into the coal bin. Then it was shovelled into the furnace door. Tom and I spent plenty of time in the cellar playing around the furnace. Uncle George brought us two old flashlights with no batteries and no bulbs. He told us that if we ran around the furnace really fast they would light. Tom's would light only when I was out of sight it seemed. I still can't figure out how that worked.

I have memories of parties where my parents would have friends over. There was lots of drinking, and the smoke from cigarettes was thick. As gross as it seems now, one of my little games was to sneak around and try to smoke some of the old butts and drain beer glasses. Honestly, I don't know how anyone can stand the taste of beer, especially warm. But, like any little kid, I wanted to look like the big people. Still, today, those memories are not bad.

One significant thing that I remember was that during one of these parties, someone at some degree of intoxication noticed me banging to the rhythm of the music with some spoons and made a comment that I was really talented musically. It may have been a joke or just some half-hearted comment, but I grasped at that and stored it in my 'personal identity' file. It was a little seed that was planted in my little mind that finally took root and eventually sprouted. Be careful what you say to little kids!

I wanted to be like the big people and I observed and imitated like most kids do. I particularly wanted to be like my father. He liked to play the harmonica; I liked to play the harmonica. He liked to work hard with his hands; I liked to work with my hands. He didn't have much use for education, having gone to work before finishing elementary school; I certainly didn't have much use for school. School! What does a truck driver need school for? I was going to be a truck driver, not one of those "college kids with their heads full of things that won't help anyone but themselves," as Dad would say. My mind was way too busy for school. Of course in those days we didn't have a lot of letters to explain why some kids learn and are motivated differently than others. You know, letters like ADD, ADHD and chemicals like Ritalin. Another problem is that you had to pass tests to advance in grades. How silly!

As a result, I unashamedly failed first grade. Well, I 'acted' unashamed! We had Miss Vernon in the beginning of first grade, and she was wonderful. Then, near the end of the year, she left and Miss Barrie came. She stood about seven feet tall, had a big wart on her nose and rode around the class on a broom being mean to little kids. And she had the nerve to fail me. Can you believe it? I vividly remember sitting on the curb on Queen Street where I knew she would be crossing. When she came I started crying. She got off her broom and asked me why I was crying and I told her that when I got home with my report card, my parents would beat me and make me leave home. I was still not a very good liar, but I was learning.

Kindergarten and those two years in first grade were spent at Bruce Public School on Larchmont Avenue, just south of Queen Street. I would walk to school about five blocks, through alleyways and streets, alone. Well, not always alone. You see, one day in first grade, or maybe kindergarten, this pretty girl sitting in front of me turned around and announced that I was her boyfriend. That was serious stuff, and as a proper boyfriend, I had to walk farther south along Pape to Eastern Avenue where she lived and walk her to school. Caroline Wilson was her name. For some reason we never did get married, but during recess I would charge around the playground with my arms spread out like Blackhawk, the comic book pilot, shooting down the "commie" Migs. She would stand on the line dividing the boy's playground from the girls and declare, "My Hero". Really!

I got a little wagon for Christmas and I would take it down to the A&P grocery store on Queen Street. Along with other boys, I would shout, "delivery" as ladies came out of the store. A woman would pick a boy and put her groceries into his wagon, and he could earn a dime for dragging their bags to their home. On one occasion, who should come out of the store but Carolyn and her mom, and who would Carolyn's mom pick but me? We headed off down the street, but when I tried to pull the wagon off the curb it tipped over distributing everything all over the street. Would you believe that she gave me a quarter? I think she saw son-in-law potential in me.

It was somewhere along Queen, near the same spot where, after looking left, then looking right, then looking left again, just like they told us, I stepped off the curb, and the next thing I remember there was a man pulling me out from under a truck. I had looked both ways, but I had not looked around the corner beside me. The truck could not stop on the ice, and I ended up with a huge swelling on my head over my left eye that actually came down over my eye.

That was the first time that I got run over by a truck. And that was the first time that our school lost its Elmer flag because of me. It was another two years before that happened to me again. You see, in those days, every school was given an Elmer-The-Safety-

Elephant flag. It flew just under the Canadian flag – the old Canadian flag. If any child got injured in an accident the school would lose their flag for some time - maybe a month or so. As I recall, it was a shameful thing to lose your Elmer-The-Safety-Elephant flag. Today they just send in grief counsellors, hold an inquiry, build a cross-walk, hire an armed crossing guard and notify litigation lawyers.

The walk from 6 Blong Avenue to the school went down an alleyway that passed by the stable door for the horses of Blantyre Dairy. I would try to sneak some sugar from home and put it in my pocket to feed the horses that would come to the door of the stable as I walked by. That was so cool! Well, not really. We didn't have "so cool" in those days, but it was fun. One reason that I remember this, is that when I got to school one time, sugar fell out of my pocket on the floor of the class and I got "the strap". I think that teachers were issued with a "quick-draw" strap that they could use on poor, innocent, little kids like me. I'm sure it was that old Miss Barrie.

I also recall walking alone along Queen Street to the Greenwood Community Centre. I think there was a swimming pool there and I sort of remember learning to float and getting some badge for not drowning or something. I would also walk west to Sumac Avenue where there was a truck yard for Smith Transport. It was fun to watch the trucks manoeuvring around the yard. I have a memory of a man painting the "Smith Transport" sign on the door of one of the trucks. It was all free-hand but it looked as good as any of the vinyl appliqué that they use today. I think my mom's adopted mother lived somewhere near there and I would walk to her house. Today, a little kid would be in danger of being abducted. Abductors likely just looked at me and said, "Nah!" and drove on to scare some other kid.

In the summers, Dad would take Mom and us three kids out to Cherrywood to a spot on the side of a hill near the Rouge River. We had one of those canvas, military style tents. I'm guessing it was about 8 feet by 10 feet, and Dad had made a folding wooden floor for it. I remember thinking that my dad could make anything and that everybody was probably jealous that we had this floor. We kept our butter, milk and other things in a wooden box that was dug into the ground on the side of the hill. It worked pretty well, except that the garter snakes would fall into it and couldn't get out. That was great for me because I didn't have to go looking for them.

There was a spot on the river where someone had made a little dam out of the rocks, and the water was deep enough to swim in. Kids did a lot on their own then, and I would head on down to the river and play by myself. That's where I figured out that if I lifted my feet and flailed my arms and legs enough, I didn't sink. Later, I started going to the Greenwood pool, as I mentioned before, and learned to float.

But there was another "swimming" event that I remember vividly after this many years. About a half mile up the Rouge River from Lake Ontario, my parents, us kids and others had a fishing spot where we would catch catfish. To this day, when I smell birch burning on a camp fire, my mind snaps back to that place on the banks of the Rouge. We had to walk over a hill, through the forest where we would see trilliums, may-apples and Jack-in-the-pulpit flowers, and on down to the river. I clearly remember the thick, grey clay coming up between my toes as I hiked to our fishing spot.

One of the first things we did was to light a fire. With the wet wood there was always plenty of smoke. I can almost smell it now. I don't remember ever having anything like a fishing rod. We had string wrapped around a little stick, a cork from a wine bottle, a sinker and a hook with a big juicy worm that we dug up somewhere. We were supposed to sit very still and be quiet so we didn't "scare the fish away"; just stare intently at the cork and wait. There were always sandwiches and hardboiled eggs, hot chocolate and oh yah, a length of kielbasa. As I recall, it rained as often as not, but that seemed to be part of the fun.

Not wanting to scare the fish, one time I hiked around a bend in the river where there was an old abandoned, mostly rotted bridge. There was pretty well no deck on it. It had piles driven down into the muddy river bed with cross-boards held on with long bolts. I don't remember falling in, but I guess I made enough noise to get Dad's attention. He came running to the rescue but instead of jumping in and hauling me out, he leaned down from the old timbers and called for me to come over to him. Now this is before I had learned to swim. I would go under and come up and go under again. In my mind, I can still see him each time as I looked up from under the water. Well, he finally grabbed me and lifted me out. He seemed kind of proud of me, but I was not impressed. I don't know if I saw my whole life flashing before my eyes or not – all four years of it, but I thought I was a goner for sure.

I am told that there was a similar episode about three and a half years earlier, just down the river, near the mouth. There is a railroad track that runs near the shoreline of Lake Ontario with a trestle that crosses the Rouge River at a place they call Ferguson's Beach. I was, so I am told, placed on a blanket near the shore to "get some sun". When Mom wasn't looking I rolled down the bank and into the river. Dad was on the trestle about 40 feet up when Mom started hollering. Good old Dad jumped off and rescued me. What he did not know, and I found out by doing the same thing about 10 years later, is that the water there is only about six feet deep. I wonder if that is the reason that Dad was only five foot seven and I never got taller than five foot eight.

CHAPTER 3

ROUGE HILL

It was probably 1950 when we moved way out in the country to Rouge Hill. We had lived for about seven years on Blong Avenue and that, for our family, was a long time. Recently I calculated that I had lived at 52 different addresses. That was before we moved to where we live now. Let's see how many of those addresses I can remember as we go along.

We lived on Woodview Avenue, a gravel road that ran from the First to the Second Concession. Actually, we lived in three, perhaps four different houses on that road. My adopted maternal, grandmother (Nanna) had moved there, and we stayed with her for a very short time before moving into a house across the road and a little south. I remember her actually standing on the road in front of the house, counting one thousand dollar bills into the hand of the realtor. When I think of Nanna, I think of food: Ukrainian food with lots of garlic, cloves and bay leaves. I could understand a little bit of the language; mostly the names of different types of food and a few words that little children were not supposed to say. She was fairly nice to us kids as I recall. Growing up with her, my mom found her less than nice. Little kids would be adopted back then, to fill in as cheap labour and I know that Mom worked very hard with little time for "childish" things. Nanna would buy old restaurants, clean them up, make them successful and sell them. My mom worked in them and before she got married she ran a sort of snack shop adjoined to one of these restaurants. I'm guessing that's where she met Dad. They were married when she was only 16, but she was definitely a grown, mature woman – and very good looking, I might add. I was born when she was just 17. It's okay, I did the math. Firstborn children need to check this out you know.

Nanna had several husbands over time. The only one I remember was Pete and I have no good memories of him. He was very fast at bringing out his razor strap. He would whip us with it often but not if my mother was around. The strap was leather, but it had a nasty metal end that really hurt. I also remember him making me kneel on dry split- peas in the corner: a cruder and more painful version of today's "time-out". You definitely did not want to get kissed by him or even hugged. The term "dirty old man" comes to mind. He apparently tried things with my mom, but she threatened to kill him or call the police.

There were several well-worn phrases in those days. One was, "Children are meant to be seen but not heard." Others were, "Speak when spoken to." "Where's your manners?" "Respect your elders." "Take your hat off/stand up in the presence of a lady." "Do your chores first." And my favourite, "Because I said so." The perfect answer to that profound question, "why?" How would that go over today? Fact is, I am so glad that I grew up then and not today. I'm tempted to break into a sermon here...maybe later. All that to say, we grew up to serve and contribute to the good of the world rather than to become the centre of it. My body, soul and spirit survived intact and without suffering irreparable damage to my little being.

From there Tom and I went to Rouge Hill Public School on Altona Road. It was a little over two miles. Fortunately, I got my first bicycle then. It was a 28 inch men's bike. I remember that I could not get over the crossbar without some personal pain, so I learned to ride it sort of sideways from under the bar.

In second and third grade (yes I finally made it out of first grade) I got a paper route delivering the Toronto Telegram. I had 81 customers on a rural route that covered five miles. The bike was a great help – in the summer. But in the winter I had to use a sleigh. From school I went down to Highway # 2, loaded the bike carrier and put the rest in a bag that hung over the rear fender. With the bike I could do it all in about an hour and a half. In the winter with the sleigh, it took from 3:30, when I got out of school to about 6:30. But it was worth it. The paper cost 25 cents a week and I got 4 cents a customer per week. I was an independent business man.

I probably started the route half way through second grade and I don't think that I made it right through third grade before I quit. One winter evening, I was so cold that I dug a little hole in the side of the snow bank and lay down on my paper bag and fell asleep. I clearly remember waking up in the cottage of a lady who had seen me there when she pulled into her driveway. She had carried me into her home, and when I woke up she was feeding me hot chocolate. When she found out who I was, she contacted my dad, who came and got me. I sort of recall that Dad finished my deliveries for me that night.

I hesitate to mention it but I remember there were about three customers together near the end of the road and it was a long way to go for three customers and it was dark by the time I got to them. For several days, I just threw their papers in the ditch. Of course, they did not pay me and my dad decided to 'help out' by going up the road to collect. I can't remember clearly the outcome but I know that I learned a valuable lesson in business integrity, the hard way.

What else do I remember about that time on Woodview? Oh yeah, the Lazelle boys. There was Bobby and Billy. They were rich. Well, their parents owned their home. I didn't know many people, other than Nanna, who owned their own home. They also had one of those pedal toys that you could ride in. It was a little airplane. I loved riding in it and was certain that if I could pedal it fast enough it would fly. At night I would dream of flying that thing up over the electric wires alongside of the road. I always dreamed of flying, even before battling it out with the Migs in the school yard at Bruce Public. But then, actually flying a real airplane was only for the really, really rich people. Right?

Sonny Cole lived on our road, and the Smith brothers over on Pinegrove Ave were also friends. Then there was Eleanor. I had to walk past her house that was on the top of a hill on First Concession on the way to school, and she would follow me a lot. I didn't know exactly why she was different, but I was nice to her and most other people weren't. Today I realize that she had Down Syndrome, although it was always called Mongolism then. Kids like her were most often kept in the house, put in institutions or publicly abused. In her case, I believe it was the latter. I remember taking some "flack" for not teasing her with the other kids. I also remember some really sad things that were done to kids that were "not normal". God was introducing me to something that would be a big and blessed part of my life in the future.

It was at this time that I had my second encounter with the front bumper of a truck. I was riding my bike down Altona Road to go swimming in the Rouge River, where it ran under the old "Suicide Bridge" on Highway #2. All I had on was my swimming trunks. I remember the front wheel of my bike catching on the edge of the pavement that was about two inches above the gravel shoulder. The next thing I remember, I was being loaded into an ambulance. One of the Hurley boys had been riding with me on his bike and rode back the two miles to get my mother. She was just arriving when I became conscious on the stretcher. She rode with me to the Oshawa Hospital.

The doctor determined that the handlebar of my bike had been driven into my back and had displaced my left kidney but did not appear to have damaged it. Of course, the worse part of all of this is that our school lost our Elmer-The-Safety-Elephant flag. The good part was, the truck driver, who was the nicest guy, would come to our home and visit me and he bought us a Hamilton Beech milkshake machine and lots of ice cream. I don't think that even the rich kids had their own milkshake machine.

CHAPTER 4

HAGERSVILLE

In 1952 Dad got a job at the Caledonia gypsum mine, and we moved to a farm about three miles from Hagersville. Uncle George, Aunt Ruth and my four cousins, George, Charlie, Barry and Frank lived in town, and we would walk with Mom to visit them or do our shopping. This was a short but "most interesting" time in our lives. During this year, we lived in a haunted house; Tom got a double hernia; Florance caught on fire; I fell off the roof and down a well; Mom and Dad split up... Let me try to recall, in some sort of order, just what happened there.

I think the name of the farmer that we rented our house from was Mr. Sprung. I remember that he had a foot missing. It seems that he tried to kick a drive-belt onto the threshing machine while it was running and his foot got caught between the belt and the power take-off on the tractor. One day while plowing, he came over and was having a beer with Dad. In an unthinking moment he said to me, "Why don't you go plough the field for me?" That's all I needed. He had left the tractor running behind the barn. At age 10, I had never driven anything bigger than Bobby Lazelle's toy airplane, but I had seen Dad push pedals, shift levers and steer the trucks. How hard could that be? There were plenty of levers to push, and eventually I had it bumping across the field. The plough had been resting on the ground, so as I bounced along it would dig in and then come out of the ground. I had no idea how to stop it, and I don't recall wanting to. With only one foot, Mr.

Sprung couldn't catch me, but Dad eventually did. For some reason I don't think I got in trouble for that. In fact, I think Dad might have been a bit proud of me. I sort of remember wondering how Mr. Sprung had made such nice straight furrows. Mine where much more "creative".

Yes, the house was haunted! We found out that some man had hung himself in the attic. No one had bothered to take the rope down. At 11 p.m. a rocking chair up there would rock. That's when any guests who had planned to stay with us over night generally decided to leave. One night as we arrived home in our 1932 Chevy, we all spotted a man in the dark who ran into the front of the driving shed. Dad, and Uncle George, who was with us, ran in after him, but when they got there he had disappeared and all the doors were locked from the inside. Another time we all came home to find that the kitchen door had been knocked off its hinges and was lying on the kitchen floor. There were chickens in the house, and things were all messed up, but nothing was missing.

We raised chickens, and Tom and I each had a pig. Dad wanted to fatten them up but I suppose that riding them around the pen didn't help that much. I can't avoid telling another detail about the pigs. As they say on TV, "The material you are about to see may be offensive to some audiences." They got to be a pretty good size but then contracted some kind of sickness. Dad decided that it was time to slaughter them since whatever sickness they had was not supposed to make them too bad to eat. Uncle George and Aunt Ruth were at our place, and, although I don't think either Uncle George or Dad had done this before, they prepared for the task. They filled a barrel with water, placed it under the branch of a big old apple tree, just outside a large living room window and built a fire under it. In the tree they had a block and tackle to hoist each pig over the barrel. The plan was to hang the animals from their back legs, which were supposed to be securely tied together. The idea was to 'stick' the pig, bleed it and then lower it into the hot water. That was so they could shave the hair off.

Well, things don't always turn out the way they are planned. It would have been a good idea to make sure the pigs had their back legs well tied, but hindsight is always... you know the rest. The first pig wriggled and squealed and let it be known that he was not in favour of this plan. With the pig thrashing around, hanging upside down over the barrel, one of the men went for the jugular. I will just say that it was not immediately successful. Mom and Aunt Ruth stood watching from inside the living room window. In the fray, a stream of blood shot across the window, and Aunt Ruth passed out. That was about the time the pig broke loose. He missed the barrel and started running. Tom and I went after him and had one last wild ride. When he finally expired, the three of us, Tom, me and the pig were covered in blood and mud and Aunt Ruth was lying unconscious on the living room floor. I can't remember what we did with the second pig. They probably just shot him.

In many ways, this was an interesting place. The Nichole family across the road had a dairy farm and we could buy a quart of "fresh" milk for ten cents. Today you would go to jail for selling milk that just comes from cows. I really wish I could have a taste of that real milk today. We loved to hang around with their kids.

As I recall, there often seemed to be someone, wherever we lived, who invited us kids to Sunday School. One day Mr. Nichole came over to ask if he could take us to their church in town. When he backed up, he drove over the back wheel of Tom's bicycle. I don't know why I remember that, except that he went and bought us a new rim and a bunch of spokes. I was fascinated to try to assemble the wheel, which ended up being a whole lot harder than I thought it would be. I think that Dad probably ended up putting the thing together. Each week the Nicholes would take us three kids to the church in Hagersville. I think it was a Presbyterian church. The lessons that I learned there had an eternal effect on my heart. Ours was not a churchgoing family, but God's love seemed to grip my soul, and I loved the Bible stories.

Our house did not have running water, inside toilets or electricity. The well was just a few feet from the house. The outhouse could be reached by going out the kitchen door, through the driving shed and there it was. Talk about convenient; you didn't have to even go outside, unless you count the driving shed as outside, since it was fastened to the house. Instead of electricity, we had natural gas piped from our own gas well on the lawn, throughout the house. There were gas lights in each room and gas stoves that looked a little like the old "Quebec heaters." Inside of them were what looked like ceramic, hollow, hand grenades. The flames flickered through them and kept the house nice and warm at no cost.

One Saturday morning the three of us kids were standing around Mom and Dad's bed in our pajamas when Florance must have gotten a little too close to the heater. Suddenly, her housecoat caught fire and she was engulfed in flames. Dad leaped out of bed and wrapped her in blankets. Fortunately, her burns were minor. Tom had his "adventures" with the gas system too. Most of the houses in that area had a pipe coming out of the ground with a regulator for the natural gas. I can't recall just how high those pipes stand out of the ground but apparently they were just about an inch higher than Tom could leapfrog over. That caused him a lot of pain, but it was made worse, a few days later, on the way to school, when the chain on his bicycle broke and he came down on the crossbar. I can't think of an appropriate comment to make except maybe, "better him than me".

I had created a series of trapezes in the apple trees. At age 11, you would think that I would know that binder twine would not be strong enough to support me hanging from my knees. We didn't have the advantage of crash helmets back then. Although I don't know if they would really protect someone who lands on his head after about a six foot drop. A helmet would have also been helpful when the chimney collapsed while I was climbing it. I fell off the roof with the bricks coming down all around me. Thinking of helmets, I suppose we would have been wise to have something like that when we rode our bikes over the chicken house. We would put a two by six plank up the back of the building that was about four feet high in the back and about six feet in the front. We rarely made it all the way over, but when we did, we didn't have to worry about the bike falling on us when we went over the front. There was a wire fence a couple of feet in front of the coop, and the bike would get caught in that as we fell into the manure pile on the other side. Like I said, we rarely made it to the top of the building. We would come storming toward the board, but often the front wheel would come off the board before we got to the top, and we would just crash into the back of the building.

Our school was called "SS No. 19 Walpole" and was about two miles along gravel roads. First through eighth grades were all in one room. The first graders were on the left side and the older kids were on the right. I was in fourth grade and sat right in the middle. This was the first time that I was ever at the top of my class. Being the only kid in fourth grade had something to do with that. This was Florance's first year in school, and Tom was in third grade. I really wish that I could remember our teacher's name. She was amazing. We had someone come once a week to teach music, but our regular teacher taught everybody everything else. I can't remember just how she did it. I'm guessing there were about 25 or 30 kids. I'm also guessing that the kids learned much more of the "Reading, Writing and Arithmetic" than kids do today. And the only way to advance in grades was to pass all of the subjects. Talk about ADHD; try teaching kids with their pockets full of frogs, bugs and whatever, while some of their pet dogs waited outside for them to come out and play. Our teacher was strict, but I seem to recall that she was also a lot of fun.

At recess the boys in the upper grades would go out the large windows that were on their side of the class. That was in the warmer weather. In the cold weather we had two wood stoves and the older boys were responsible to bring in the wood and have the fires going in the morning when the rest of us arrived. We would climb into the rafters of the driving shed which held the firewood and eat our lunch there. We would also try to lasso the girls from the rafters. I suppose that the teachers, and even the parents of those days would end up in jail these days for allowing such things. I'm sure there were things to complain about but most of my memories are good ones. Well, that was at school anyway.

Dad would be away for days at times and there was this "Frenchman" who took a special interest in Mom. He would take us all in his car with the rumble seat. As little kids we didn't realize that this man's intentions were not "honourable". I don't have much memory of all that happened but when the school year was over Dad left Mom and took Tom, Florance and me to live for a while with Aunt Phyllis and Uncle Clarence.

CHAPTER 5

BACK TO TORONTO

We all lived in what had been the house of Grandma and Grandpa Mitchell. This is where Grandma stayed in a room at the top of the stairs. She had been bed-ridden for several years at this time. The house was on Torrens Avenue in Toronto. My cousins, Andy and Johnny Sims were just little guys when we lived there. One not-so-nice memory was of Andy losing his eye. He was out playing in the garage and found a garden hose hanging from the beams. Unfortunately, when he pulled it down, a pair of hedge clippers came down with it. Anyone who visited that house would remember the huge cherry tree in the back yard. You just couldn't give away all the cherries that that tree produced, and I loved (still love) cherries.

I am sure that having her own two boys and now the three of us kids along with Dad, while at the same time caring for Grandma Mitchell was a huge challenge to Aunt Phyllis and Uncle Clarence. A can of Campbell's soup could go a long way if you just kept adding more water. I remember feeling some injustice that Andy and Johnny seemed to get a little special treatment and perhaps an extra cookie, but after all, they were her own kids.

There were a couple of other boys closer to my age and we use to go down to the Leaside Bridge that ran over the Don Valley. According to Google it is 143.8 feet high. The beams under it are about 8 inches wide with "N" members going from the lower beams up to the bottom of the bridge. We loved playing on the beams and would travel across the bridge on them. There were a few cement pillars supporting it, and we would rest on those and eat the lunch that we would bring along with us. I sort of recall dropping the crusts from my sandwich and trying to hit the workers on the ground below.

Although we were dirt poor, somehow we three kids got a trip to the Canadian National Exhibition (CNE). It was the largest exhibition in Canada and was famous for several things. One thing that it was infamous for was polio. Many people who attended in those years (this was the summer of 1954) came away with this killer disease. Florance and I were among them. I was just very sick but did not seem to develop any paralysis. Florance was not so fortunate. Most of the left side of her body was affected. Partly because of the trauma of this event, Mom and Dad got back together.

CHAPTER 6

ROUGE HILL AGAIN

By the time school started we had moved, this time back to Rouge Hill and again we lived on Woodview Road. It was a tiny two-room house on the east side of the road. If we were dirt poor before, we were dust poor now. Florance was recovering in this tiny house. It was all we could afford although that is where we got our first TV, and it was a beauty.

There was a man whose name was either Mr. Clark or Mr. Watson. I can't remember, but he owned a glove factory and I know that there were glove factories owned by a Mr. Clark and a Mr. Watson, so I'm guessing that it was one of them. Details are definitely foggy, but somehow he found out about our need and came to our house. I vaguely recall a doll that was dressed in money. Then the TV arrived. It was a Dumont 21 inch and paid for by our rich patron. Each of us kids still remember the first picture that came on. It was a formation of jet fighters zooming across the screen. Then there was the "Singer Four Star Theatre". The TV sat on the kitchen table on the west side of the main room. The one door to the outside was on the south side. The wood-stove was against the back wall on the east side right by the doorway that went into the other room where all five of us slept.

Tom and I were quite proficient with a cross-cut saw. The back of the small plot of land was against a swampy forest. We would take our axes into the forest and cut down some tree or cut up some fallen tree. Of course for eleven and twelve year old boys, cutting down a tree was way more fun, although less practical, than just taking what had already fallen. One of my most powerful, life-lesson memories comes from that experience. Many times in later years I would remember and would get the strength and courage to carry on because of that memory.

When cutting a length of log, we would have to judge just how much we could carry or drag home. Cut it too long, and it would be too heavy to get up onto your shoulder. Cut it too short, and you ended up carrying less than the max, which meant having to make more trips. We seldom cut a piece for the two of us to carry because the standing trees were close enough together to make it difficult to maneuver. To carry the log, we would first stand it on end, then determine the spot that was just forward of centre to balance it. Since our strongest muscles are in our legs, we could squat down and let the log lean back onto our shoulder and then struggle to stand upright. This is when we normally found out how accurate our judgement had been in gauging the length. Once the log was up, it was not that hard to balance it – for a while! Then the trick was to pick our way over dead-falls, through mud or snow, back to the pile at the house.

To this day I can vividly remember the frustration of feeling that I could not make another step, but at the same time knowing that, if I dropped it, having lost so much energy already, I would never get it back up. It was that feeling of, "I can't possibly make another step, but I can't possibly quit." And somehow, you take another step... then another. Then I would find myself at the bottom of a slippery, snowy slope having to climb up it, when my legs wanted to refuse to work. Just because you can't do it does not mean that you don't do it. Impossible is no excuse! How many times in my life have I known for absolute certainty that I could not go on; the job was way beyond my ability and strength and knowledge? And yet not going on was not an option. Some of those times will be mentioned later in this tome.

One of God's greatest gifts to man was the chainsaw. I remember when we got our first one. It was a big old Remington, and the thing was not light. But that was long after this time. The "buck-saw" or "Swede-saw" did the job on wood that was less than eight inches in diameter. It was the good old cross-cut saw that did the heavy stuff. Today you more often see them nailed up on the side of a shed or barn – good place for them! If you don't know, it is just a long saw blade, about six feet long and about ten inches across at the centre. It tapers to about five inches at each end with a wooden handle, about fourteen inches long, fastened to each end. It can be operated by one person, but it sure wasn't meant to be! The log has to be supported off the ground normally on what we called a sawhorse. Ideally the log lies across the X's that the sawhorse is made of at about waist height. That way you don't have to bend or reach too much. Now, unlike any other saw, you don't push but you pull on the handles, each person pulling in turn. Sounds simple eh? Well, this is one of the greatest instruments made by man to teach the principle of cooperation. If you get a little rambunctious and want to speed things up, you may be tempted to push. That often ends up with a bow in the blade, on your side. One of the most important things to know about using a cross-cut is that the blade has to stay perfectly in line with the cut. If there is any bow on the side going into the cut, it will bind and the poor guy on the pulling side has way more work. Of course, if you and the guy on the other side are not getting along all that well, you may just want to put a little bend in the blade.

After school Tom and I would have to cut wood. I didn't have a paper route then. It was during one of these evenings that the "rich" man who bought us our new TV, happened to be visiting. For some reason, we did not have a regular axe. The one we had had a regular, full-size head but a handle that was only about 18 inches long. I was splitting the pieces of log that we had cut into lengths of about 14 inches. I think Tom was putting them on the chopping block and I was swinging the axe. There was a clothesline that ran across the yard just over our heads. We had not noticed that, as we were working with the chopping block, it was moving little by little, and that now it was right under the clothes line. As I swung the axe down, the line caught under the head of the axe. The axe stopped but my hands didn't. I fell forward while the axe spun off the line and descended into the crown of my head. When I started yelling, Mom was talking to the rich man. To assure the gentleman that everything was alright, Mom, jokingly said, "Oh, one of them probably hit the other on the head with the axe." I don't remember what the reaction was when I came into the house covered in blood, but I suppose there were looks of confusion at least.

This was the same house where we rode out Hurricane Hazel. It was October of 1954. Mrs. Willoughby came running into class, well as much as she could run, with her wooden leg. She was almost in tears. She told us that we had to hurry straight home because a terrible storm was coming. I would have been 12 years old. To us kids it was the greatest fun. We would stand out on the road with our jackets open to catch the wind and lean forward into it. Then we would slide backwards along the road until we hit something and then we would just go tumbling. As I recall, the wind was from the South, so it helped blow us home. I don't know how we would have made it if the wind was blowing the other way. By the time we got home the rain had started and it really came down hard. Shortly after arriving, the water started to rise. There were two or three steps up into our house, and the surrounding land was lower than the steps. By the evening the water was coming through the door. Although it was October, the rain and the wind were not cold. The whole thing seemed like a big, fun adventure.

Sometime during that year we moved from the two-room house about a quarter mile south on the same road to a chicken farm. Mr. O'Cane, an Irishman, owned the farm and lived at the back of the property. We lived in the house near the road. It was a pretty good size place with a lovely big porch on the front. There was a long row of chicken houses running east and west with lots of windows facing south to catch the light and heat. I should mention that it was normal for boys at about age eight or nine to get their first BB gun and then about age twelve to get a .22 rifle. Tom and I were pretty good at picking off tin cans, and Tom became particularly good at shooting out chicken house windows. The only other thing that I remember about that place was that one night a lot of horses broke loose and ended up running all over our lawn. I don't know where they came from.

CHAPTER 7

CHERRYWOOD

From Rouge Hill, we moved to Cherrywood. That was actually walking distance from where we had just left. From the "chicken farm house", you could walk north along Woodview Road to the Second Concession, (that's called Finch Avenue now) east to Altona Road, north to the Third Concession, then west to the Markham Town Line and we were the first driveway north, across from the old Hutterite meeting place; just a little over 3 miles. Again, we did not have running water but Tom and I would put a five gallon pail on a stick between us and walk down the hill to a spring to fetch the water. Then we would fill a barrel or a tub back at the house. I can remember Mom hauling that water by herself lots of times.

Dad drove a cement mixer. He did that for quite a few years. The driveway was close to a quarter mile long and part of it went through a swampy forest. Often, at the end of a job there would be quite a bit of concrete left to get rid of. There's no way of figuring how many loads of concrete went into that swamp, but it seemed that vehicles were always getting stuck there.

The three of us kids would walk to the Cherrywood Public School in the little village of Cherrywood. Come to think of it, I don't remember if Florance was well enough to go to school then or not. There were probably ten or fifteen houses, a school of about four classrooms, a general store and I think there was a blacksmith shop behind the store and across the road from the school. If you walked out of our driveway and down to the road leading into the village, it was about a half mile longer than walking across the fields. It was hard to get a bicycle through the field, so we generally rode the long way home if we had a bike.

I don't remember any of the school kids there except a girl that I liked named Barbara. She was one of 18 kids in her family, and when I met her, her mother was expecting another. They were a happy family as I recall, with a big garden, a cow and a little house where all the boys were crammed into one room, the girls in another and the parents in another. The older girls cared for the younger kids, and the older boys worked in the garden. My brother was kind of interested in another one of the girls named Sheila.

The old place where we lived was a big field-stone house and the walls were well over a foot thick. I remember the three of us sitting on the inside of the windowsill watching huge thunderstorms. They were particularly spectacular, partly because we had no electricity and each time the lightning flashed, it went from almost pitch dark to extremely bright. I have always loved thunderstorms – well maybe not so much when I was flying through or around them – that's for later!

There were several great apple trees in front of the house and one big mulberry tree. I loved mulberries. We were not limited to how much of the fruit we ate which was wonderful. But I wished someone would have told me that mulberries are about as powerful a laxative as you can get. Fortunately, the outhouse was not very far from the house. There was a big old barn on the far side of the apple trees, and it had plenty of hay. What more could a kid want? In recent years I drove up to the old place and walked in the overgrown driveway to find that the house and barn had been torn down.

Like I wrote in the early part of this tale, the same event can be viewed in totally different ways by different people, equally involved. Well "Scampy" (I'm not sure if that was its name or not) is one of those cases. Up at the Third Concession, the Altona Road has a great hill and the road was paved – perfect for a go-cart/push-cart/coaster/glider or whatever you want to call it. I loved making these vehicles. Sometimes it was just a plank with a rear axle nailed across the back and a two-by-four on the front with big spikes, acting as axels to hold the wheels on. The two-by-four on the front had some sort of mechanism to allow it to steer, and generally there was a rope fastened near the front wheels to steer it and to pull it back up the hill. Sometimes it was much more sophisticated with a shaped "cockpit", some sort of windshield, even fenders and tin cans nailed to it to look like headlights.

Scampy was one of my more sleek models. I think it even had a fancy steering mechanism. The rope went through the sides of the 'engine compartment' and wrapped around a stick to which was fastened a 'steering wheel.' The biggest problem with trying to build one of these was finding wheels. Wagon wheels were sort of okay, but spoked, baby buggy wheels were the best. Well, Florance had this nice baby-doll buggy but it was going to be hard to get them without a little 'horse trading'. The deal was that she would get to ride in Scampy first. If you were to drive down Altona Road today you would notice that there is a little bit of a curve where it crosses the Third Concession. Well, in those days the road came straight down to the cross road. Then you had to stop, turn right along the concession and then left again to continue down the hill. The good part of that is, if you couldn't make the turn, you just shot across the road, over the ditch and hit a wire fence.

Really! It was no big deal! I should mention that our emphasis was always to get the most speed, and brakes do not contribute to speed, so if there were any at all they were just a piece of wood that pivoted on a nail on the side of the cart. When you pull on it, the bottom end would drag on the ground and maybe stop it. Well, as part of the deal for the wheels, Florance got to be the first driver of Scampy. As I recall there was no crash, in fact I think she just ran into the ditch before she ever got to the turn. But to this day, the story is that I was trying to finish off my little sister by putting her into a piece of equipment that may not have met all the requirements of the Highway Safety Act.

I really wish that I could remember the name of the farmer who rented us that place. He lived several fields away, where he had another barn by his house and three Clydesdale horses, Prince, Royal and ......? The only motorized vehicle he had was a 1925 Star car that had not run for years. I was told that he tried to repair the carburetor by carving a wooden choke valve. I got to work with the horses. No way could I handle a plough. If the tip hit something and the horses kept pulling, it would throw me right over the plough. I ran the buck-rake and the hay wagon. He had an old thrashing machine but I can't remember how he powered it. There was a horse-drawn machine that cut the standing grain and tied it into sheaves. I learned to follow him and "shook" the sheaves by standing them together with the grain on the top to dry in the fields. The farmer would let me ride Prince into town. There was no saddle. I don't know if there was ever a saddle made big enough for a Clydesdale. Prince seemed to enjoy being ridden, and sometimes all three of us kids would ride him together. We would have his collar and bridle on. The bridle to "steer" although he worked just as well with a "gee" or a "haw". Then the collar was to hold on to. He was so wide that our legs pretty well just stuck straight out sideways, so without the collar, we would just slide off. Then we would have to walk him over to a fence so we could get back on.

In the spring, I was helping the farmer load piles of manure that sat out over the winter into the manure spreader. We were just finishing a big pile when one of us, I can't remember which, lifted up a fork full and exposed a nest of yellow jackets. I ran, waving my arms and swatting at the little beasties, to the creek and jumped in, splashing like crazy. The farmer just stood still, but the horses took off across the field at full gallop, spreading manure and parts of the manure spreader all over the field. I got over fifty stings. I think he got a couple. He then took a gooey handful of what we were loading and spread some all over the stings that I had. He said that would draw the poison out. I wonder how much poison came out and how much went into my hide.

He lived in a big, old house with his sister. To me they were really old. To a twelve year-old someone over 40 seemed really old. One day Dad and I were over at his place to help him with something. We went into the house, which was quite an experience. I had been in there before but I don't think Dad had. The sister was a little taller than she was wide but not by much. It was evident that the two of them wore the same clothes day and night. The table had every dish, plate, cup, spoon, fork etc that they owned, piled up on it along with much of their food. Remember there was no refrigerator or anything like that. She asked Dad if he would like a coffee. Now Dad did not have a very strong stomach but he said yes. I remember that she picked up a very well used, very seldom washed cup. She looked into the cup and realized that it was not clean and would not offer Dad a dirty cup. So she simply spit into it and wiped it out with the corner of her, what used to be, white apron. I can't help laughing even today, when I think about it.

CHAPTER 8

FAIRPORT BEACH

Next, we moved down to Fairport Beach. But we missed the old farm, so Tom and I would get some guys together and walk up to Cherrywood to play in that barn. It was just over five miles (that's eight kilometres) each way. It was always good to have Tom along. If we boys got hungry, we would send him into a farm house along the way to see if the lady of the house would give us something to eat. He must have looked particularly sad and hungry because I can remember him coming back out to the road with food. In fact, I sort of remember getting a pie one time.

I can remember five different houses that my parents lived in in Fairport Beach. I only lived in three of them, because I joined the Navy during that time. I figure that I lived there for five and a half years. Grade seven and eight were at the Dunbarton Public School just north of Highway 2. Depending on which house we were in, it was about a two mile walk. That two mile track held many adventures. To start with, the 401 highway was built about that time. Back then it was a four-lane, divided, 60 mph highway, the biggest of its kind in Canada. We walked – well I guess we ran – across it every day going to and from school. Like most roads, Fairport Road was gravel, and the crossing at the 401 was level; no crossing guard, marked walk-way or light. No, I didn't cause our school to lose our Elmer-The-Safety-Elephant flag this time!

Wow! The memories of Fairport Road! I've got scars to help me remember. After crossing the 401 and then highway 2, we went up behind Crook's grocery store and gas station, by the little old church and there was Dunbarton Public, a school that also brings back many memories. Our school colours were gold and royal. I don't know why that was particularly important but for some reason it was important to me. Although we moved a lot, somehow loyalty became a very important thing to me.

Poor Mr. Bunting was my main teacher. He was a great guy and really spent himself trying to help me. At one period of time, he strapped me almost every afternoon for something. I wasn't a rebellious kid, in fact I really liked him, but it just so happened that sometime nearly every day, I did something that deserved the strap. One day when I reported for my regular strapping, Mr. Bunting was almost crying and he said, "Art this doesn't seem to be working." It was clear that he did not enjoy having to do this. I felt so sorry for him. I wanted to say, "It's Okay. Just strap me. It's what we do!" I was never a star in any sport but he would work it out that if the softball team was going somewhere I would be able to go along. What a great guy! One time I even got to go to see the Toronto Maple Leaf, professional baseball team play against the Montreal Royals. And I am pretty sure that I didn't pay.

The principal, Mr. Parker was my main teacher in eighth grade and he was a pretty special guy too. When he gave the strap he would say he was giving the "stinger". Yes, he took over for Mr. Bunting. Funny how things pop back into your mind! When I remember Mr. Parker, I recall one time when he was out of the room, and Bobby Crosier was chasing me...or I was chasing him, who knows? Anyway, someone threw something, and I ducked but when I did, I fell forward and hit the back of a chair with my face and drove my top tooth through my lower lip. Good old Mr. Parker came in about then and got out the first aid kit with the iodine. He washed out the cut well by putting the glass iodine applicator through the hole in my lip. It was kind of fun to be able to close my lips and blow blood through the hole to "gross-out" the girls. Of course the event was finalized with the customary application of the stinger.

    The grade seven and eight classes had a euchre club, a square dance team and a tumbling team, and I was in all three of them. The dance and tumbling team would travel and put on performances. I can't remember who we performed for, nor can I imagine anyone other than our parents wanting to see us jumping around. At that time, girls were kind of a "curiosity". I lost no opportunity to show off or do something that would "gross them out," and I enjoyed any attention, but I was not too sure what I felt about them. I was definitely a show-off, but I didn't know whether to pull their hair, dip it in the ink well or take their books and hide them. I was sort of like a dog chasing a bus. The chase was fun, but what do you do when you catch the thing?

    There was the time in the beginning of the square-dancing lessons when I had to "touch" a girl. She was the prettiest girl in class, and I had to put my hand on her waist! I know that I sweated and probably turned a few shades of red. My self image was pretty low. After all, I was one of the poorer kids, and because we moved so much, we sort of always felt like the outsiders. I also felt that I was too short and my head was too big and my nose was too wide and...I don't remember the girl's name. I think it was Sheila but, either way, Caroline Wilson was "ancient history" now. I acted cool but I was about as shy as you could imagine. I wondered if she enjoyed making me squirm. Since she was my square-dance partner, I always found time for practice. I also remember one time, I was at the movie theatre with Rick Finlay and she came in and sat by me. That was bad enough, but when I put my hand into my popcorn box I found her hand in there! I think that I almost passed out. Growing up has its terrifying moments.

    I mentioned the scars that remind me of walking home along Fairport Road. Well, it also had to do with a girl and a knife. Jean was one of the nicest girls in our "gang". She was one of the only

Christian kids that I knew. One day she had had enough of my pranks. I hate to admit it now but I was a real brat at times – okay a lot of the time. One day when the gang, about eight or ten of us, was walking home, I ran up behind Jean and grabbed her purse. I was going to dump it out on the road when she pulled out a pocket knife and slashed at me. Wanna see the scar? I was always trying to get the girls attention. I sure got her attention that day.

Along the east side of the road was the telephone line. It was one of those thick bundled lines about two and a half inches thick. Normally, it was high enough off the ground but when the heavy snows came, and especially when the ploughs piled it up, we could jump up and catch the wire. Four or five of us would hang on and start bouncing up and down. We could get quite a distance off the ground. The idea was for all but one person to drop off at the bottom of a bounce, leaving one person to be launched like an arrow off a bow string. The difference is that an arrow has the string behind it, so it flies off cleanly. However, a kid hanging from the wire is being pulled rather than pushed by the wire.

This means that, at the top of the bounce, you need to try to be offside a little, or you crash into that heavy bundle of wires and that really hurts. Also, if you don't let go, you could end up upside down holding on for dear life and then you are likely to hit the wire on the way down. Landing was normally not a big problem because the snow was generally deep enough to prevent getting too bruised up. I don't think that getting injured doing that would qualify for losing the Elmer-The-Safety-Elephant flag.

But sliding down the snowy road while holding on to someone's back bumper likely would. Just south of the 401 was the railroad track. I suppose while it was legally a level crossing, it actually ran along the top of a ridge. So the road rose up higher than the surrounding area to cross the track. It was easy to lay down in the ditch, beside the road, just out of sight of traffic coming over the track. In winter cars sometimes had to struggle to make it over the rise, which was perfect for us. Once over the top, vehicles could accelerate down the other side and carry on. The trick was to spring out of the ditch late enough to not be seen by the driver but early enough to grab onto the back bumper. If you were too close to the side he might see you in the mirror. Crouching nice and low, right in the centre was the best spot because if you were behind a tire it could throw up snow or slush on you. Things worked pretty well unless your boots hit a dry spot on the road. When it was gravel, it wasn't quite so bad because you might be able to still slide but once the road was paved, it could mean a lot of torn trousers and sometimes torn skin.

Down close to the lake was the Community Hall. Some people had started a "youth club" there where we could go and make crafts and listen to stories. I don't know who was responsible but those stories were Bible stories. Not only was it okay to teach kids Bible stories in a community club, it was common to have Bible stories in school. Every kid in any Ontario public school memorized, the Ten Commandments, the Lord's Prayer and the Twenty Third Psalm and likely got marks for memorizing other Scripture as well. Many of the stories in the early Ontario Readers were straight from the Bible. Hmm! We had great times at the Community Hall. Someone started a "Junior Police" boxing club and I really loved that. I did not join in a lot of team sports, mainly because I was afraid of always being chosen last when they were picking teams, but I enjoyed things like gymnastics, boxing and swimming.

On most Sunday mornings, we kids would find ourselves at the little church; the only church in the area. It too was on Fairport Road. It seemed that sometimes it was a Brethren work and sometimes Baptist. I sort of recall different people coming to preach in the earlier days. During the week they had the "Teenagers Club." Again, there were crafts, Bible stories, memorizing competitions and a clear and consistent presentation of the Gospel. There was also Sunday School with much of the same. I don't remember many of my friends going except Bobby Crosier.

He got to run the 'magic lantern'. That was a big projector with a bulb so powerful that you could almost heat the place with it. There were glass slides, about six inches square, with words and pictures that would project onto a screen on the platform. In those days, even us "heathen" kids knew more hymns and Bible songs than some churches have in their repertoire today. "Climb, climb up sunshine mountain", "The B-I-B-L-E, yes that's the Book for me", along with "Rock of Ages" and "In My Heart There Rings a Melody". I've always loved singing, probably more than others loved hearing me sing.

Pastor Victor Mornin is the first actual pastor I remember there. He was a tall, thin man, almost like a beardless Abraham Lincoln but he spoke with a Jamaican accent. He was born in Jamaica and had served as a fairly high government official. Perhaps I think of him like Abe Lincoln because he was a humble, servant of a man with great wisdom and an unquenchable love for us kids. Good characteristics for a pastor! It's hard to resist love like that.

"Toby's hill" was a favourite play area. I have no idea who Toby is or was but this hill was where we would drag our sleds, toboggans, skis and other home-made contraptions. I can't remember if it was Scampy that had somehow survived from Cherrywood, or another one of my creations, but in the winter I took the wheels off it. Probably Mom made me give them back to Florance. And I nailed some old wooden skis onto it. That really was a disaster. It was fun as long as it didn't roll over but it always seemed to roll over and it was heavy and hard enough to cause some bodily damage. Can you picture a kid with most of his or her body inside and just from the chest up, sticking out the top? When it flipped, the part of the kid sticking out of the "cockpit" was susceptible to being broken off. In the summer, I took that same creation, pulled off the skis and nailed it onto two pieces of cast-off telephone pole and launched it into Lake Ontario. The poles were long enough that it worked fairly well although it still had a tendency to want to flip. By this time I was a pretty good swimmer.

And that brings Petticoat Creek to mind. We spent lots of time down on the beach at the mouth of the creek. In the warm weather, it was a great place to swim. A big old willow hung over the water that you could swing out on and drop, hopefully into a spot that was not too shallow. As summer wore on, the water got shallower, and at times the mouth of the creek would close completely. In winter, of course, it would freeze solid and we could skate and play around on it. But spring was when the real fun happened. With the melt-off, plenty of water poured down the creek, and as the ice broke up we would ride down stream on the broken pieces. The idea was to jump off before it flowed out into the lake. Well, that was the idea anyway.

One time "Mort" and I were on the same ice-cake. As we approached the lake, it broke in two and Mort ended up on the big section. He somehow managed to jump off in time, but I got forced out into the lake on mine, which was not really big enough to support me. The current was really strong, and before I could do much about it I was way off shore. I was wearing hip-waders and as the ice began to tip I found myself on the lower, underwater part trying to run up the slippery, wet ice and sliding backward into the freezing water. Don't ever try to swim in hip-waders. Tom's job was to paddle around off-shore in a leaky old rowboat that we had for just such an occasion. Although we were maybe one hundred yards out, the current was still quite strong and as I tried to swim across to his side of the current, he tried to paddle to mine. We missed each other a few times before I finally caught the boat and scrambled in over the side.

Back on shore, we had a fire going. We rarely went down to the beach without lighting a fire. Even though there were girls there, I stripped down to my long-johns and hung my clothes on sticks around the blaze to dry out. Petticoat Creek now has a bridge over that spot but otherwise, it hasn't changed a lot. More recently, I drove my motorcycle there and went for a hike up the swampy valley. It seemed like the same old acorns were lying right where they were almost 60 years ago, and I could see the old trees where I had built tree-forts.

Tree-forts! I built plenty of tree-forts, but one building project was the most memorable. It was in the same forest, on the side of the hill leading down to Petticoat Creek, just below Mr. Parkinson's house. We chose a lovely old oak. I had a camper's hatchet and I was well up in the tree, trimming small branches to make a good place to start the fort. Bobby Crosier was down below, nailing pieces of wood to the trunk of the tree to make a ladder. Need I say more? Hatchets are much more dangerous than axes, just like pistols are more dangerous than rifles. Hatchets and pistols both have a tendency to flip around a lot and unlike their bigger types, they are not held with two hands. As I reached out and swung at one branch, my wrist caught another, and the hatchet was knocked, spinning from my hand. Gravity did the rest. But the hatchet was not damaged at all since it landed, blade first on the back of Bobby's head. It did get a lot of blood on it though. We were close enough to Mr. Parkinson's house and his kind wife helped clean up the mess. I would not have wanted to go home with a bloody hatchet.

Looking at Googlemaps today, things don't look a lot different in the original Fairport Beach area, but all around it is totally built up. The first house we lived in, like many of the houses we lived in, is now torn down and replaced. It was at the corner of Park Crescent and Surf Avenue. Like many folk at that time, we had an outhouse but I think there was indoor water. The next place was on Marksbury Road, just south of Tullo Street. Then we lived on Beach Point Promenade at the beginning of the sand spit. I just looked at the map again and it looks like every home we lived in down there has been torn down. I am also quite sure that all those street names were not the names back then. They have even changed the name of Fairport Road to West Shore Boulevard.

Come on! North of the 401 it is Fairport Road and it goes to Fairport Beach! And while I'm at it, who said they were allowed to build all those houses on Toby's Hill?

During our family's time there, we had two fairly well known dogs. It was always embarrassing when people asked the name of the red haired, sort-of-spaniel. Mom named her "Beauty." Okay she was not ugly but "Beauty?!" At least she didn't get me into trouble. Then there was Jerry, the beagle. In those days very few dogs were kept fenced or leashed. If they were not running free, how could they ever come to meet you when you were on the way home from school? Most dogs stayed on their own land, unless they were out walking with their master or looking for them, and everyone seemed okay with that. Unlike today, the average dog cost less than $25 to buy, if you paid anything and they mostly ate scraps. Those were the days when dog was "man's best friend". They guarded the property, protected the family, fetched sticks and balls and maybe the odd neighbour's cat and knew that man was their boss, owner, master. [I began writing a comparison of those dogs with the "little darlings" we see today. No, I better not go there.]

When we lived on the shore, on what is now called Beach Point Promenade (how posh!), there was a swamp across the road from our house and since it was built right on the beach, Lake Ontario was our "back yard". In the autumn I would get up early, before going to high school, and take my 12 gauge shotgun out to a bit of a blind that I had in the swamp. The ducks, heading south would fly right over that spot and I had some decoys set out to attract them.

One morning, all the ducks ignored my little area. It might have been because there was a big, old Great Blue Heron strolling among the decoys. Normally, it is easy to scare a heron away but this guy just could not take a hint. As I walked back to the house, dejected, that bird decided to add insult to injury and he flew just about fifty feet, right over my head. Well, I hadn't unloaded my gun, and to "scare him away" I just pointed upward and shot. Much of the time, when I aimed I missed, but this time, without hardly looking...well...you know!

Now I had to get rid of the evidence. I went to the edge of the swamp and tossed it as far as I could into the reeds. After breakfast, as I came out the door to walk up to the 401 to catch the bus, there was Jerry, all wet but ever so proud. He had somehow managed to find this bird, drag it home and display it in front of the house. Now, although I might be late, I had to go back in, get my boots on, find something heavy to tie to the bird and re-hide it where the fish and turtles could help me dispose of the incriminating matter. "Man's best friend" indeed! For those who may not know, there has never been a legal hunting season for Great Blue Herons.

Despite the trouble that I caused Mr. Bunting and Mr. Parker, they both passed me. I wonder if they were just afraid of keeping me at Dunbarton Public School. Recently, when I drove by the location, I noticed that this school has been demolished. Just for the record, I didn't do it. But it seems that someone has torn down most of the houses I have lived in and now the school I attended. It could be that they are trying to erase any trace of evidence that I was really there.

CHAPTER 9

AJAX HIGH

Ajax High School was, of course, in Ajax about six or seven miles away. Although Mr. Bunting took an interest in me, I think that I can safely say that I was not generally missed by most teachers. High School was no different but now I had several teachers in each grade to share the load. I did fairly well in the important classes like music and shop but not so well in the less important ones like, math, science, French, Latin, and commerce. In those days, every student chose to follow one of three tracks; "Academic", which lead to university (no way was I going there!) "Technical" (but that required sciences) and "Commercial" (that had a lot of girls and not many guys). One day Mr. Black, who taught Latin and other Academic courses came to me and suggested that I would make a very good Commercial student. I don't think that he conferred with Mr. McGuire who was the main teacher in that department. So Mr. McGuire got me!

Looking back, that turned out to be a blessing, and not just because there were lots of girls which definitely made the classes more interesting. Typing and bookkeeping proved to be a lot more useful than Latin, although in later years I developed a real interest in Latin. Typing was not word processing or computer science. There was no such thing as a computer in any high school in the 1950s. If you made a typing error, you could not just "backspace" and do it over and if a word was misspelled, no dotted red line appeared under it like constantly seems to happen as I type this document. To make more than one copy you needed to have several sheets of paper in the typewriter with carbon paper between them. Then, of course, any correction had to be made on each sheet separately. To make more than a few copies, you would type on a stencil. The little hammer that smacked the stencil as you pushed the mechanical key removed material from the stencil. Now if you made a mistake, you had to use a pink, gooey fluid to cover the strike, then blow on it to dry it and carry on. Then the stencil was put onto a machine that made lots of noise and produced copies. Isn't this exciting stuff? The whole point of this is to impress the reader and make you feel sorry for me. Is it working?

My buddy, Bobby Crosier ended up in the same department. As I recall, we were the only guys in the typing class. How cool is that? Of course, with all those girls to impress, how was a fellow to get good marks as well? One day, when Mr. McGuire was out of the class, I took all the keys off all those old Underwriter typewriters and put all the 'As' on one, all the 'Bs' on another and so on. The girls were impressed, but Mr. McGuire didn't seem to catch the humour in it when he returned to see me standing on a desk, trying to pull one of the keys from a machine. He knocked me right off the desk. You could do that to a student in those days. I wonder if he didn't want to go and knock Mr. Black down as well. He must have been born for punishment because he and the rest of my teachers conspired to fail me and had to have me for a second year in grade nine. Also in those days, they made you pass your exams to move into the next grade. Seems a bit legalistic doesn't it?

Dr. Lindemann was our music teacher. That was a class I really enjoyed, and it was not just because I got to sit next to Darlene, although I didn't mind that at all. I played trombone. I took the trombone home for practice much more than I took any books for study. Playing music gave me a sense of accomplishment and joy, but in my mind I felt that I could never consider music as a career as much as I would have liked that. I could not have dreamed that in a short time my life would be immersed in full-time study of this wonderful field.

Mr. Reifenstein was our shop teacher. Since there was no homework and I got to use my hands as much as my brain, I did quite well. Again, who would have known that, while I was making little pieces of furniture and sheet metal items, I would one day be building aircraft and buildings?

Anyway, after two years in grade nine and at the beginning of my second try at tenth grade I went to Mr. Ramsey, the principal. I was fairly well known to him by this time. I made a deal with him, that, if I maintained a 75% grade in all my subjects, he would let me take Thursday afternoon and all day Friday off each week so I could work. I tried something totally new, studying. And it worked! I began bringing home more than just my trombone from school. It cut into my fun-time but allowed me to drive a truck, which was then my main purpose in life anyway. I worked at the IGA in the store on Thursday afternoon and driving a delivery truck Friday and Saturday.

This was definitely not my first job. During sixth grade, in Cherrywood, I earned a bit by working for the farmer. Most summers I picked berries to earn money, and, while living in Fairport Beach, I had a job at a garden centre up at the corner of Highway 2 and Whites Side-road. Early in the year I would do budding and grafting on thousands of rose bushes and fruit trees. Then through the summer it was mostly weeding fields and helping customers. I have always loved working outside in the summer heat although the work with the rose plants was not fun. The grafting is done about two and a half inches above ground which means you are bent over, like you are tying your shoes, all day long with no shade.

From about age 15, I paid for most of my own clothes. It was good to feel that I was old enough to contribute. Dad never made much money, but he worked very hard and being able to earn my way was important to me. It also allowed me to buy my first car at fifteen years of age – a powder blue Pontiac, Silver Streak with a "torpedo back" and a flat-head six. Dad found it for me for $125.

The deal was that I would work on it and learn how to care for it but not take it on the road until I was old enough to have a driver's licence. I drove that car all over the place, but I don't even know if I still had it by the time I turned sixteen.

One time I got pulled over by the police when I was taking my friends for a ride. I have never struggled with being too tall, and I suppose I was pretty conspicuous looking through the steering wheel. When the officer found out that I didn't have a licence, he told me to drive straight home and that the ticket would be in the mail. You can bet that I made sure that I checked the mail each day before anyone else could. I think that the fine was $35 which meant a lot of hours working in the hot sun. For the next 55 years I never got another driving ticket. Well, there was Zaire, but we will cover that later.

I mentioned that Dad worked hard, and we never had much money. I thank God for both my father and my mother, but they did have problems. Even though we could not afford luxuries or even some necessities, both of them smoked a lot and loved their beer. The beer truck would deliver right to your home in those days, and our house was well known by the drivers. I can't guess how often Dad stopped on the way home at the hotel beer parlour, probably two to four times a week. Mom would be there to meet him sometimes. If we kids were with them when they went shopping or visiting, they would make their regular stop for "just one" which normally turned into quite a few. We spent many hours sitting in the back seat of the car in the hotel parking lot, summer and winter. At one of our favourite hotels, there was a cafe at the side of the parking lot. It was our favourite because sometimes we would each get a dime, or on a good day a quarter, and with that we could sit in the cafe at the counter and sip on something. The cafe owner knew why we were there, and he was kind enough to let us take as long as we liked, sitting in his warm building.

I have seen a lot of pain in the lives of a lot of people because of alcohol. I definitely was not a "good" kid growing up, but I never thought of drinking as fun. Oh yeah, I wanted the other guys to think that I was a big guy so I talked up a big story of wild exploits, but I can't remember ever paying money for any type of alcohol. I had seen a lot of slobbering, falling-down drunks and even helped them find their way home. Somewhere I once heard someone say, "There is no such thing as an alcoholic who didn't take a first drink." Yes, I did have a few over the years, but I have no idea what it is like to be drunk.

I think that I could have become a very good thief. Different people have different weaknesses, and one of mine has been a temptation to steal things. Remember, it is not a sin to be tempted but it is to yield to that temptation. Jesus was tempted in every way, but did not give in. Stealing goes well with lying, and I was already pretty good at that. To this day, I will see something, and something goes off in my brain that says, "I could grab that and no one would know." Whenever I see butter tarts, I remember standing in stores with my lunch bucket hanging open next to the display of Vachon butter tarts and casually sweeping them into the bucket. I can still taste those tarts. I sort of remember stealing bottles of Bee Hive Golden Corn Syrup, and then I would drink them like pop. There was the time that a local kid stole a bicycle from some other place and left it in the ditch. He said that someone must have left it there. Not knowing that he stole it, I told him it was mine and claimed it. I even got others to back up my story.

CHAPTER 10

EVERYTHING CHANGED

As I mentioned earlier, it seemed that most places where we lived someone showed up to invite us to church and/or Sunday school. In those days, almost any church preached, believed and tried to live by the Bible. So going through my teen years, I had a fairly good handle on what people called the Gospel. I knew for sure that they were right when they said that I was a sinner. I had also heard enough about God to know that He would not and could not let any dirty old sinner into His perfect Heaven. I knew what Hell was all about, and there was no doubt in my mind that that is where I was heading. People told me that God sent His Son into the world to live a sinless life and to give His life to pay for the sins of the people. But I was not a good person. Oh, they told me that He died for me too, but they didn't know how bad I was. If they did they would know better than to offer this 'salvation' to someone from my side of the tracks.

Even at the age of sixteen or seventeen, as a tough "fearless" kid, I would lay on my bed when no one could see me and cry and try to stay awake because I felt that life was so short and Hell so certain that I didn't want to waste a minute sleeping or risk falling asleep and not waking up. At church, the preacher – at that time it was Pastor Mornin, would plead for people to believe and accept Jesus. I believed everything they told me about Jesus, but it made no sense to accept Him because He wouldn't be willing to accept me. Why would He? What would He get but someone to mess up His beautiful Heaven? This went on for a long time. I had a very low self esteem and felt unworthy of anything good from friends, teachers, neighbours and especially God.

Then one Sunday morning – even today, I am overwhelmed when I think about it – Don Whiteside showed up! He told the few boys gathered in the basement of Fairport Beach Baptist Church about his life. He robbed his boss at age 13. He served his first jail time in 1944 at age 15 and he found that exciting. By the time he was 17, as a young merchant seaman, he got put ashore in Australia for threatening a shipmate with a gun. He lived from one place to the other by stealing. He was charged with breaking and entering and fraud and passing counterfeit money and spent time in Guelph Reformatory. After that he ended up in Collin's Bay Penitentiary for armed assault in a robbery plus other things.

To impress his parents and the parole board, he started attending church. According to Don, "I got down and prayed and asked Jesus Christ to come into my heart and save me from my sins." By the time I met Don, that Sunday morning, he had received a Queen's Pardon (the first in Canada) and was serving as a missionary in South America. When I saw that God could save and use someone like him, I had no more excuses. I prayed with Don, and like him, I asked Jesus to be my Lord and Saviour. I gave Him what there was of me and all eternity was changed for Art Mitchell.

That morning, as I ran home, I felt I was not even leaving footprints on the ground. "Happy" is a poor word to describe it. Crazy, ecstatic, perhaps! I have seen people find salvation in Christ. Some have been joyful, and some didn't express any wild emotion at all, but I felt like I weighed almost nothing at all. To me it was the most traumatic, exciting sense of freedom imaginable, and I remember it vividly more than fifty years later.

CHAPTER 11

ROYAL CANADIAN NAVY

In the summer of 1960 I was looking for a job and was wandering around downtown Toronto. I sort of remember seeing a recruiting poster and found myself at HMCS York. I ended up getting an interview and audition with the Bandmaster there. Each year at our high school, the Royal Canadian Air Force band would perform. I loved music and especially the music they played. I also had a fascination with the military, perhaps because the person I was named after served and died in the Canadian military. Of the three services, the Navy held my greatest interest. The interview and audition seemed to go okay, but I didn't hear from them, so that is when I found the job driving for the IGA.

As I mentioned, I worked out a deal with the principal of Ajax High so I could continue to go to school and take a day and a half off each week. My grades were higher than ever before, and I was also enjoying my newfound faith, although I was definitely no "super saint". Then in mid December, I got a letter from the RCN telling me to report to HMCS York to be sworn into service, just before Christmas. A few days after New Years I was to catch the train to Nova Scotia.

Dad took me to Union Station. It was the first and only time I can remember my father with tears in his eyes. I didn't realize the train I boarded was also a special train in another way. I was told it was the last official, coast-to-coast, steam powered locomotive. On the train I met several other Navy recruits who had boarded farther west and others joined as we travelled east. I wondered as

IN HIS EXCITING SERVICE

we rolled into different stations along the way, why there were so many people out to see the train. I think that our last stop was Greenwood Air Force Base in Nova Scotia. Up to that point we were still on our own. There we were herded onto an old blue RCN bus for the last leg of the trip.

Elvis Presley, long sideburns and lots of Brylcreem (or Vaseline for us poorer kids) were popular. Almost all the recruits had long greased-down wavy locks. They were the picture of "cool" and each one tried to impress and out-lie the other. Tough guys! Ready for anything! Well, almost anything! The bus arrived at HMCS Cornwallis. As it turned into the main gate, a huge parade square met our gaze and an enormous sign on the wall of the '"drill shed" on the far end of the square that read, "Learn To Serve". We all learned that in the Navy there was very little distinction between the words "serve" and "slave."

After the old blue bus went through the gate, it turned left, went about fifty yards, turned right, went another fifty yards and stopped at the front door of the barber shop. I have no idea where these "barbers" got their training, if they actually did have any training, but the recruits who walked in the front door looked very different from the ones who walked out the back. Lesson one: humility! Humility, or more accurately humiliation, was liberally bestowed on each one of us, especially in our first two weeks in "Basic Training". Remember, this was the beginning of January. It was cold and very damp. With our freshly shorn, fuzzy heads, we were "marched" to a building where each of us was issued with a couple of sets of "Number Fives".

Each uniform had a number. Fives were denim work clothes. Ones, Twos and Threes were regular sailor uniforms: Ones had gold badges, Twos had white badges and Threes had red. Number Fours were the white, tropical uniforms. More about that later. We could only get Fives because the others had to be tailor-made. That was a great thing about the Navy. The Army and Air Force were issued uniforms, "off the shelf". We had people come and measure us who sent the measurements away where our uniforms were custom-made somewhere in Quebec. It took at least two weeks for them to arrive. For those two weeks, we lived in virtual segregation. Old timers, like the guys who had been in training for more than two weeks, strutted around like they had been at sea all their lives and mocked us "pussers". One of the first things we were told was, "If it moves, salute it; if it doesn't move, pick it up; if you can't pick it up, paint it." In those first two weeks we learned many manly skills like embroidering our names and service numbers on all of our kit; ironing, rolling kit, polishing boots and making beds.

    I had some experience embroidering in high school. One of the cool things in my teen days was having a powder blue, denim jacket with the collar turned up and every one of your friends' names sewn onto it. It was important to see your name on as many other people's jackets as possible. Anyway, by the time I joined the Navy, I was pretty good with needle and thread. Some guys had names like "Cain" to sew, but others had to stitch on "Cowperthwaite" or "Brocklebank". I made some money helping them with theirs. Along with our name we had our service number. Mine was 47589H.

    Basic training involved lectures on the heritage of the Royal Canadian Navy, which was mostly the history of the Royal Navy. The three stripes on our collar represented the three battles of Trafalgar. The big collar hanging down our back was for the old sailors to wipe their hands. You see, the "old salts" as sailors were called, handled ropes that were preserved from the salt and sun with tar, so the sailors always had black hands. Another name for sailors was "tars". There are some other things that they were called, but I dare not include them in this wee story. You may notice that the other armed services salute with the hand facing forward. Not the Navy. Because of the black hands that the old timers had, they (we) salute with the hand facing downward with a nice straight line from elbow to finger tip. The bell-bottom trousers had a double purpose. It was very easy to roll them up so you could get on your knees to scrub the deck, and if you went overboard you could trap air in them to help you float. When the wool was wet, it would hold air fairly well. We learned to take off our trousers in the water, tie the cuffs closed, go underwater and blow air into them and tuck them under us to form a type of life preserver.

Boots had to be laced in a way that they could be quickly cut off so they would not weigh you down in the water. To cut them off quickly, we all carried a special knife with a sharp blade and a marlin spike. The knife was known as a "pusser's dirk". We wore a white "lanyard" around our neck that was supposed to hold our dirk. The lanyard wrapped around a "silk" that was quite interesting. It was made of black silk, 12 inches wide, folded in a special way to create a two inch band that could be wrapped around your forehead to prevent sweat from getting in your eyes while you were "loading the cannons". It was also sewn with a twist and to a specific length to form an arm sling if you broke your arm in battle. The silk was tied to the uniform "jumper" by a "tidily bow".

Shortly before I joined, they changed the trousers to a zipper front instead of the old 13 buttons. Great idea! Each piece of the uniform had to be ironed in a very special way. Although we learned the "seven seas" method of ironing the trousers, we didn't need to do that. We did have to iron them inside-out along the side and inner seams so that, when worn they would spread out as much as possible. Several guys ordered special, extra-wide cuffed bell-bottoms so that when they swaggered down the street they would really stand out. You sort of developed a street sweeping swagger.

Our hats (caps) were very special. Copied from the Royal Navy, they were bright white with a black band. Over the black band was the "cap tally" a silk band with the name of your ship embroidered in gold lettering. Ours read, "HMCS CORNWALLIS". HMCS stands for Her Majesty's Canadian

Ship. The land bases, as well as the ships, were referred to as ships. In times of war sailors wore black caps with no tally, so that if their ship was sunk the enemy would not be able to know what ship they had sunk. The black was to make them less visible. Since I served in peacetime, we wore white. They were referred to as Port & Starboard caps. Inside was a red band on the left and a green band on the right. I guess it was so that when the sailors went ashore and imbibed, they knew which way to put their caps on.

It took a couple of weeks to learn all the traditions concerning what we wore and why. By that time our nice tailored uniforms arrived, and we were deemed worthy to wear them. For the next thirteen weeks we marched and studied and marched and cleaned and marched and ran and marched and swam and marched and learned all about our weapons and went through the toughest 'assault course' in the Canadian military and we marched some more. We learned a lot about seamanship, things like navigation, sailing and how to tie all sorts of knots. We learned port, starboard, stem, stern, bow, quarter-deck and the difference between a rope, line, painter and hawser. We learned how to scrub, scrape, swab and paint the deck and anything else that our superiors thought needed scrubbing, scraping, swabbing and painting, even though they had been scrubbed, scraped, swabbed and painted by the class that went before us.

We were taught a word that has lost most of its meaning today – OBEY! The line-of-command was very clear. Each rank from Admiral Of The Fleet to Ordinary Seaman was extremely important. We learned who to salute; how to answer people of different rank; where you fit into the whole system. That was easy. At that stage we were lower in rank than the Captain's dog. And yet there was a huge sense of pride in being even a tiny part of such a great organization. An interesting sideline: Each Sunday we were marched to church. I was serious about my new faith, but

I was still trying to figure out how it would work out with this new career.

Near the end of March we graduated, and were assigned to our areas of specific service, or "branch". We had been the class of Assiniboine 1/61. That particular class of 69 recruits had 21 Bandsmen assigned to HMCS Naden, just outside Victoria, British Columbia. It was my first time in an airplane, other than the one that Billy Lazelle use to let me peddle along Woodview Avenue in Rouge Hill. In those days Trans Canada Airlines, now Air Canada, belonged to the Canadian government and all military personnel were shipped by TCA. They had three types of planes: the Vanguard, DC8 and Viscount. I got to travel on all three types as I made my way from coast to coast, arriving on Vancouver Island. I remember Bob Wallace and me climbing the stairs onto the DC8 in Malton Airport, now Lester Pearson, YYZ. There was a big red ESSO truck fuelling our plane. We shouted to the driver challenging him to race us to Vancouver. Several hours later we landed there, and guess what we saw waiting for us! Yes, there was a big red ESSO truck. How'd he do that?

In high school, I had played the trombone and a little bit of trumpet, so I assumed that I would be assigned to a brass instrument. Well, at the Royal Canadian Navy Academy of Music, they had all the brass players they needed. They gave me my choice of clarinet, flute or oboe. I figured that everyone played clarinet. I had the idea that flute was more for girls, but I didn't know what an oboe was. So that's what I requested, and I was never sorry that I did. We were each assigned a sound proof room, about eight feet by eight feet, with a mirror, a music stand, a chair, a small table, a stack of music and a window. Our group, "Class 17", was the last all-Navy class to go through the academy. Although we were all sailors, our class eventually had instructors from all three services.

My instructor was Staff Sergeant Reid, who had served in the Royal Marine Academy of Music, in Britain. I remember, very fondly many of the lessons he taught me. Most had to do with music but many concerned becoming a man. He demonstrated patience, wisdom, endurance, and just plain hard work. He was a brilliant, professional, natural teacher and a great musician. It's easy to learn from a man you admire!

One of the problems oboe players, and other reed players have is finding a good supply of quality reeds. He made reeds for people all over the world and taught me to make them too. The quality of an oboe reed is extremely important. If you ever listen to an orchestra tuning up before a performance you will hear the clear perfect concert A sounded by the first oboe. Then everyone else tunes to it. Concert A is 440 vibrations per second, not 441. Unless the reed is perfect, the tone is imperfect, and the whole orchestra would be out of tune. Kind of makes you feel important, or stupid if you don't have it right.

I found so much pleasure studying and playing that I was determined that professional music was my life-time calling. The course took 22 months. Every month we were examined in theory, aural and instrumental. If you failed any test, 66 in all, you were released from the academy into some other branch. At the end of our course there were only four of us left: Bob Wallace, Johnny Larson, Burt Hamer and myself, and I was the top of the class. My graduation solo was Handel's first oboe concerto in B flat. The main adjudicator was Captain, Dr. Gaffer, the man who wrote the music for Queen Elizabeth's coronation. Funny, how I failed so many grades in school and excelled in this. No wonder I wanted to stay in music the rest of my life!

I very much enjoyed swimming, which was great for anyone in the Navy. Bob and I joined the Royal Lifesaving Society and worked our way up the different levels. At Cornwallis and Naden there were Olympic size pools that were available to us at almost any time. We would draw a box lunch from the galley each day and spend the noon hour doing "lengths" and practicing towards the progressive awards. We had to do at least 55 lengths of the pool before eating our lunch. It seems strange today but in those days there was no thought of "mouth-to-mouth resuscitation." To revive a drowning victim, we would lay them out in different positions and lift their arms and compress their lungs while straddling them on our knees. As I recall, it was called the Holger Neilson method. It was nowhere near as effective as the CPR used today.

When I first arrived in Victoria, I got a letter from Pastor Dave Holmes back at Fairport Beach Baptist Church in Ontario. He encouraged me to go to Central Baptist Church in Victoria and introduce myself to Pastor Bob Holmes. I figured they must be related and, if I didn't go Pastor Dave would sick Pastor Bob on me, so I went. Bob Wallace, one of the final four, who also graduated with me, went too. Wow! God had a plan! For those 22 months Bob and I would make our way into town each Sunday for church and Thursday for prayer meeting. On most Fridays we would attend the youth meetings. Very often on Sunday afternoon we would take a handful of Gospel tracts and go to Beacon Hill Park and try to talk to anyone who would listen about Christ. Pastor Bob and others invited us home on Sunday afternoons for lunch and a great time of learning and growing in our faith.

Central Baptist had a wonderful youth group. In those days, there was no such thing as a Youth Pastor. The youth elected a president, vice-president, secretary etc. from among themselves and did things together. Some groups just had social times with maybe a Bible reading. When we first arrived at the church it was a bit like that, but the leaders, people like Jimmy Sadler and his brothers, Eugene Benner, Don Richardson and others, were totally sold out and eager to share Jesus with anyone who would listen and some who would rather not.

All of the folks in the church seemed so welcoming and encouraging. I really looked forward to going and many times walked the full distance, about four miles, from Naden to the church. In the beginning, I have to admit that one of the key "perks" of going to this church had something to do with the young ladies and their attraction to the uniform. As I write about different stages in my life, I wrestle over how much to mention about the "sweet young things" that caught my attention. Of course, I was so spiritually mature that I never really noticed them – right? NOT! In fact, as I look back, I think most of the girls might say that I was most often a gentleman but sometimes a jerk. More of that later, perhaps.

I will admit that, when I first started attending the church my thoughts were influenced by one or two of these girls. The leaders were patient and very encouraging. Gene Benner put Leo Williamson on our case to make sure that we did not just come for the girls. Leo was definitely used by God to keep us on track. By my second year there, Bob became president and I became the vice-president of the group and we became more excited about sharing our faith. Besides "witnessing" to people in the park, we would visit seniors' residences and sing and read for them and just try to bless them. Prayer meeting became one of my favourite times. Bob and I and some other sailors like Doug Seymour helped to form a chapter of The United Naval Christian Fellowship, a worldwide group that provided Christian hospitality and encouragement for sailors from many countries. Those on the base would get together for times of prayer in one of our cabins. We shared our faith fairly boldly with other sailors.

One night, we were together when another bandsman came into the room, quite drunk and crying. He was being discharged from the Navy for being a homosexual. I was very nervous, but the others agreed to pray for me, so I went into another room with him and we talked. As I prayed, he somehow became completely sober and coherent. By the end of our time, he had prayed very sincerely and clearly to invite Jesus Christ to be his Lord and Saviour. I had no idea what might happen after that. Within a day or so, he went to visit Pastor Bob at Central and told him what had happened. I should mention that this fellow had been a Sunday school teacher in a very liberal church in town although he knew almost nothing of the Bible. To jump ahead in the story, he left the Navy and the last I heard he was serving the Lord in a church back in Ontario.

The next Thursday, I arrived at the church prayer meeting and was shocked when Pastor Bob called me up front to explain what had happened and how this man came to Christ. Prayer meeting then had at least 150 people, and to stand in front of any group, especially without my oboe was a terrifying experience, but I shared. It may have been about that time that Pastor Bob got it into his mind that I should go to Bible college. I had my music and loved it very much; perhaps too much, but I had no intention of being anything but a musician – certainly a Christian one but a musician!

I was a sailor and had all of my seamanship training, even qualifying as a coxswain so I could sign out Navy sailing dinghies or whalers. However, the only time I was at sea during my whole time in the Navy was when I crossed the Bay of Fundy on the east coast or the Straights of Georgia on the west coast, on the government ferries. One time I went on board a German submarine that was tied up in Esquimalt. Some sailor! Although I never sailed the seven seas I did get involved in some military action, well almost action.

It was during the Cuban Missile Crisis of October, 1962. The USSR was determined to land and plant nuclear missiles on Cuban soil and the USA was just as determined to not let it happen. Most historians agree that this was the closest that the world came to MAD (Mutually Assured Destruction) during the cold war. We, along with the whole world held our breath wondering who would blink. In the end some historic agreements were made, and the crises ended. In the mean time, we were "at the ready." When I stood duty at the docks, there was real ammunition in my rifle, and my job was to use it on anyone who did not have a legitimate right to be anywhere near my station. The possibility that some Russian would suddenly pop his head up from under water was certainly remote but EVERYONE was very nervous, and we believed that war was moments away. That was the first time I stood alone with a loaded gun, prepared to use it on someone. True, the likelihood was slim, but some nine years later I stood with a gun ready and quite sure I would have to use it, on several people. Later....

I remember hearing of one incident on our base. Apparently, a Commodore arrived at the North Gate in his chauffeur-driven car, and demanded that the young Ordinary Seaman open the gate. Because of the seriousness of the situation, our passes were changed often. The sailor requested to see the Commodore's current pass. The Commodore however felt he was too important for such things and told his driver to go through. It is reported that the nervous sailor pointed his rifle at the car and said, "Excuse me sir, I am new at this. Do I shoot you or your driver first."

This was just before the time in Canadian military history when someone came up with the crazy idea of uniting Navy, Army and Air Force into one homogenous lump. Everyone would wear the same uniform. The proud, traditional Navy uniform was traded for a sort of greenish suit that looked more like something the mailman might wear. There had been a distinct sense of pride in each branch of the armed services. The Navy, of course, was the best in every way – according to any member of the Navy.

About the same time as the Cuban Missile Crisis, there was a track and field meet at Work Point Barracks between the three different services. Believe it or not, I was representing the Navy in pole vaulting. In those days we used a very stiff, aluminum pole and twelve feet was a great jump. I don't remember what I did but I didn't lose to those "Pongos" or "Pigeons". We would almost rather lose to the Russians than one of these "inferiors". Historically, the Navy has always been the "senior service". I never lost, but then I never won either because it was at that moment that we were all recalled to quarters because of the Cuban threat.

CHAPTER 12

THE LADIES

Okay! I suppose I should go into my exploits concerning the fairer sex! How should I deal with this? Well there was this girl, let's call her Sharon. That's appropriate since it is her name. She was a lovely Christian girl from a great family. Note: It seems that I always got along very well with the families of the young ladies. Each summer, I would make my way home to Fairport Beach on leave, and each summer (in my nice uniform) I would enjoy the pleasure of some "sweet things" back home. No one, especially me, looking back, would accuse me of being a stable sort of guy. I "fell in love" with many and of course, each one was "True love".

One summer I decided to buy a motorcycle, a 1958, 650 cc, Triumph, Thunderbird and ride it home to Ontario. Now with a uniform and a motorcycle, life was great; in fact too great. I spent time balancing between Pat and Sheila and at the end of the two weeks got engaged to Valerie. In the mean time, back in Victoria, Sharon waited faithfully. Please understand that even though I was a sailor, with all the "reputation" that goes with it, to me, making love meant holding hands, maybe hugging and a kiss before leaving. I was way too scared for much more than that.

Anyway, when I got back to Victoria, Sharon found out about Valerie. I think that Sharon had told her parents we were going to get married, and they were quite happy with that. It was not a pretty scene! Val's parents paid for her to come out to Victoria for a while, and she stayed with the Stevensons, some of my friends from the church. The week she arrived, there was an evangelistic crusade at our church, and about the second night she went forward and accepted Christ. She was baptized at the end of the week. I was able to get a ring for her when she was there. Then she went back to Ontario, and I continued with my music studies.

After graduating from the academy, I was assigned to the band back in Cornwallis. Life was great! I was 21, engaged and living the dream, as they say. When we played concert music, I played the oboe. When we played military music, I played percussion. We played everything from fancy balls and farm fairs to stirring parades. That brings me to July 1, 1963, my "day of glory".

If you check the records, which I just did, you will find that July 1 was the hottest day of the year in Ottawa. I recall that it was 104 degrees Fahrenheit, although the record shows 97 at the airport. Back then, instead of rock concerts, every year there was a military tattoo on Parliament Hill. Many of the Army regimental bands along with the Air Force and the RCMP bands paraded through the streets of Ottawa and up to the parliament buildings. They were led by the Royal Canadian Navy band and guard, where we performed the "Sunset Ceremonies" for the heads-of-state, dignitaries and the general public. As I said, all the bands and guards were led by the RCN band. The person in the front rank on the left in the band is the person that everyone lines up on, and just guess who that was! Man it's hard to be humble when everybody is following you! I remember there were TV cameras everywhere.

But remember this was the hottest day of the year. Bandsmen from every group were fainting. We in the Navy, wore our number fours. That's the white uniform designed for the tropics. I don't know who designed them, but they were anything but cool. They were a type of tarpaulin that trapped the heat very well. Then we wore gaiters. They go over the bottom of your bellbottoms and the top of the boot. On top of that as a percussionist (actually I was a tenor drummer, and we hardly hit the drum, we mostly just spun the sticks on little straps) but as percussionists we wore gauntlets that not only completely covered our hands but went about 6 inches up our arm over the canvas jumper. We haven't got to the bad part yet!

Over the uniform, certain ones of us wore a full sized, actual leopard skin that was lined with red felt and with the head hanging down our back. It gets better. Over all of this we had two inch wide drum harnesses supporting the drum. Are you in tears yet? I hope so. We didn't have enough fluid left in our bodies for tears. We had sweated so that the red die in the lining of the leopard skin ran through our number fours where the belt and harness made contact. By the end of the evening I was not sweating because there was no sweat left in me. Can you imagine what it was like for the Army guys who were wearing those big bear skin "buzzbees"? Many people passed out and were carried off. After the bus ride back to HMCS Gloucester I was ready to drink anything. Someone gave me a bottle of beer – warm beer. It went down and came right back up. I can remember that taste to this day. I have never liked the taste of beer before or since that day. Enough! If I keep this sad story up you will not be able to read through the tears.

Valerie and I were supposed to get married sometime in August, I think. We wrote most days. Then one day, out of the blue, a letter arrived with the ring in it. Now what? Maybe I was getting what I deserved. I had left some girls with the idea that I was going to marry them, although it was not what I had intended. I certainly was not the example of a romantically mature young man. Hurt? Confused? Humiliated? Way too immature? All of the above!

I loved my time in the Navy band on the east coast. Because HMCS Cornwallis was the Basic Training location for the RCN, we spent a lot of time playing on the parade square for the recruits-in-training as they marched and marched and marched.... It was nice being on training staff and not a "pusser". There was no limit to the amount of time we had to practice. Imagine doing something that you absolutely love and getting paid for it. Well, sort of paid. I think we got about $60 every two weeks but our food, clothes and travel was free.

Even back then, I had a desire to fly. A fellow bandsman, Pat, had a 1960 MGA and we would drive up to Greenwood Air Force Base, look through the fence and drool over the airplanes. Somewhere I bought a *From The Ground Up* manual and used to spend hours studying it and dreaming. Interesting that, many years later, that was the same manual that I used to learn and later teach flying with. It was also many years later that I bumped into Pat, who then had his own business buying and selling aircraft. Back then flying seemed like an impossible dream but I was living a dream already and finding fulfillment with my music.

CHAPTER 13

FROM RCN TO NBTC

Throughout that time, as I recall, Pastor Bob Holmes continued to challenge me to go to theological college. I should mention that right after graduation from the music academy, Bob Wallace managed to somehow get a release from the Navy to attend Northwest Baptist Theological College. That left only three of us from a class of 21. I don't remember a lot of details, but I finally decided to see if the Lord just might want me in theological college. I somehow got the paperwork, and on September 15, 1963 I formally applied for release from the Navy. I was told, very clearly, that the Navy had invested a lot of money in our class and got very little in return, and that the possibility of me being released was about nil. I had already applied to NBTC, and for some reason, was accepted. During the process of applying to get out of the Navy, the application had gone to my Commanding Officer, who wrote, "not recommended." Then it was passed on to the Captain of the base, who wrote "not recommended" and finally to the Chief Padre, who wrote "not recommended". The hopeless application was sent to Headquarters in Ottawa.

On October 15, just one month later, I arrived in Vancouver and made my way to NBTC. Somehow, someone in Ottawa did whatever was required, and I received an "honourable discharge from Her Majesty's Canadian Navy for the purpose of continued education" at no cost at all! In fact, I was granted rehabilitation leave for several weeks, with pay. "Out routine" that normally took at least a week, was accomplished in a couple of afternoons, and I found myself out on the highway, hitch-hiking my way to the Digby ferry, to cross the Bay of Fundy and on across Canada.

I had the strong impression that God wanted me in Bible college and the devil did not. There were a few adventures as I made my way across Canada. I decided to go through the States to Toronto. In Skowhegan, Maine, I ended up standing under a big tree in a rain storm in the middle of the night when a family of skunks came trotting across the road and paraded right past me. On the other side of the road was a State Police station. I had seen the lights go out earlier but decided to go bang on the door. A trooper answered, and since they did not have any "accommodation" he took me into the town, and they put me up in the jail.

In those days, a Canadian military person could get accommodation in American jails – really! There was a reciprocal agreement for American military in Canadian jails. The procedure is the same as being locked up for a crime. You get "booked" but the crime was, "foreign military accommodation". My belt and bootlaces were removed and the cell was locked. The next morning I tried to get the attention of the officers upstairs, but since there were no other 'prisoners' and there was no charge sheet on me, no one on duty knew I was there. The State Trooper, who had dropped me off the night before, happened to come by and ask about me. That's how I finally got released. He put me in his cruiser and dropped me off on the highway right by a "No Hitchhiking" sign. "No problem" he said, " this is the best place to get a ride."

I made my way to Fairport Beach to spend a couple of days with my family and then back on the road, this time over the north of the Great Lakes and across the Canadian prairies. Hitch-hiking back then was one of the best ways to travel, especially in uniform. Salesmen would pick you up and jump into the back seat of their car to sleep while you did the driving. Often a farmer would take you home over night and set you back on the road with a lunch.

Anyway, things went fairly well until I tried to get by Banff, Alberta. It was getting dark, and I was about 10 miles west of the town, where the Trans Canada Highway runs parallel to the river. There is no lack of wild life around there, and I was feeling quite vulnerable. There were very few vehicles, but eventually I saw a car coming from the west. I decided to cross over and try to get a ride back into town. A classy car stopped and a very attractive young lady picked me up. Her dad was drunk, asleep in the back. As we arrived back in Banff, she offered to have me stay with her overnight. The sailor's uniform may have conveyed a message I did not intend. I convinced her to drop me off at the RCMP office in town. That's when I found out that Canadian police do not provide "accommodation" for Canadian military. They told me about a boarding house down the road. I didn't have enough money but I carried a post office bank account passbook. The owner of the boarding house agreed to let me stay, with a promise that I would not leave town without going to the post office and getting the money the next morning. I never really carried money with me on the trip.

I was awakened the next morning by a girl, who came into my room in a black negligee, offering me her services. I never had anything like this happen before I decided to go to Bible college. I got up and out of there quickly, got the money for the boarding house from the post office, along with bus fare to Vancouver, and continued on my way.

From the Vancouver bus terminal, I got a city bus to Fraser Street and Marine Drive. Since the college was on Marine Drive I decided to walk the last little distance. Well, I had no idea how far it was. I arrived at my destination drenched in sweat with my suit case and duffle bag and was sitting in class on October 15. I should mention that since I was quite certain that the Navy would not release me, I applied for release on the very day that school started several thousand miles away. Looks like God wanted me there!

CHAPTER 14

NORTHWEST BAPTIST THEOLOGICAL COLLEGE

As I try to get started writing about NBTC, I hardly know where to begin. The very idea of Art Mitchell going to 'college'! One of my life heroes was Dr. J. H. Pickford. Not only was he the President of the college, he was one of the main professors, an author and a family and personal counsellor. He was a model to all of us of spiritual passion, godliness, wisdom, knowledge and in my case, long-suffering. He apparently only slept 3 hours in 24. He was totally focused on the moment. I remember that some of us put a whistle in the exhaust of his car. That afternoon, he jumped into the car, started it up and went down the road and out of sight but we could hear the whistle long after we lost sight of him. The next morning we could hear the whistle coming back. He drove into his parking spot outside college hall, shut off the car and walked into the building with no indication that anything was unusual.

I often spent time in his office, sometimes voluntarily, sometimes not. I don't know how much I should mention about the non-voluntary times. It seemed that when I went to see him about anything, though he was one of the busiest men I ever knew, he always seemed to have plenty of time. He acted and spoke like there was not another thing in the world that was more important. For me, a guy who was used to being considered of little value, this had, and continues to have, a huge impression on me. I do not understand, to this day, why he didn't throw me out of the school.

As I write, my mind bounces from one "adventure" to another. "There was the time...." Where do I begin? To keep tuition down, each student had work to do on campus. We raked leaves, cut grass, washed dishes, painted, scrubbed, peeled vegetables and many other things that I can't recall now. With all that work, and study as well, how could anyone find time to get in trouble? It's all a matter of priority, and it seems that getting in trouble must have been one of my main priorities. My motorcycle was not all that noisy, but whenever I would race it around the lawn and jump it down into the valley, students and teachers would gather at the classroom windows. Then Wally let me drive his 1947 Harley and I could not make the turn beside the chapel and took out the flower garden. Bob wasn't too happy when I dropped the water balloon on him from the men's upper bathroom roof. Larry seemed a little upset when we lowered his Mini Minor into the dry swimming pool. I dropped way down on Tim's list of nice people when I "tried to fix" his watch with my hunting knife and a hammer. There is really not enough room to record all the crazy things that, if I was the school president, I would have likely kicked out the perpetrator. As I recall those days, my mind is way too full of pranks and silliness, that I am not all that proud of today. If any of my old classmates ever read this, I am sure that they will have plenty of other tales that will likely be embellished with time. Unfortunately, most will probably remember those frivolous events much more than the times when I was buried in my books, studying – and not without good reason.

While I very much admired Dr. Pickford, there were other wonderful men of God who taught many great lessons. More than that, they demonstrated godly character and modelled powerfully and passionately what they taught. Not many of them had doctorates in those days. That is not to say that they were any less brilliant than those with rows of letters sprinkled behind their names. They did not teach courses on the "Theology of Church Growth." We were left fairly ignorant of how to set up hugely expensive audiovisual "theatres". Much more emphasis was placed on building churches that built up believers who would go out and boldly live the Christian life, than creating places where "seekers" would feel comfortable. Yet, in those days, I remember the churches being full and many new believers catching the excitement of living and witnessing for Jesus. The professors instilled in us an unquenchable desire and a sense of excitement for God's Word. Systematic Theology was not taught as a science but a living, unveiling of the character of our God, in three relevant Persons. There was no course on Spiritual Formation.

MINISTRY ASSIGNMENTS

What we learned in class was much more than theoretical knowledge. From the beginning, each of us was given ministry assignments. In my first year, among other things, I had a Sunday school class at Ruth Morton Baptist Church. On Sunday evenings, the student body would go together to different churches and sing and share our testimonies. In each of those four years I was part of the traveling choir, and for a time I led the male quartet that represented the college in western Canada.

In my second year, I worked with Pastor Howard Philips at Marpole Baptist Church. He was unable to get out much because of his health and age, but he had a passion for door-to-door evangelism. Since he could not do it, he would send me out each Saturday to different neighbourhoods to bang on doors and try to share the Gospel with people. At the end of each day, I would meet with him in his house to discuss what had happened at different homes. I still remember going up to houses in different areas. Some were warm and receptive, some were polite but closed, and others were "not interested", but in general there seems to have been much more openness than there is today.

Pastor Philips was sort of a "pastor to the pastors". He was what we would today call, a mentor. He and his wife would have hot chocolate and some "goodies" for me when I came to give my report. He would ask questions and give suggestions and encouragement. I had a Sunday school class, and my main task during the Sunday morning service was to read the Scripture. It seems that I never read without messing it up somehow, but he kept on having me do it.

At the beginning of my third year at NBTC I was assigned to Metropolitan Tabernacle, and I continued to work there, under Pastor Bill Clayton for several years, even after graduation. Today, my assignment would be called Youth Pastor and Worship Leader, but neither of those "titles" existed then. I worked with the youth from high school through young adults and led the congregational music in the different services. Among the youth, there were several lovely young ladies – not that I noticed! Not to mention the great selection of female theologues and those seeking a 'Mrs.' degree at the college. As it turned out, I ended up marrying the pick of the crop from Met Tab.

When I was still in the Navy in Victoria, I was encouraged by the youth group at Central Baptist to go out into the parks and give out Gospel tracts and share Christ with anyone who would listen. I convinced a few of the students at NBTC to join me on the streets and in Stanley Park. We gave out thousands of tracts and spoke to many people about Christ. It was sometimes a bit scary but so encouraging when we got together after to share what God had done.

In those days NBTC was on Marine Drive near Boundary Road in Burnaby. There were three buildings: "College Hall", "Braeside" and the Chapel. College Hall was a lovely old, stone mansion that had been owned by some lumber baron. It was three stories high plus a basement. The two top floors were the men's dorm. Classes, the library and offices were on the main floor. The dining hall, kitchen, laundry and storage were in the basement. The stone walls were covered in ivy.

Braeside was the name of the ladies dorm and the residence of the cooks, who acted as guards for the ladies from the inhabitants of the men's dorm. It was also an old ivy-covered mansion and I believe it was originally occupied by the second-in-command of the lumber company. The chapel used to be the coach house in the old days. That is where most of the classes were taught. There were beautiful lawns with plenty of mature maple trees. The men were responsible for cutting the lawn, cleaning up the leaves and any other outdoor jobs to keep the place tidy. A stone wall separated the parking area, near the road, from the grounds. The driveway came in the western end of the wall, passed in front of Braeside, then College Hall and up through the eastern end of the wall. Behind the main buildings the land dropped off to "the pit". It was a lower area that had been tennis courts and more lawns with a swimming pool, that in our day, was overgrown with thorny blackberry bushes. The drop from the main lawns to the level of the pit was likely fifteen feet; a perfect jump for my little motorcycle. Below the pit was a forest that ended at the Fraser River. If you hiked down to the river you could run out on the huge log-booms that were tied up, waiting to be processed in the nearby mills.

NBTC was only one chapter in my life, but it would not be hard to expand that chapter to a book. Many of my life's dearest friendships began there. There were two friends named Bob, Larry, Tim, Wally, Joel, Paul, Fred, Ken, Warwick, Baldy, Don, Johnny...and many more. Conspicuous by their absence are the names of ladies with whom I may have had some connection. Way too dangerous to go there! It would be fun to write a chapter on each one of those men, but then they might write something about *me*. That is just too risky!

Oh, the adventures! I would be tempted to go into detail about the time when we were preparing for exams and a bunch of us marched through the library and over the tables, each one "playing" musical instruments that we did not know how to play, with poor Haptain Wong yelling, "You guys gonna frunk out." Or the time I tried to scare a mouse that was living in the hollow rafters in the ceiling of the study hall by luring it along, tapping with my fingers and then smashing the rafter with *The History of Christianity* by Kenneth Scott Latourette. Unfortunately, the light fixture got between the book and the rafter. Professor Richards came into the room, and seeing me standing on the study table, holding the book on top of my head to shield me from the flying glass, he said something like, "I'll leave for now while you concoct your explanation."

Because I arrived for my first year one month after classes started, I could not catch up with first year Greek. Somehow, I managed to handle the other subjects.

Since I needed four years of Greek, as well as two years of Hebrew, I had to take both Greek 3 and 4 in my final year. As a kid who hated French and failed it every year in high school and was also "invited to discontinue" Latin, I was definitely not gifted in languages, especially ancient ones. I wish I could say that because of my lack of scholastic aptitude, I worked extra hard, but there are too many witnesses 'out there' who could be quick to correct that statement. I loved many of the subjects and admired the professors, but I could have demonstrated that love and admiration a lot more effectively by spending more time in the books.

Somehow after four years I had passed all of the required subjects for a Bachelor of Theology degree. In some cases, this may have been just by the skin of my teeth. Since I had not graduated from high school, I was granted a four year Bible Diploma. I was advised that since I was 25 years old, I qualified as an "Adult Student" in B.C. If I attended an approved college and successfully completed certain academic subjects, equal to first year, I would have the equivalent to high school graduation. I found an apartment in a home, across the street from Vancouver City College where I took History, Geography, Economics and can you believe it, English and German? God was beginning to give me a love for languages. I didn't know how important that would be in the future. With the credits in hand, I went back to NBTC and was granted my degree.

CHAPTER 15

SUMMER JOBS

I did not have the money to pay for even my first year at Northwest. They allowed me to finish that year with some debt. During each summer break, I was able to work, so by graduation in 1967 I had paid all my school debt. In the summer of 1964 I went to Waterways (now Fort McMurray), Alberta. I did several jobs around town and helped Pastor Art Hoehne at the Waterways Baptist Church. Then I was offered a job up in Fort Chipewyan, working for Canadian Fish Producers. I ran a small outfit that rented boats to the Indian fishermen. I had a couple of young men working for me. Mugler Peche and Wilfred Ratfat would chop ice from the ice-shack and pack it into tubs full of fish that I had bought from those who rented the boats. An old Norseman, Mark IV float plane would fly up from Waterways. We would paddle out with the tubs of frozen fish, pile them in, wipe the oil off the side of the plane and off it would go. No freight was ever tied down - just open steel washtubs stacked on each other. I sort of recall that we put 22 tubs of fish at 88 pounds each on board. That was the plane that flew me up to "Ft. Chip".

I knew little about planes then, other than that ones like Billy Lazelle's peddle plane really didn't fly. Even with my limited knowledge I sort of felt that the instruments on the panel were supposed to be working. I noticed on my first flight that the oil pressure, fuel gages, RPM, VSI and magnet compass were the only things on the panel that worked. That far north, the magnetic compass is not worth much since it is trying to point downward more than any direction. I sort of recall that the pilot's name was Walter Goulet or something like that. I believe he was a Christian. He apparently was not afraid to die anyway. He only flew "contact" (VFR) since there were no operating gyros. Sometimes with the low ceilings and visibility contact meant the floats were almost contacting the water or the trees. On that first trip I left my previously ingested breakfast in a little tobacco tin that was between the seats. Not realizing the danger I was in, it sort of spurred my desire to fly.

My brother Tom came up there and during part of that summer we went off into the forest along the trap lines and cut firewood. We lived under a tarpaulin in fairly primitive conditions. Do you know if you boil a tea bag in a can of water over a fire long enough you can get several cups of very potent "tea"? We would cut and stack cords of wood along the trails and put a mark on each pile. Our mark was two squares, chopped into one log on the top. Then we would go into town and sell the wood where it sat. Trappers would buy it, sight-unseen, trusting that it was an honest cord and where we said it was.

For a few days the fish company paid me to camp out in the Wood Buffalo National Park. I can't even remember what I was doing there but each day I had to report by two-way radio. One day I saw a buffalo scratching himself on the pole that was holding up my radio antenna and had to chase him away.

During the time that I was living in town buying fish, the local Northern Canada Evangelical Mission (NCEM) missionaries had to leave for health reasons. They were burned out! They asked me to carry on the ministry while they were away. Not a lot of people attended but I had a chance to preach and visit. While Tom was there with me, there were forest fires burning up in the Northwest Territories. You didn't have to volunteer. The forestry people just conscripted every able bodied person to fight the fires. A Beaver aircraft on floats took us along with a few other men to the fire. One disadvantage of a float plane is that you cannot fly at night.

We took off after 11 pm and landed just before 1 am. Since it was summer it never got dark that far north. We fought fires for about a week and then were flown back to Ft. Chip.

Near the end of my second year at NBTC, Art Hoehne, the pastor at Waterways (Fort McMurray) was in need of someone to take over the church work for five months while he attended to other things. A few of the students applied but somehow they called me. I remember that at the end of the college choir tour, we were somewhere in eastern BC when the tour broke up. Warwick and I hitch-hiked to Calgary where he lived. He went home and I continued on. Just north of the city the snow was blowing, and it was after midnight, so I dug a bit of a shelter in the snow bank on the side of the highway and settled to sleep for a while. Some time later, a couple of police woke me up and took me to a cafe. After the warm up, I got back on the highway and caught a ride to Edmonton in an 18 wheeler. The visibility was horrible in the blowing snow. I think the driver just wanted someone to help him stay awake.

I had enough money to buy a ticket on the Northern Alberta Railroad, the "Muskeg Special", from Edmonton to Waterways. It was fun to stand at the back of the train and actually watch the rails rise up after the train had passed over. That was the summer of 1965 and it was one of the most challenging, wonderful summers of my life. Art and Ella Hoehne were still there, which was such a blessing. I got to preach every Sunday morning, Sunday evening and Wednesday prayer meeting. I also had a Bible class on Sunday before the morning service and taught a group of young boys every second Thursday. Gib taught the alternate weeks.

On one of those evenings, Gib didn't make it, and it was his turn to teach. I played with the boys for a while in a local park, and eventually decided that we better go back to the church where I shared some totally unprepared "talk" with them. I don't know what I said but to me it was just something to fill the time. At the end, because I didn't know what else to do, I asked them if any of them wanted to accept Christ. I sort of recall that there were nine boys and that five of them stayed and prayed, most sincerely to become believers. One had bandages on a knee from some surgery and insisted, along with the others, to pray on his knees. I have prepared a lot of messages over a lot of years but I can't recall a response like that. Humbling!

The memory is not as clear as I wish it was, but I recall one of the first "jobs" I had after arriving there was to go and minister to a couple, whose two year old son had wandered too close to the sleigh dogs and was killed by them. If I thought that being called "Pastor" was heady stuff, I was very wrong. The people were very appreciative and encouraging, but if I learned anything, it was that I had a lot more to learn. The church paid me what they could but it was not enough to pay for the next year at college, so I worked in my spare time driving taxi, school bus and a concrete redi-mix truck. I also ran a D9 bulldozer on night shift.

Waterways was very different in 1965 from 1964, when I first went there. In '64 Ft. McMurray had a hotel, some government buildings and a few stores and that was about it. The road went from the Athabasca River to Waterways and not much more. People told me about the "tar-sand" and if you walked out into the bush much you would see it here and there but there was no processing of it, just talk. In '65, when I returned, things were very different. They were building a bridge across the river and several companies had contracts to build sections of the new highway that was to come up from Edmonton. It had become a 'boom-town'. Some of my college buddies came up to cash in on the job opportunities. I think Larry and Brian were among them, and about midsummer Ann and Elaine also arrived to help me with the children's groups.

There were some adventures with my part-time jobs. Like the time I had the drunk in the taxi who wanted to fight, or the time the driveshaft broke on the cement mixer when I had a full load of concrete, and we had to weld it back together on the spot to make the delivery before the load went solid. There was this little kid who would sit behind me when I was driving the school bus. His dad was the manager of the airport. To make it up the hill to the airport, you had to put the bus in second gear and floor it. A couple of times, the kid would wait till we were almost at the top of the hill and would reach forward with his foot and kick the bus out of gear. That was a long hill on a narrow gravel road and backing down it was more than a little challenging. One day, in the interior mirror I saw him slipping down in his seat to try it again. A metal lunch pail was handy and I used it to make a nice groove in his shin bone. I'll bet he still has a scar today. So sue me!

Growing up, I never went to any sort of organized kid's camp, never mind a church camp. A part of the ministry of Waterways Baptist Church was to run a Christian camp at Anzac, a few miles from town. In those days there was not a lot of published curriculum, so I was sort of winging it. The boys that attended this camp were mostly from the local Indian reserve. I had arranged some cool crafts like making miniature birch-bark canoes. These were not the sort of boys who sat in little circles and listened attentively to the nice leader. During "activity" time, they went into the bush and rounded up wild horses. They would chase them through an old barn, where others were waiting in the loft to try to drop on the horses as they came running out the end of the barn. After that summer I went back to college with a much greater desire to pay attention to my instructors and with an acute awareness of my ignorance and limitations.

During the summer of 1966, after my third year, I stayed in Vancouver and spent much of the time working, as a "swamper" on a Coca Cola delivery truck. That was probably the year that I found my place on the Amway pyramid – the bottom. I also remember selling Watkin Products, door-to-door. There was one customer who always bought plenty of Watkin's liniment. I don't think he had a problem with sore muscles. It may have had something to do with the alcohol content of the product. My work at "Met Tab" with the youth and young adults continued through the summer along with these other adventures.

I believe it was near the end of my last year at NBTC that I started working "graveyard shift" at a plywood mill down on the Fraser River. In all my life, I have never been a good "union man". I operated a veneer dryer. Logs were brought up from the river, into the mill on a chain ramp to a lathe-like machine that spun them and shaved off thin sheets of wood, sort of like opening a giant scroll. These sheets were graded and stacked on pallets. The pallets were then carried by forklifts to the dryers where operators would feed them into stacks of rollers which then carried them through what looked like multi-layered ovens, or kilns. There the moisture was removed in preparation for laminating them into plywood. I operated one of about four dryers.

On graveyard shift there was not a "quota" of work to do, like during the day and afternoon shifts. At the same time, I sort of enjoyed seeing how much veneer I could process. My father had taught us a work ethic that required doing your best for your boss so that you would make him look good. This was considered a better way to keep your job than to rely on shop stewards who treat the employer as if he were too rich and greedy. I recall the mill being shut down one time when a worker was sent home for being very drunk while he worked over a conveyor belt that carried wood into the "chipper". Had he fallen...well it would not have turned out well. There are unfair employers and there are also workers who hold employers hostage while they produce the least amount possible.

I was told a couple of times, "People who work too hard, might get hurt." One night I was waiting for a new pallet of veneer when a fork lift driver, with a load weighing about a ton drove it against me, crushing my left leg against a steel pillar. I passed out over the load and he drove away. Another forklift driver saw me there and was able to dig me out. The next day, in the hospital, a union rep came to visit with some goodies. He reminded me of the danger of working too hard and making the "brothers" look bad. After the worker's compensation ran out, I returned to the mill but didn't stay long.

After finishing my fourth year at NBTC, I spent that summer back in Ontario. Part of the reason I went back 'home' had to do with a young lady, who had moved from BC to Toronto. During the summer I drove a paving truck. After a few weeks the company bought a couple of old Euclid S-18 scrapers. You know, those earth moving machines that look a bit like a dinosaur. I got a couple of hours training and started moving dirt, lots of dirt. To this day, that was the highest hourly wage I have ever earned. It was a staggering, $3.60/hr. How could a guy even spend that much money? The tires were seven feet high. In those days there was no safety cage or even a seat belt. The engine screamed so loud that it was almost impossible to be near them without earplugs. I remember one day arriving on the site without ear protection. I had to pull up some grass, crush it into wads and jam them into my ears. Even with that I was almost deaf at the end of the day.

I had purchased a car with some of my new fortune. It was a sleek looking Triumph Herald Coupe. It looked pretty but it was no BMW. The panel was pressed paper, which made it easy to install any instrument. I just had to cut a hole with my pocket knife. From the windshield forward it rotated forward to access the engine. That made it exciting when the hold-down fasteners failed when you applied the brakes, which they had a habit of doing. The driver would be staring at the inside of the 'bonnet' which totally blocked all forward visibility. I decided to drive it the 2700 miles back to BC. Along the road I picked up a hitchhiker, who ended up getting stuck with me in Wawa, northern Ontario, when a piston rod started knocking badly. I had to pull out the crankshaft, order a new rod, piston, rings and bearings and hitchhike to Thunder Bay to have the shaft machined and return to reassemble the motor. Two days and we were back on the road.

Now, I had finished my last year at Northwest and was studying at Vancouver City College. I lived with another single guy, just about a block from the student nurses' residence at Vancouver General Hospital. One morning, after work, I came home to find my roommate running around on the sidewalk in front of the house where we lived. When he saw me he came running, saying that our landlord was in the garage, dead. His wife was in the driveway and his car was idling just outside. I ran into the garage, expecting to see his body lying on the floor but instead, was shocked to see him hanging from the rafters. On the workbench was an open book with an illustration of how to hang a deer for cleaning. A drawer from the workbench was lying against the bench, that he had apparently been standing on. He had been dead for well over an hour. Eventually, the police came and after taking their pictures, cut him down. After that, I found an upstairs apartment on Twelfth Avenue right across from Vancouver City College and coincidentally about a block from the nurses' residence. Do you notice some repetition here? More about that later...

Somewhere along the line I studied for and got my insurance agent license and worked for Abbey Life and then Life of Alberta. My office was on the eleventh floor of an office building in downtown Vancouver. I could leave the office at noon, drive across the Lion's Gate Bridge to Seymour Mountain and ski, then be back in the office to work in the afternoon. After I sold insurance to most of my friends and family (lucky people) my insurance career ended.

It was probably about then that I started selling cars at Trapp Motors in New Westminster. "Nine acres of new and used automobiles - the biggest Pontiac, Buick, GMC dealer in western Canada." They taught us the "turn-over" system of selling cars. It had been developed by a psychologist and some actors in

California. What a system! There were seven steps that you took your client (victim) through. If at any time it looked like they might get off the hook, we would apologize for not being able to help them and "turn them over" to someone else who would continue through the process. Then you would split the commission. I learned a lot about manipulation and deceit (sales). One thing we were trained to do was to go out to some large mall parking lot and put notes on the windows of certain cars. The notes would be written on a torn, brown paper shopping bag and they would read, "Sorry I couldn't wait. Please call me about your car." And there would be your name and phone number. The "victim" would call, wondering what happened to their car and we were to say, "Are you the one with the white Chevy." (or whatever type of cars you had tagged that day) Then we would explain that the dealership had promised a car just like that to a customer, who was coming in soon. But another salesman had sold it off. "Have you thought of selling your car? We really are in a fix and would offer almost anything for it." That was called the "set". The hook would then be swallowed and away we go with the seven steps to get them into a new car. And it really worked! When offering them a new car, we were to use lines like, "If I can make you a deal that will satisfy you in every way, will you drive this car away today?" Believe me, there is no safe way to answer that question. Throughout the presentation, we worked in the "Highball - Lowball - Highball." The system worked so well that often the buyer left the lot with a vehicle that they did not really want or need, paying more than the sticker price and thinking they had cheated the dealership. Anyway, being a pastor and a salesman for Trapp Motors had, shall we say, some sense of conflict? It was definitely not my "calling" and I ended up buying a car at "employees discount" that was actually more than it was worth. But it was pretty! It was a 1967 Pontiac, Firebird and it was fast! Pretty cars attract pretty girls. What a deal!

CHAPTER 16

WILLIE

This was about the time that this really pretty girl came into my life. She was more than just pretty. She was the catch of catches. Why she ever took any notice of me I'll never know. As the "youth and young adult guy" at Metropolitan Tabernacle I worked with some lovely young ladies and being so 'mature' I took turns falling in love with them, well at least wondering which one might be the right one. There was something very different and special about Wilma Lloyd!

I had met Willie a couple of years before when my roommate, Larry brought her into the Tab. She was attending Vancouver Bible Institute in Surrey, while waiting to enter nurses' training at the Vancouver General Hospital. Yes, the place with the nurses' residence about a block from where I lived. Now she was attending the Tab and as time went by, although she was sort of shy, she stood out. I learned early on that she had a passion to serve God from her youth. That was great but she was convinced that she was being called to Africa. I should mention that after graduation I had spoken to different mission representatives and felt "called" to South America.

Actually, at my graduation ceremony, the main speaker, who could not return to Bolivia for health reasons, announced that he had found his 'replacement' and that I was it. I did have a sense that some mission representatives seemed more desperate than divinely guided. However, since I was likely going to South America and Willie was aiming for Africa, it did not seem wise to allow myself to get too interested. But she was so wonderful that I thought that I should 'line her up' with some of my buddies. We went on a few double-dates; her with one of my buddies and me with some other girl. I had no idea that she was happy to be on these dates but not with the buddy. If she was interested, she kept it a good secret while I was getting more and more interested. I warned myself, "Don't get yourself involved with someone who is totally out of reach."

We were together at many youth events and although I may have been with another girl, it was hard not to notice her. There was that time at Qualicum on the beach! Then at that costume party in North Vancouver. She was dressed up as an old "hay seed farmer" in coveralls and my date came as a "Greek goddess" but I had a tough time paying attention to the one I was supposed to be with. But oh, that time at Boundary Bay, she wore that little red swim suit and I probably bumped into things because I was not watching where I was going.

Then there was that night! The youth were out visiting shut-ins and carolling one Christmas and Willie and I were riding together in the back of Hughie's car. I sort of slipped my arm up behind her on the top of the seat above her shoulder. She didn't move away or give me "the glare". After a little while, I let my arm drop down - just a bit onto her shoulder. No adverse response! So far, so good. Then, I dared to put my arm right on her, expecting her to pull away, glare at me or hit me. But instead she snuggled up. Wow! Willie? Really? Even as I write this, I remember the excitement I felt. She could do so much better but she was interested in me! I still wonder why she "picked" me. There were others who were eager to catch this treasure. Others had already asked her to marry them, great guys, mature guys with good backgrounds and the ability to give her a comfortable life. Did she know she was going to end up living such a challenging and at times risky life? She could have had stability and security.

If I was counselling her then as an outsider, I would have likely tried to talk her out of getting involved with such a gypsy; a fly-by-night, fickle, poor, immature, "pass by the skin of your teeth", twenty five year old boy. In fact, I know there were those who tried to do just that. Even Pastor Clayton, my mentor, who unfortunately knew me quite well, sort of indicated that she was much better than I deserved. I remember even after marrying us, he pointed his finger at me and said something like, "You take care of that girl or you'll answer to me." For years after we were married, Willie would give him a report on our anniversary.

But I am getting ahead of myself. Before that fateful evening, and after my job selling people automobiles that they didn't want and couldn't afford, I got a job driving for Mair's Charter Bus Line. That was a fun job. They had about a dozen coaches and I don't think that there were two of the same kind. I would take skiers up to Alta Lake. Today that is Whistler Mountain but then there was little more than a gas station, a parking lot and a chair lift. I enjoyed taking sports teams to tournaments. Trips to North Vancouver Island were great. Much of the trip involved sitting on the ferry and resting in some hotel during the competitions – and getting paid for it! Wherever you stop the bus for a meal, the driver eats free. Growing up as I had, "free" was always one of my favourite words.

One night, Willie was riding along with me on a "shift change" to the Riverdale Mental Hospital. I would go through New Westminster picking up staff, deliver them to the hospital and take the ones going off duty, back home. This particular evening I had quite a cold and had taken some Dimetapp antihistamine. We were on the return part of the trip, driving past the penitentiary when a big white street sweeping machine crossed in front of me. I stopped the bus to let it pass. Most of the passengers didn't notice but Willie did. She asked me why I stopped and I told her that I was letting the machine pass by. She informed me that there was no machine nor any other vehicle within sight. The bus driver, me, was hallucinating. Maybe I had taken more Dimetapp than I needed.

Way back in high school, Bob Crosier and I talked about joining the police. In those days, policemen were respected by almost everyone. [*My computer grammar checker says that I should not use a gender specific word like "policeman" but use "police officer". Sorry grammar checker, in those days police officers were policemen.*] Bob went on, after school, to become an Ontario Provincial Policeman (OPP). But even after hanging by my knees and lifting weights to stretch myself, I could not force myself past five foot eight, the requirement back then. While driving bus, I saw an advertisement for Federal Correctional Officers. That was pretty close to being a police officer so I applied. After the required checks and interviews I was accepted as a "CX2" (Correctional Officer level 2) at the British Columbia Penitentiary in New Westminster.

There was a minor problem. There would not be a training college for six months. So for six months I worked in all the positions with minimal training. In fact, after the formal, Correctional College training, I did no more or less than I had done before. Before the college I took "on-the-job" courses on weapons, physical restraint and self defence, security, law, and also trained to become a K9 officer.

I can now say that I served two years in a maximum security, federal penitentiary. Fortunately, I didn't have a number on my uniform and I went home after each shift. Over all, I enjoyed most of my time there. I had plenty of time to sit and talk with inmates. I found many of them very open to the Gospel. On the "outside" it is very hard to convince people that they are sinners. On the "inside" although many insist that they are innocent, they generally accept the fact. Since it was an ex-con that led me to Christ, it was a very special privilege to share Him with these men. And there were those who prayed to accept Jesus as Lord and who displayed evidence of His life in theirs.

When I finally got to attend the correctional college, which was held in facilities just outside the prison wall, it was not a real challenge. Others, who attended from all parts of western Canada came with very little idea of the operation of a penitentiary. In fact, during an evening class, a supervising officer came into our class declaring that there had been a possible breakout. Being evening, there was limited staff on duty and they needed men in the towers, that were not normally manned after lockup. Other positions needed staff and regular on-duty officers needed backup. Two recruits manning number three tower for over an hour, while the rest of us searched inside and outside the walls, eventually called down to one of the searchers on the ground. They were wondering if the rope laying over the wall was "normal". Umm! Waddayathink?

In the two years that I served, there were not a lot of problems. Most of the time things were "quiet" but when things went wrong they went very wrong. We had a couple of escapes, some attempted killings, beatings, two riots and a hostage taking that ended in one civilian employee being killed.

At night, after lockup, there was only one officer who was on duty, outside the buildings and inside the wall. That was the K9 officer. We were equipped with a Police Positive 38 caliber revolver with five bullets, a two-way radio and our dog. The dog had a leash about 8 feet long and we often carried a fifty foot riot leash. If you saw anyone outside any building they were assumed to be escaping inmates. Any officer who wanted to go from one building to another had to radio the K9 officer, who would stay out of the sight of the officer to observe that he was not acting under the duress of an inmate.

The dogs that we used were not like police dogs that are trained to be kind to the public. These animals are trained to respond to their handler *only*! Even the people who train the dogs cannot approach any of them when they are 'on duty' without being severely mauled. During the course that I took to become a dog handler, one of the trainers did not follow the required protocol and the dog turned on him. They were trained to protect and obey their handlers at all cost. It was not all that frightening to be alone at night on the prison grounds. Once an officer was wounded and they had to shoot the dog to get at the officer to help him. At the end of a regular shift, your animal was returned to its kennel and if you did anything at all that was not the proper protocol, that same dog who moments before would die for his handler, would now happily and viciously attack him.

One shift I heard shouting and banging coming from inside a covered corridor that ran from one cell block to another. I can't remember what the problem was but a group of about fifty inmates were rioting. They were in the middle of the corridor, trying to break through the wall to the outside area. I got a call from inside warning me that they were attempting to break out of the building and the walls were thin enough that they could possibly do it. I only had the five bullets that were issued with the gun. By the way, we were not issued our own weapons but each shift we drew weapons according to the job we were doing. I was definitely feeling vulnerable. The dog could likely disable more people than I could with my gun. If they got out and got to me I would need to make sure that I had used all my ammunition or they would use it on me. I stood there aiming at the place where the most noise was coming from. The dog seemed to be really looking forward to the action. Fortunately, the officers inside were able to put down the situation. I think they used water hoses.

Another thing that I remember was the haircuts. There were several trades that inmates could learn. Given the choice, they would have liked to take lock smith, gun smith or long distance running but for some reason those were not available. Several trained as barbers. It cost me $6 per year to have my hair cut and I went every two weeks. In the beginning, I have to admit that I felt rather disadvantaged when I realized that they also used straight razors. When they had new officers, some of them enjoyed slowly stropping the razors while glaring at the throat of their nervous "customer". My hair has always been fairly thick and they liked to use me to practice for their exams.

I have to take a break from the prison story to discuss another event that concerned Willie. You see, I was engaged to her longer than she was engaged to me. Here's how that works. I had proposed. She had said yes. We were engaged, right? Well she promised to marry me but I didn't have the money to get a ring, yet. According to her, the hardware was the proof. Anyway, as soon as I could I went into Rose Jeweller's in Vancouver and ordered the ring. At this time, Willie had finished her RN and was working in Powell River. She was planning to visit her sister Karen Newton in Surrey, just about the time that the ring was ready. She did not know that I had ordered it. I was working that day in number four tower on the front wall of BC Pen. I got my brother, Tom to go to the store and pick up the hardware. I called on the phone from the tower to the front gate to let them know that he would be approaching the wall. He came out to the penitentiary and I lowered a bucket on a rope to receive it.

That evening, November 8, 1969, I went over to the Newton's place to see Willie. I had no idea how I was going to make the presentation. So, I asked her if she wanted to go out for a drive. We went to Dairy Queen and bought Dilly Bars. On the way back, I told Willie that I thought I heard a 'ring' in the engine. I stopped, looked under the hood and returned with the ring. I know. That's pretty lame. But for ever after, November 8 has been "Dilly Day" in our family. In Africa, where there was no Dairy Queen, Willie and the kids started a new tradition. They would somehow find a big dill pickle and decorate it with whatever they could find to make some little creature. Today, Willie generally has one of the grandchildren help her produce the annual Dilly. If I forget Dilly Day, it is almost worse than forgetting our anniversary. Although I was "engaged" to her before that, it became "official" on that day for her. It's all about the hardware.

A posting for an "inmate counsellor" came up and with my degree in theology and pastoral experience, I was qualified to apply. I was turned down because as an experienced officer I , "had been exposed to the prison environment, and might be biased in my dealings with the inmates." Really! There were some great "perks" in working at BC Pen. We got to eat in the officer's mess and the food was the best you could imagine. In later years I ministered in logging camps where the food is unbelievable. In the prison it was even better. We ate the "leftovers" from what the inmates had the previous day. There were steaks that covered the plate, butter only, margarine by doctor's orders only. If and when the inmates were served spaghetti or macaroni, it was thrown on the walls and officers were threatened. It was definitely no Hilton but the food was fantastic. That made it hard on my new bride. It was during my time at the prison that we were married. I would arrive home where Willie had prepared something special for dinner, like fried chicken. The problem was that I had just consumed a steak or two with all the trimmings at work.

We were married on August 22, 1970; more about that in a moment. My father could not make it out to BC from Ontario for the wedding because of "some sickness". A few months later, we found out that he had cancer. I approached the administration at BC Pen about taking leave to see Dad. They told me that I could take time before he died, or after for the funeral but not both. Willie still had not met him. I was assigned two inmates for transfer from BC Penitentiary to Kingston. That covered the cost for me to travel. Then they bought a 'spouse' ticket for Willie that, in those days, was a very reduced fare. I had to pay them back for her ticket.

We could not sit together in the plane or even acknowledge each other. The RCMP escorted me and my prisoners to the back row, on board. I handcuffed them to their seats and then the rest of the passengers were boarded, unaware of the "special guests" on board. Willie came on with the other passengers and sat near the front. During takeoff and landing, my charges' handcuffs were removed, according to law. No one, especially my special travel companions, knew that I deliberately put my revolver in my carry-on baggage, stored above me. The crew were aware of our situation but they also thought that I was armed. I believe that there is no good way to use a gun in a pressurized aircraft and having it on me could possibly make it accessible to the wrong people. They could see the lump under my jacket from the holster and that was enough.

After landing in Toronto, we waited until all the passengers disembarked and the RCMP officers came on board. They escorted us to the cells at the airport. We waited until the uniformed escort from Kingston came and received the inmates. By the way, to keep our presence on board the plane inconspicuous, I wore civilian clothes. Interestingly, there was no such thing as an Identification Card or even a badge, issued to Correctional Officers in those days. I did have all the paperwork for my two "friends" but how did the police know that I was not one of the "bad guys"?

Willie and I spent a couple of weeks with Mom and Dad. Up until our arrival, no one had told Dad that he was not going to recover. We visited him in December and he died in January just after his 54th birthday. That was the only time that Willie ever saw him and he was in horrible shape then. Smoking, driving the old coal trucks and working in a gypsum plant had contributed to the lung cancer and the alcohol, lifestyle and family genes produced the colon cancer. She had never experienced his great sense of humour or been exposed to his teasing. Any girl that I brought home got "the treatment" from my father. If he really liked them, he would really tease them. If he didn't think much of them, he was "politely silent". He would have really given Willie a hard time.

After working at the prison for a year, I was eligible for marriage leave. Like I said, we were married in the summer of

'70. While Dad could not come, Mom, my sister Florance and her husband Ron did make it. By this time I had rented the basement of a small home in Surrey, BC. There was an "L" shaped room for kitchen, dining room, living room, bedroom, ballroom, whatever.... To get to the toilet, sink and shower, we had to go out into the unfinished part of the basement, across from the workshop. I lived there for a few months before the wedding to prepare our little "nest". I never met the owners before we were married. They were away and their daughter rented the place to me.

Mom, Florance and Ron arrived on the Thursday and stayed at the "nest". I worked Thursday afternoon shift and then did a "double". I worked right through the midnight shift as well. When I got home in the morning, the four of us drove to the ferry. To get from Surrey to Powell River, where we were to be married, you have to drive though Vancouver and North Vancouver to the BC Ferry at Horseshoe Bay. We boarded and I found a place to stretch out and catch a little nap. When I woke up, I realized that all the people I saw were coming on the ferry. I staggered to the windows and realized that the ship was preparing to depart. I raced down and off the ramp just as the last vehicles were boarding. Eventually, I saw my car sitting up in the parking lot. Not being able to find me, Ron drove the car with the others off the ferry.

An hour and a half later we arrived at the second ferry and eventually made it, late Friday afternoon to Powell River. There was the rehearsal and regular preparation. I'm afraid I was too tired to remember but I'm told we had a great time. I slept, that night on the couch at Willie's sister, Jean's place. Well, I really was afraid to sleep. You see, I had not been "nice" to some of my friends, before their weddings and I was scared that they were planning some evil to get even.

The wedding was in the old Westview Baptist Church, a few blocks from Willie's parent's home at 4752 Joyce Avenue. That was the same home where Willie had spent her whole life, up until she went to Vancouver for nurses' training. By that time I had lived in at least 25 different places. The girl had no idea of what she was getting into. That church building was later sold to Mormons to Willie's great horror. Pastor Clayton "tied the knot". The vows were very traditional. I still remember "plighting my troth". Old vows or not, the deed was done and she was mine! "Signed, sealed and delivered" as they say.

The reception was at the Powell River Motor Inn just behind the Lloyd's home on the land where Willie played as a little girl. No way did I want to go back on the ferry after the wedding. Not with all our friends. We did not let many people know but I had planned for us to fly back. At the Westview airport, the photographer wanted to get a nice picture of the two of us standing on the boarding stairs. To do that, we had to wait until everyone else boarded, including a couple of our friends. Of course, when we finally got in the plane there was one seat in the front and one in the back, with our smiling friends in between.

I had hidden my little VW Beetle in the Vancouver Airport parking lot. I had good reason to fear that my 'buddies' might have found it and sabotaged it. They did, but we didn't know it until the next day when I turned on the vent and confetti flew out all over the car. We drove from there to our 'nest' in Surrey, stopping by a Chinese take-out on the way.

The next day, we drove up to Mara Lake, in the Shuswap area of central BC. The parents of a nursing friend of Willie had offered us their cottage on the lake for $25 for the week. It was beautiful! A neighbour took us all around the lake in his boat. The weather, scenery, hiking, swimming, cottage and bride were perfect.

After the honeymoon, we settled into our little home. I went back to prison and Willie got a job at the Royal Columbian Hospital, quite close to the BC Penitentiary. Both of us were on shift so it never was practical to drive to work together. I don't remember how long we were in our little basement apartment but we eventually rented a "normal" apartment near the Guildford

Mall. In the mean time, Willie left the hospital and started studying towards an LTh. degree at Northwest Baptist Theological College. It was a three year course but with the credits that she already had from Vancouver Bible Institute, before her nursing school, she was able to do it in two years.

CHAPTER 17

IN HIS EXCITING SERVICE

In Willie's final year at NBTC we were both helping out at the Langley Baptist Church, where my old college roommate Paul was pastoring. At the same time, we were continuing to pray about serving in missions. Peter Stam was the director of Africa Inland Mission Canada and he was speaking at the college for a few days. We arranged to meet with him. When we told him that we wanted to find what work God had for us and that other mission reps seemed more interested in fitting us into their mission than helping us find God's will, he made a comment that I will never forget. He let us know that he was more interested in helping us find God's will for our lives, where ever that might be, than to fill a "vacancy" in his mission. His response had such an impression on us that within days we applied to Africa Inland Mission.

After all the paperwork, interviews and references, we received a letter from Mr. Stam, declaring that we had been accepted as "missionaries under appointment for service in Zaire." The letter was written May 2, 1972. Just days before that, we received another bit of news. We were going to be three! On June 1st of 1972, I wrote the first of very many "prayer letters". In the letter, I excitedly announced that the Mitchell "family" were stepping out in faith, believing that God was calling us to Africa. At the end of the letter, without ever realizing the significance of it, I signed it, *"In His exciting service, Art & Willie Mitchell."* Each of the letters that we wrote from that day on was signed this way. How could I have dreamed just how 'exciting' it was going to be?

With Willie about three months pregnant, we travelled from BC to Toronto to begin AIM candidacy training. We stayed in the basement of the mission office at 1641 Victoria Park Avenue in Scarborough, Ontario. Don Walcott, another candidate lived with us. I remember poor Don going out in the middle of the night with me to find potato salad for Willie. When a pregnant lady has "cravings" for something in the wee hours of the morning, there is only one thing to do, if you want to get some sleep.

I can't remember everything we did during the Canadian part of our candidacy but I know that we spent two weeks going through, "psychological profiling" with Dr. Stan Skarsten at the Institute for Family Living. By that time in my life, having studied some psychology and counselling, I had developed a distrust, or maybe it was just fear of those weird guys and their funny tests. By the end of the two weeks of really intense sessions, I developed a profound appreciation for this godly man and the valuable things that we got a chance to learn about ourselves. Of all the training that we did in Canada and in the States, the thing that probably had more to do with our success overseas than most, was the time spent with Dr. Skarsten.

Everyone in the group 'broke' somewhere along the way. Rather than being threatened by that, we learned about our strengths and just as importantly, our weaknesses. Knowing where we were most likely to fall and how to recognize the indicators that we were approaching our limit, allowed us to establish strategies to avoid many problems. Later, on the field, when I remembered that, life was a lot more successful. When I ignored it, I generally paid the price.

After the "psych prep", we spent four weeks at the Toronto Institute of Linguistics, learning how to hear, transcribe and reproduce sounds that were often very unfamiliar to our ear and tongue. In that time we were taught how to learn a foreign language, as well as how to "fit in" to a strange culture. In the last two weeks we actually learned to read, hear and even tell stories in the Pidgin language of Papua New Guinea. After that we did our first "deputation", where we took six meetings in one day in Minden. "Deputation" is a word that strikes terror in the minds and hearts of many missionaries. We had very little training on just how to do it but God was faithful.

Then through August we attended the formal Mission Orientation in Pearl River, New York. For the first two weeks we had classes, seminars, Bible study and fun. We learned more about the ministry of the mission and just where we would best fit in. The final week was spent in Newark, New Jersey. The male candidates slept in a down-town mission with the men off the street. Our clothes were taken from us and fumigated. We slept dormitory style, locked up in the large, very hot room. For breakfast we had porridge that was cold and slimy. Then we loaded into vehicles and were driven out through locked, barbed wire gates through the streets to our assignments. The painted centreline on the street divided the Puerto Rican from the Black population and no one dared cross that line. Kids with almost no clothes sat on the lawns watching expensive TVs next to Cadillacs that sat, stripped on cement blocks, at the curb. It was a time when racial tension was very high in America. Black Christians drove us through the neighbourhoods. As they did, they were shouted at and accused of being "Oreos". The women candidates got to stay in private homes, which was better but not great. A man was killed the previous night on the lawn of the home where Willie and Dorothy stayed.

Through the day, we gathered kids off the street and set up a "Vacation Bible School" in a local park. I remember, when we were registering them, we had this little black guy. When we asked him for his name, he said, "Tomato". "No, what do your parents call you?" "Tomato mister." "No, what name is your real name?" "All I know is Tomato mister." And the other kids confirmed that was the only name they knew him by. Our time there was excellent for cross-cultural training.

For the next several months we travelled and visited as many churches and individuals as we could. We had to raise our prayer and financial support before we could leave. Normally, it took about a year to do this but God proved His faithfulness, and that He was going to be our Provider for the many years of service that followed. When we were not traveling, we were packing. Everything had to go into steel barrels that were then welded shut. Seven copies of the contents were listed in French and English with their estimated value and whether they were new or used.

As the time got closer for the birth of our baby, we had to stop living "on the road". The Foster family in Delta, BC gave us a room in their basement where we stayed for the birth. On December 9, 1972, Hope Louise Mitchell was born at the Surrey Memorial Hospital at 2:45 a.m., one of the most wonderful days of my life. Our commissioning service was held on January 15 at the old Langley Baptist Church. Since he had already been a very big part of our lives, Bill Clayton preached, challenging us and those present.

A few weeks later the three of us were back on the road. Traveling through northern BC, Hope often slept in a dresser drawer, sometimes with a heating pad under her blankets. The three of us hit Prince Rupert, Smithers, Burns Lake, Houston, Prince George, Edson, Edmonton, Lloydminster, Saskatoon, Fort McMurray, Drumheller, Crossfield and Calgary on one trip in an old, borrowed car that was definitely not ideal for the winter trip. Some of the speaking engagements were not even confirmed before we set out. In 34 days, we had 25 meetings and covered 4,600 miles. By the time we finished that trip, Hope had pretty well spent half of her life on the road.

At the beginning of April, we took a "step of faith" and rented an apartment in Neuchatel, Switzerland, where we were to begin French language training. A couple of weeks later, discouraged, I took a temporary job in the forest at Powell River. On about the third day on the job, Willie drove out to the worksite to tell me that a Church in the Bahamas had heard about us and were providing the remaining amount of monthly support for us to leave. When I got home that afternoon, Willie met me at the door to announce that an anonymous donor had sent in $1,000 towards our "outgoing expenses" and later that day we found out that someone else gave $100. In 1973 that was a huge amount of money; more like about $10,000 today.

CHAPTER 18

SWITZERLAND

About three weeks after that, we arrived at our new apartment in Peseux, near Neuchatel, Switzerland, with our heads spinning. Hope was just five and a half months old. Now you have to remember that in high school, I never passed a French test and I was sort of proud of that. After our studies at the Toronto Institute of Linguistics, I was eager to learn. In high school, I was only interested in learning what might make me a better truck driver. French did not seem important. Now, I really wanted to learn because I would need this language to be able to communicate effectively. The business of a missionary is to communicate. My motivation was totally different. I attended classes full time and Willie found a tutor so that she could study and take care of the baby. The city of Neuchatel is between the Jura Mountains and Lake Neuchatel – very Swiss! We studied hard but there was time for hiking and over our time there I owned several 'moped' bikes and eventually a Vespa 125 motor scooter. With Hope in her backpack on Willie's back and Willie perched behind me on the Vespa, we took time to enjoy the beautiful country side.

It was hard but I really enjoyed learning the language. To learn to speak another language well, you have to be able to laugh at yourself. I had plenty of opportunity to do just that and to provide a good laugh for others around me. I had been trying to find one of those baby walkers; you know, the circular plastic things that the baby sits in, with a sort of tray to lean on and castors that allow her to scoot around. Like so many things, I think some clever lawyer managed to have them recently declared too dangerous. Anyway, in those days they were still legal. Someone told me that they were available in a certain store nearby.

My ability to communicate was still quite challenged so I didn't want to talk too much to anyone. I waited until it was dark so I could look into the store without being noticed. I thought that I could locate the walker, dart into the store, point and grunt, buy it and retreat. I waited until everyone in the store seemed busy and entered. As soon as I did, a little bell rang and it seemed like everyone there turned to welcome me. Without making eye contact with any of them, I quickly made my way to the back, where I had spied the item. Pointing and sounding like a cave man, although a French cave man, I got my prize. The nice lady offered me a carton to carry it home in and showed me the instructions on how to disassemble it so it would fit in the box. Since I am so mechanical, I decided to take it apart myself to save the nice lady all that trouble. She kept telling me how simple it was. Again, being so capable with things like this, I had it all in little pieces in no time. I guess I must have really impressed her and the others who were gathering around to watch. It was about then that I realized that she was offering me one that was already disassembled and in the carton. Amid the snickers and comments that fortunately I could not understand, I reassembled the unit, paid for the one in the box and slinked out of the store. For the rest of our time in Peseux, I never returned to that store.

Two young girls, aged 16 & 17 came to live with us and to attend a local school for Canadian girls. One was a fairly new believer and the other accepted Christ in our home shortly after arriving. Willie and I were really working hard at our French studies and beginning to communicate more. But our evenings got quite tied up with Bible studies. We had study time with the girls on Monday and some Tuesdays. Wednesday evening other missionaries, who were there studying, came to our place for Bible study and prayer time. Friday evening we hosted a French Bible study. Some of the students became very close friends.

The local people were so helpful. One couple had access to a beautiful chalet on the Italian side of the country and invited us to spend a week with them and another missionary couple, high in the Alps. At another time, during a two week break from school, I got a job in a small 'factory' in the mountains near Peseux. For the entire time, I had to drill two little holes in thousands of small pieces of brass that were about 1 1/4" x 1/2" x 1/8". I had no idea what the items were for and no one else in the place knew what the things they were making were used for, other than that the company made some parts for spy equipment of some sort. We were not to look at the work of others or discuss our work with them. With the money I earned from that I was able to buy the Vespa.

Hope had her first birthday on December 9, 1973 and the explosion happened on the 10th. At about 4 p.m. each afternoon I would arrive home on my scooter. I drove into the narrow lane by our house, parked the Vespa and went up to the third floor of the building. Willie was standing in the kitchen with Hopey in her arms, about three feet from me. I was still in the hall. Suddenly, almost all the windows in our building blew out. I did not hear the full volume of the blast because I was in the concussion and the pressure plugged my ears. Willie got the whole noise. I ran back to the window and saw rocks, parts of telephone poles, wires and dirt falling everywhere. I ran down the stairs and out front to where I had just passed along the road. A three story, stone house with walls 18 inches thick was mostly gone. It was two houses from us and all the houses there were joined together.

I was the only one conscious on the street. One man lay dead against the PTT building (post office). A shoemaker eventually came staggering out of the bottom of the wrecked building yelling that a woman was buried in a car. I could see a part of the car and I started pulling the rocks and dirt with my hands. After a couple of minutes others started arriving and someone joined me to help dig out the car. At one point, I realized that the place where I was throwing debris had a pair of blue jeans sticking out of it. Then I realized there were running shoes at the ends of the legs. There was a child, mostly covered in rocks. I quickly started uncovering her. The man with me just grabbed her by the hips and ripped her out of the rubble. It was obvious that her back and many other parts of her body were broken so I went back to uncovering the car. With the material on it, it was compressed to about two feet high.

By this time some emergency people were arriving and someone had one of those metal cutters that work with a chain saw engine. They cut the pillars holding the roof on the car. When we ripped the metal roof off, the fabric liner was still covering the interior so we could not see if anyone was inside or not. For a moment no one touched the liner. It was as if each person did not want to know what was in there. Finally we looked and the car was empty. There had been a woman standing beside the car but the blast had thrown her across the street where both her legs were broken by a stone planter on the sidewalk. She was laying outside a small coffee shop just outside our front door. There were several people sitting in the shop with all the ceiling material down all around them. They were in shock and no one moved until the police arrived several minutes after the blast. They were mostly parents of children from the nearby school, who each day would meet their mothers or fathers on the way home. If the explosion had happened moments later, several of those kids would have been killed. If it had occurred about two minutes earlier, I would likely have been killed.

Amazingly, only one man was killed. The child, somehow survived with back, arms and legs broken and a fractured skull. The lady with the two broken legs and a few people with minor injuries from the coffee shop were the only other casualties. Big pieces of the building had flown over the top of a seven story building about three hundred meters away. The explosion was attributed to a gas leak.

CHAPTER 19

AFRICA

On July 14th we left Neuchatel by train and travelled to the French border. There we had to switch trains, which would not normally be a problem but no one told us the train we were to catch, was at another station. By the time I found out, we had to run as fast as we could dragging our baggage. The customs official saw us coming and just opened the gate and stepped aside. The train was already moving. Willie and Hope got on as I was running along throwing things onto the steps of the last car. I finally grabbed the hand rail as my feet could hardly go any faster, and made my way up the stairs to my cheering family.

We spent the night in Brussels and flew out to Kinshasa, Zaire, by way of Cairo, Egypt. At 10:30 pm we touched down for the first time in Sub-Sahara Africa! We were expecting someone to meet us but the people there hadn't received our communication – surprise #1. When it looked like they were going to shut the airport, I figured we better see what we could do. It was very hot and humid. No one looked like an official but everyone acted like they were. Someone declared that he was in charge of customs and demanded that I open our bags. He proceeded to take items out and give them to others, who just took them as their own and walked away. Things were going downhill very quickly and there was no one to whom we could appeal. With nothing more to lose, I started shouting and claiming that we had been invited to this country and that important people were expecting me and they didn't know who they were dealing with. It worked!!! To my surprise, our "official" sent people running to retrieve our stuff. Then he put a white chalk mark on each bag, ushered us out of the "terminal" and locked the doors.

Someone who claimed to be a taxi driver started carting our things to an old car. Never let these guys put your things in the locked trunk of their car! The only place to go was into Kinshasa but we had no idea where after that. The driver suggested that there was a mission guesthouse that he knew of. We arrived in the middle of the night at a locked gate to a compound. The driver then demanded way too much money and we only had Belgian francs. Since he had our baggage, we had little choice. Someone there allowed us to put our things in a screened in storage room and we climbed in and from what I recall, we just slept on top of our things until morning when we met the managers. Sure enough it was a Mennonite guesthouse and the people where wonderful. We spent the next few days finding our way around the city, getting visas, registering with the Canadian embassy and arranging our flight to the opposite side of this vast country. There were no representatives of Africa Inland Mission in the west of Zaire but we met other missionaries and people from a Christian travel agency, who were very helpful.

We flew with Air Zaire (also called Air Zero or Air Maybe) to Kisangani and the crooks were waiting. We checked into the Wageni Hotel. It was famous because that was where missionaries had been killed a short time before while trying to escape the "rebels." I learned over our years in that country, that "rebels" was an appropriate name or description for many groups including members of the actual Zairian military. I left Willie and Hopey in the hotel and went out to find something to drink. I was able to buy some Coke but they would not let me leave with the bottle. I went back to the hotel and got the others. When I arrived at our room, they were standing on the bed to avoid the huge scorpion beetle that was zig-zagging all around the floor. We went out into the streets to find something to drink and check out the place. We "just happened" to walk by a compound where there was a white man working under the hood of his vehicle. I wish I could remember his name but he was a missionary and he invited us in where we joined a wonderful bunch of missionaries who were having a going-away party for one of their own. They were all so welcoming and helpful.

The next morning, at the airport we continued with the crooks. We were charged a 'special' fee because they thought that we had left Europe over weight, although we were not overweight there. Willie and Hope were put on the plane while I dealt with the crooks. The amount was determined just as the ramp for the airplane was about to be pulled away. They apologized that they did not have enough time to give me a receipt because the engines were started and the plane was leaving! Just like at the French border, a few days before, I had to run to catch up with my family. This was mid July and Kisangani is in the middle of the jungle - hot - humid!

Touching down in Bunia, in the centre of the AIM region was a powerful, emotional experience. We had arrived! But the crooks were waiting. In Kinshasa, our passports were taken and we were issued a paper with lots of stamps on it. According to the very angry, local "officials" in Bunia, this was worthless. They demanded that I show up at their office later so they could determine the consequence of this violation. This time, on arrival, some of our own AIM missionaries met us and we were released into their care. They prayed and later, took me back, where after getting quite a lecture from the official, he put one more stamp on our papers and declared it officially acceptable. We were treated royally by the AIM folks in Bunia. I even got a chance to preach for the first time in Africa, although it was translated.

After a few days we went by "road" to Rethy, a mission station where we were to live while we learned Swahili. Rethy had a printing press, a hospital (with no doctor) and the missionary kid's school. The altitude was over 7,000 feet, so although it was not too far north of the equator, the temperature was comfortable and there was no malaria. We had spent 15 months studying French in Switzerland. In about three months, our Swahili was almost as good as our French.

Our "final" destination was Linga, just one hour through the rolling mountains from Rethy. During our language study, we had the chance to make some visits there that made us study all the harder. The need was so great in Linga. Before ever moving, I was designated as the station repair man and teacher in the Pastor's Training School and Willie was to spend the main part of her time at the medical clinic, which took care of the villages in the local area. The Grafe family was there and Betty Wilson, a veteran missionary who ran a school for women, where they learned Bible, basic health and home making skills. All of the mission staff would be leaving shortly for furlough and we would need to be there to take over the work.

In late November of 1974 our barrels from Canada arrived at Linga. We were about to receive them when Willie suddenly began having pain. By two-way, HF radio it was determined that she needed to get to Nyankunde Medical Centre as quickly as possible. At the same time, Hope and I had our first case of malaria. By road that would be a very rough, one day trip. There was a Mission Aviation Fellowship (MAF) airplane in the air, not too far away. The pilot, Hank Warkentin, landed within a couple of hours and after a 35 minute flight we were at the centre and Willie was being prepared for surgery to repair an abdominal hemorrhage. While they were at it, Dr. Tommy Westcott removed her appendix, since it was acting up. I was so impressed with the amazing medical care in much less than ideal accommodations. I was also impressed with the work of MAF! Imagine being able to fly these "bush planes" into remote places, saving lives, delivering critical supplies, Bibles, evangelists, health workers and evacuating the sick and wounded! Wow! But only the most skilled, courageous, spiritual super-heroes could do something like that, right? Certainly, it would be a ministry that I should never even dare to dream of.

From what I have heard and experienced, Zaire (the former Belgian Congo and the Democratic Republic of the Congo today) has never had a time of peace and even today, as I write, parts of the country are considered by the United Nations to be the most dangerous place in the world for women. The eastern and northeastern region has traditionally been the worst. In conversation with senior missionaries, they referred to the timing of events as "before or after the second or third or whatever evacuation." I have to limit many of my 'stories' and experiences because most people would not believe them and any credibility I may still have would be threatened.

At Linga, we had some wonderful times and some very unwonderful times. The three main tribes in the region were continually at war, sometimes openly but often through hateful secret acts. Tragically, even some of the families attending the Bible school, where I was teaching, were suffering and those causing the suffering were sometimes other student families. Things that we said, even in the Bible School were reported to the MPR (Popular Movement of the Revolution, the one and only political party). "Official reports" went out that the missionaries were hoarding limitless quantities of money that had been sent for the Africans but were intercepted by these cruel white people. They were told that everything that was in our homes actually belonged to the people and if they could get rid of us, money would pour in to eliminate all the poverty. In fact, anything that we did bring into the country with us had to be declared as the property of the church and the church was under the direction of local bishops, some of whom exercised their authority and claimed things like the generators, vehicles and other equipment.

At the same time, there were wonderful godly Zairian men, who stood against the corruption, propaganda and evil. For some of them, it was a costly stand. They were examples to us of the power of God in lives profoundly changed by the Gospel. Some of these godly men may not have had the formal training or degrees that we had. In fact, some didn't even own their own Bible, never mind a personal library. But the wisdom they had was very much worth seeking, especially by us "newbies" and we did.

Remember that back in high school, I was no teacher's favourite student, especially French teachers. I did not demonstrate any gift for language learning. So it was particularly amusing that my first actual ministry assignment in Linga was to teach *French* in *Swahili* to the Bible School students. Don't tell me that God doesn't have a sense of humour. Eventually, I taught more subjects.

There had not been a course in Christology so I put a curriculum together and began teaching it. The students were training to be pastors. Some had already served as such with the limited information that they had. Overall, they were very tolerant and somehow understood what I was saying. But one day things got very confusing. I was teaching about the miraculous virgin birth of Jesus. I guess, the way I was teaching made it even more miraculous. You see, there are two words that sound very similar; 'birika' and 'bikira'. It is a very minor difference, don't you think? However, 'bikira' means virgin and 'birika' means tea kettle. They didn't laugh or even correct me. They were too polite for that, but some of them did look confused.

While I taught at the school and did other things on the station, Willie spent much of her time at the dispensary. Our house was one of four that circled the top of the hill. The dispensary was about 300 meters down the hill towards the village. The Bible School was near the mission houses and the students homes were in a couple of rows on another side of the hill. Most of the local people were friendly, even though according to the MPR, we were supposed to be hoarding all their wealth under our beds. It was not a place where anyone felt safe. Quite often, in the middle of the night someone would come knocking at our door to tell Willie there was an emergency at the dispensary. Most often it was a maternity case that was going badly. Sometimes, I was away on a trip and Willie would be alone with Hopey. In the beginning, the other missionaries were around and sometimes Willie would have to leave Hope with them and go down to take care of a patient in the middle of the night. When we think back now, we wonder where the courage came from. God protected them both.

In Rethy, the station nurse Carolyn Saltzenberger, had taught Willie to do a procedure called a symphysiotomy. In that region, because of poor nutrition, many women had pelvic cavities that were too restricted for their babies to pass through. Caesarean sections were much too complicated but by cutting through the cartilage in the front of the pelvis and allowing it to open a little, many babies were safely delivered that would otherwise have died, often along with their mothers. Registered Nurses in Canada are not trained or even allowed to do any procedures like these, neither are they permitted to diagnose and prescribe any drugs but that was just part of a "normal" day's work out there.

I had to do, or hire others to do, any maintenance and keep any machinery going. On the station, we had a three kilowatt, single cylinder diesel generator. We would turn it on at 6 p.m. for three hours each day. There was a device to turn it off "automatically" that was made of an alarm clock with a string tied to the alarm winder that pulled a teeter board. On the board was a bag of bolts that would then fall off and, through a couple of pulleys on the ceiling, pull the lever that shut off the fuel to the generator. It worked great but more times than not, we forgot that it was getting close to 'lights-out' and we would be fumbling around in the dark looking for candles.

For a few months, the Grafe family was still there. Three of their children were away at the missionary kid's school in Rethy but the youngest, Marky, who was a little younger than Hopey was around as a playmate. About the time the Grafes left, a family up north were looking for someone to care for their pet chimpanzee,

"Rosie" while they went on a one year furlough. Rosie moved in with us. Well, she was not supposed to be in the house but.... I would tie her to the mud-walled shed out back but she could untie almost any knot. She would make her way into the house, "piddle" on the floor and come looking for us, handing us her rope, knowing that she had done wrong and needed to be tied up. I had built a play-area in the middle of the hill with slide, sand box etc. where Rosie and Hope would have tea parties and play together.

Hope had different babysitters that would take care of her while I was teaching and Willie was busy seeing patients. One day, the sitter arrived with a long string of locusts. They had been "skewered" and were wriggling. When Willie asked what they were for, she was told that they were for baby "Opi". Willie then asked, "To play with?" "Oh, no! To eat." was the answer. They actually taste pretty good but I only tried them fried. Hope our 'mini missionary' likely spent more time in the village than we did. She spoke a funny mixture of English, French, Swahili and Kilendu. I could not always understand her but that did not slow her down at all.

For some time, little Hope had no missionary kids or siblings to play with. However, for a short time she had an African "sister". Life was considered cheap and death was all too common. A young woman had died in childbirth in a nearby village. The "dead" child was taken from the body of the woman and left in a corner of the hut with other garbage. Several hours later, someone noticed that the pile of junk was moving and that the baby was alive. She was brought to us and Willie was able to clean her up and treat the injuries, which included cuts on her head and pressure ulcers from the violent birth. Hope would have been three or four. She took on the role of "big sister". Somewhere we have pictures of the two of them together.

I can't remember how long she lived with us but soon some people, who had earlier rejected her, now seeing that she was alive and doing well, came to claim her. In one way we felt happy for her but by this time we had grown close and had thought of the possibility of keeping her as our own. Because she came to us on a Sunday, we named her " Baby Sunday." We never heard much about her after she was taken away but we were told that she was then named "Tsethasi." Africa Inland Mission, in those days had a policy that missionaries were not allowed to adopt Zairian children. That may seem hard but there were good reasons for that policy. Today, I have several friends from Africa who have adopted children and it has turned out wonderful.

The Early Years

Probably about the time I started dreaming of flying.

Art, Florance and Tom

Edna and Charlie

Art, Edna, Charlie and Tom

Mom and I. Seems there has always been a church in the background.

Charlie, Tom, Florance and Art

6 Blong Avenue as it was 75 years ago

The teen years

The Navy

The four 'survivors' of Class 17, Royal Canadian Navy, Academy of Music.

HMCS Naden, wearing his Number Fives

Able Seaman, 47589H

10th from the left, back row

On Parade at HMCS Cornwallis

Northwest Baptist Theological College

Hard at work. College days.

Correctional Officer, Graduation and Wedding

CX2, Officer Mitchell – I can say that I served 2 years in a maximum security, federal penitentiary.

How did this ever happen?

This pretty young thing had no idea what she was getting into.

IN HIS EXCITING SERVICE

Africa

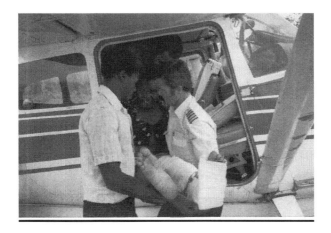

Air ambulance

A common runway for getting in and out of villages

Why we use aircraft

My favourite office in my favourite bird (Victor Juliet).

My favourite bird, "Victor Juliet".

A few of the children at a local village

The Bible school graduation in Katshungu.

Regular engine inspection on a Cessna 206.

Nose strut

A few pictures from many newsletters over the years.

Common to have huge crowds come to meet the plane.

Andrew helping Art plan his load (Victor Juliet)

Willie, Amy and Andrew entering a small jungle village

We worked hand in hand with local mechanics to keep the 'birds' in the air

"Thirty Flight, Thirty Flight, Victor Juliet!" That would be the call that Willie was waiting for as she recorded my flights for those years.

Hope and Rosie

The Puppet Ministry team in Dodoma, Tanzania

Flypass

This and the one above were promotional photos for Flypass Ltd.

"110 mile per hour half ton pickup".

The dedication service for the first missionary CH 801, for Venezuela

Michael Dawson, the first CH801 missionary pilot, addressing folks at the dedication.

The 801 leaving Flypass hangar for Venezuela

Assembling Michael's 801 in Venezuela

VY-33X, The Venezuela 801 during flight testing in Puerto Ayacucho

Both my plane and my plans came to a crash

John Morgan

Breslau Country Manor

Shantymen and The Flying School

The Shantyman float plane – Found (FBA2C) CF-RXI at a logging camp

CHAPTER 20

FILL'ER UP

There were always shortages of just about everything. Diesel fuel, kerosene and gasoline were seldom easily available. One time, when we were almost totally out of diesel, I heard that there was some at Oicha, a mission station near the equator. I think that I will just copy the prayer letter that I wrote on November 1, 1975. Here goes:

"A couple of weeks ago I had to make a trip with our borrowed Land Rover. It started out as quite a normal event. One sick person had to be transferred to the medical centre at Nyankunde and from there I planned to go on to Oicha to pick up some kerosene and diesel fuel. The whole trip is about 120 miles 'as the crow flies'. An hour after we were supposed to leave we were ready, with five extra of the sick person's friends who just had to go "a few kilometres down the road."

Since it hadn't rained for three days around here, I left my rain clothes, boots and chainsaw behind. A couple of hours later, after having cut through several trees across the road with machetes, we came to a 'detour'. By this time the rain, that I was sure would never come, came. As we travelled along the detour, the trail continued down, down, further and further. One of the Africans with me assured me that it was a good road. He had been over it only 22 years before and had no trouble. Suddenly, we came to a low valley with several trucks, cars and Land Rovers. Many of them had been stuck for days and assured us that it would take a few more days before they could get through.

I decided to go all the way back to the detour sign (a pile of bushes) and try the 'bad' road. After about one hour along this road, I found out why it had been closed. We found, at least, 300 people laying trees through a swamp that used to be a road. I worked with these people for a while, then sat on the hood of the Land Rover, to relax and get out of the slop and muck. Other vehicles had arrived by now, one of which was a beer truck. Much of its cargo was now consumed by the others waiting and the women who are always there at such times and who were making the rounds of the drivers, trying to earn a little money. One of the leaders of this immoral lot decided to approach me. With all of her friends there, she received not what she was after, but the Gospel as clearly as I could say it. She and her friends later thanked me and I noticed that she left her drinking and sat alone quietly until I left.

Four hours later I was on my way again. Finally, these folks who "only had to go a few kilometres", had reached their destination. By the time we arrived in Bunia, where I was supposed to buy some things for folks further down the road, all the stores were closed. It was now dark, but I had to get on to the medical centre in Nyankunde with my patient. The road was so good that I could get up to around 35 miles per hour now. Suddenly, at this incredible speed, I hit mud again. The vehicle continued down the road sideways. I was waiting for it to flip over when the wheels caught solid ground and shot into a bank on the side of the road. Fortunately, it was a bank of sloppy muck rather than rocks. We were all shaken up but there was no damage. At the end of the trip the patient, who had promised to pay for the transportation, decided that he couldn't afford the full price. He was far from poor.

I stayed at the medical centre that night. Next morning I woke early, only to find that the hydraulic clutch system was dry (no clutch). After bleeding it and not finding any leak, I started out to finish my 120 mile trip. Most of this day's trip was through the Ituri Forest, which surely deserves being called a tropical rain forest. Just before entering the forest, the clutch just stopped working. When travelling, it is not hard to change gears without a clutch, but when stopped it is almost impossible. You guessed it! I got into some mud again and ended up well grounded. To try to move was unthinkable with no clutch.

Finally, a little Mbuti Pygmy came along. I asked him to pump the clutch while I dug a hole to lay in the slop under the vehicle to bleed the clutch. The Pygmy was afraid to get into the Land Rover "that thing that is only made by man's hands" so he just stuck in his little leg to pump the pedal. In the process I used up all my spare fluid and still had no clutch. I drained a little from the brake system and got enough clutch to change into four-wheel drive and get out of the hole. I finished the 120 mile trip in only 16 hours on the road, which was a few days faster than most others.

When I got to Oicha, I was told that the fuel that I had come for was not there. I would have to go on further to find some. Since leaving home I had not refuelled. Nor did I have extra with me and my tank had just enough to get me to the next place, if I didn't get stuck. Having spent one day at Oicha, rebuilding the hydraulic system, I went on in search of my fuel. On arriving in the next town (Beni) I was told that they had not had diesel fuel for over six weeks. Now what?

Well I don't think I have ever spent such a time of concentrated prayer in my life as on this trip, and this was no time to stop praying. A young fellow, who had come along from Oicha for the ride suggested that we might try a trucking operation in Beni that was run by a fine Zairian Christian named Victor Ngezayo. I was able to get a little more than enough for the return trip, but it was well over the going price.

The next day I left early with my precious load of fuel and kerosene. I travelled through the forest in a convoy of trucks. Just as I arrived at the medical centre the clutch went again. This time it only took about 45 minutes of adjustment and I was on the road again. When I arrived in Bunia, the stores were just closing, so many of the things I was to buy, had to be forgotten. I also found *that a lot of people were expecting a ride home with me, but because of my load, I had to leave some good friends to find another way. I wouldn't have gotten stuck again if there had not been another truck stuck. By trying to go around him I got into it once more. Two more hours with the truck and on I went. It was starting to get dark but I thought I would try to get home, after all, what else could happen?*

While rounding a bend in the road, at almost 10 mph, my head lights struck the form of several people standing on the road. I supposed that they would move as I got closer. Then I saw that they each had a rifle and they were pointed at me! With the vehicle stopped and prayer continuing I asked what the problem was. They were drunken soldiers with their 'weekend women' and some cases of beer, and they were angry. They wanted me to unload my barrels and passengers and take them for a ride. After some negotiations they decided they could just get in with my load. As it turned out, only two soldiers, one woman and one case of beer was able to squeeze in. When I asked who should be charged for the broken springs, one pointed his gun at my head to show he meant business and growled, "Pole pole Bwana" or "just take it easy."

When the soldiers in the Land Rover decided they had gone far enough, they told me to stop. As I opened the back door they got out into the road with their guns and their woman. Then as one tried to get their beer out past the barrels, the other started fighting with him. We grabbed their precious stock from the vehicle, put it on the road and took off home. That's sort of a rough outline of the trip. I have left out a few juicy details. I suppose muck can be called juicy.

It was more than just a trip for me. It was a tremendous time of learning. I began to learn that, my Lord really does know the way through the wilderness. I had a chance to really see God perform and He allowed me to share in a learning experience that no amount of money could pay for. I can recall praying several times along the road, *"Lord, don't you think I have had enough for one lesson?" The Lord just loves to show us how great He is and how feeble are our plans and efforts.*

While the snow is piling up back in Canada, we are entering our hottest time of the year. Hopey will be having her third birthday on December 9. Then, even though Christmas is not supposed to be celebrated here, we are praying that our friends will, at least be able to remember the birthday of Christ in their hearts. Pray for them! It is business as usual for the Zairians on Christmas day. We have been enjoying unusually good health. So much is happening as a result of your prayers. Please continue. Praise the Lord also that you can still celebrate Christmas openly - others cannot.

In His exciting service,
Art, Willie & Hope Mitchell"

Life in Linga was becoming much more challenging. Some local church leaders were put out of the church because of corruption. Some were being threatened and poisoned. The Grafe family had left and Betty was preparing to leave. That left us alone. Witchcraft was very present in many ways. Politically, no one was in command but everyone seemed to try to take command. There were two Zairians plus Willie and me, trying to teach and Willie still had all her medical responsibilities while my station responsibilities were much more than I could handle. I was teaching courses that had never been taught in that school, mostly because we had never had a fourth year. About 30% of the AIM, Zaire staff were leaving the region, either for furlough, for assignments elsewhere or were just quitting.

The churches were going through growing pains and it was becoming more difficult for our mission leadership to enter into it without being accused of being "colonial" or "patronizing". We were increasingly being threatened by armed men from different sides. "Officials" felt free to just walk into our house, especially when I was away, and 'liberate resources'. Then one day, with "soldiers" all over the station, a 12 year old missionary girl, staying with us, was "handled" by soldiers. There was nothing we could do.

CHAPTER 21

WHAT NEXT?

That evening, after notifying our directors in Bunia by radio, we left with two suitcases, a duffle bag and a few books. We dropped the traumatized girl off at her home in Rethy and continued driving the rough mountain roads to the Uganda border. On the way, we dropped off our borrowed Land Rover, named "Ebenezer" and picked up a car that belonged to a lady, Millie Colton, who had left earlier and was waiting in Kenya. We drove through the night and after passing through the Uganda, Kenya border, we tried to sleep in the car on the side of the road. It was too cold so after an hour, we continued towards Nairobi.

As I write this account, I have been reading through more of the prayer letters that we wrote during those days. One of the things that stands out is the amazing amount of prayer that our friends back home were doing. We experienced some fear and frustration but over all of that, we had a wonderful sense of peace that God was not unaware or unconcerned. We had no way of knowing just how intricately He was orchestrating all the details.

We were about one hour away from Nairobi, passing a road that led to the Rift Valley Academy (RVA) in Kijabe. This was about 22 hours from when we had left Zaire. At that precise moment, we spotted some friends, turning onto the highway from the Kijabe road. One minute sooner or later would have meant missing them entirely. We had not seen them since we were together in Pearl River, New York for mission orientation. They stopped and we learned that they had been at RVA for a break and were just starting the two day drive back to their station in the Northern Frontier District (NFD) in the northern area of Kenya, towards the Sudan border. Right there, they asked us if we could join them for a while at Loglogo, their mission station.

We knew that it would take about two weeks to arrange our departure from Nairobi to Canada and we had no plans for that time. Their Land Rover was completely loaded and we had to deliver the car we had to Millie in Nairobi. They turned around and we all drove back to RVA, about 20 minutes off the highway where another missionary, I think it was John Barnet, immediately offered to drive us to the NFD. This was not, "just around the corner." This would cost him about five days. To this day, I cannot understand why he felt led to do this. We spent the first night at Ngurunet, where his brother lived. We had left the car at RVA for another person to take to Millie.

This was nice, but it made no sense to us. We were exhausted, confused and totally unaware of what God was up to. We spent Christmas in the dessert among the scorpions, camels and cattle of the Samburu, Rendili and Maasai people. It "just so happened" that a missionary pilot, Barry King with Sight By Wings, was flying through in a couple of days on a tour of the stations in the NFD and "for some reason", the missionaries at Loglogo had arranged for me to go along with him. I certainly didn't object!

Now I have to remind you that from way back in my childhood days with Billy Lazelle's toy airplane, I had always dreamed of flying. In fact, in my sleep, I frequently dreamed that I could fly over trees and around my friends, who were ground bound. In the Navy, I sometimes visited the Greenwood Air Force Base and stared through the fence at the planes and imagined flying them. In Linga, I had attempted to build a hang-glider from bamboo and cotton. I remember talking to Willie about the possibility of learning to fly but we came to the conclusion that it was something absolutely out of my reach and that I should, once and for all, get the silly idea out of my mind. Even in discussions with the Canadian director of AIM, Pete Stam, he told me clearly to make up my mind to abandon any thought of flying since "AIM would never become involved in aviation".

While flying with Barry to the different stations, I realized that the dialect of Swahili that I had learned was very similar to what the people there understood. The Christmas that we had planned on spending in Linga, Zaire was spent in Loglogo, Kenya. Our time in the desert ended and we made our way back to the city to await our departure. The night before we were to fly home to Canada, the AIM mission directors in Kenya asked to meet with us. There, they told us that they would like us to return to Canada where I was to get a CPL and A&P and return to Kenya to do TEE in the NFD. *(CPL = Commercial Pilot Licence. A&P = Airframe and Powerplant Mechanic Licence. TEE = Theological Education by Extension).* I wasn't completely sure what all those letters meant. Although AIM did not have a flight service at that time, they were planning to start one in the near future.

Our minds were swirling. We were confused, depressed, traumatized and frustrated, feeling like useless failures over the situation that we had left behind in Zaire. I tell people that after leaving, we were not interested in even talking about it and we certainly knew that we would never return to that seemingly hopeless country. Now we were being asked to do something that was as wild as planning a trip to the moon. After buying our tickets to Canada we had a grand total of $500 along with the two suit cases and one duffle bag. Even the few books that we had taken from my library in Linga were left in Loglogo, where we learned they were later destroyed by a flood – yes a flood in the desert!

CHAPTER 22

CRASH COURSE IN AVIATION

We flew from Nairobi through Amsterdam to Toronto on our way to Vancouver. In Toronto we spent some time with the AIM folks in the Canadian headquarters. In those days there was no Post Traumatic Stress Disorder debriefing but they were all very supportive. While spending some time with family, I visited Dunfair Baptist Church (formerly Fairport Beach Baptist) where my whole adventure with God had begun. That was about the time they were changing the name to Bayfair Baptist. Jack Hannah was the young pastor, fairly fresh out of seminary. When I shared our story, Jack was incredibly understanding and encouraging. I suppose I was expecting to be reprimanded and shamed for being a "quitter". He promised that the church would continue to support us, not only with the prayer and financial support that they had faithfully provided from the beginning, but in whatever God was doing in our lives in the future.

A short time later while in Vancouver, I found a 1949 Piper, Clipper, PA 16, registration CF-GNC. I knew so little about planes but I could see that the noisy end was in the front and the dirty side was down and it had wings; so it looked good to me. My brother-in-law, Bob Boodle, was a private pilot with about 100 hours experience which was infinitely more than I had. Together, we spent a few hours checking out the plane. When I got home, Willie asked me the "most important" question. "What colour is it?" I couldn't remember.

The price was $5,500. I had $500. I called Pastor Jack, back in Ontario and he said, "You get the plane and we'll get the money." A couple of weeks later, the little congregation took up an offering, where most of the members gave one week's salary and sent me the $5,000. I owned an airplane! You see, in my "best days" as a young liar, I could not have made up this sort of story. Art Mitchell, the poor, trouble making, insignificant, educationally challenged, no-future kid was being swept along in the flood of God's love and purpose. I had a plaque installed in the plane that read, *"This airplane was purchased for the work and to the glory of God by the people of Bayfair Baptist Church."*

Not only did I have very few answers, I really didn't know the questions. I quickly found out that the Clipper was not the right airplane to learn to fly. I could not find an instructor around Vancouver or Victoria who could or would teach me in it. It was referred to as "a twitchy tail dragger", a fabric covered, four seat, clipped wing Piper.

Pause for a quick lesson in aircraft design: You will notice that almost all airplanes have three "landing gear"; two "mains" that carry most of the weight and one either in the front or the back. If it is in the front it is a "nose wheel" and if in the back a "tail wheel" or "tail dragger" (still referred to as conventional landing gear). So what? Well to keep it simple, a nose wheel plane tends to go straight down the runway on take-off or landing but a tail dragger would prefer to spin around and go backwards. Just trust me! All that to say, young instructors, which most of them are, do not like machines that seem to want to self-destruct. When the Clipper was designed they were the most common configuration, so "everyone" learned in tail draggers. Another thing, AIM only intended to buy nose wheel airplanes. It seemed that I had made a serious mistake – but God knew!

I finally found an old instructor, Bill White, in Campbell River, on Vancouver Island, across the straits from Powell River, Willie's old home town. I moved her parent's little camping trailer to the airport and settled in, leaving Willie and Hopey with her folks on the mainland. On March 5, 1976 I started my first lesson in the plane and within 20 minutes I was "soloing". Yeah, really! One thing I had not noticed was that while this plane had dual "sticks" and dual rudders, it did not have brakes on the co-pilot (instructor) side and that made Bill nervous. He showed me how to taxi around the ramp. Then he got out and turned me loose to taxi while he watched from the safety of the coffee shop. After about an hour, he got back in and we went flying.

As I look at my old log book, it shows that I had 14.5 hours of dual flight instruction when he finally got out of the plane and let me fly solo. In a tail dragger, or any plane, that was not bad. No way, can any pilot ever forget his or her first solo. I sang and prayed most of the way around those first three circuits. This was not a dream and it was not Billy Lazelle's toy peddle plane. This was "the real thing" and I was ecstatic and terrified at the same time. I was a "pilot." Ace McCool, step aside! Now if any captain on a 747 had a heart attack and needed help, I was ready!

Ever heard the expression, "Pride cometh before a fall?" After successfully defying gravity all by myself, I went home to Powell River for the weekend. I was back and raring to go first thing Monday morning. Bill got in with me and we did a take-off, flew the circuit (or "pattern" as the Americans say) and landed. He got out and told me to spend an hour doing "touch and goes". The take-off was great. I climbed straight out; turned left at 500 feet; turned left again onto the down-wind; levelled off at 1000 feet; made the "down-wind" call, reduced power and turned "base" and then turned "final". "I hope you're looking Bill. I'm sure you are impressed." Beautiful approach right to the centreline. Remember what I said before about taildraggers wanting to spin around and go down the runway backwards? The safest way to touch down is with the "stick" right back in your lap and all three wheels making contact together. Well that is for "beginners". A lot of pilot accident reports start with, "I was a little high, a little fast and a little long." And I was. The main wheels touched down and then bounced back up and then touched down again and then up and then... well you know. The plane was twisting to the left and as I bounced along. I realized I was heading for a row of parked aircraft, tied down in the grass. It did not seem like a good time to try to go straight so I let it continue to spin around. I came to a stop in the mud, about 30 feet off the side of the runway, facing in the direction from which I had just made that lovely decent.

Slowly, from the coffee shop, Bill came strolling. He eventually said, "Well, among taildragger pilots there are those who have ground-looped and those who will. Now that is taken care of." We pushed the airplane out of the mud, checked for damage, had a coffee and a discussion and went back flying for another hour of "dual".

On average, it cost me $10 per hour to operate the plane and $10 per hour for instruction time. That was much cheaper than having to rent a plane and it also gave me freedom to do long cross-country flights through the mountains. Although it was somewhat cheaper, to me it still cost a huge amount of money. Throughout all the training for the different ratings in Canada and in the US, God provided in ways that were beyond imagining. Most of the time, I would "book" flight time and instruction without the money to pay for it. By the time each flight came due, the money had arrived. I cannot remember ever having to cancel a flight for lack of funds or going into debt to cover it. The Clipper worked fine for the initial training but later I had to rent other planes to finish the advanced training.

I got my Private Pilot Licence on May 18 and Willie and I were able to fly through BC, Alberta and into Saskatchewan, visiting friends and supporters. The mountains, forest and challenging weather made for great training but the place where we were supposed to work in northern Kenya had very few mountains, a few thorn bushes and relatively predictable weather. Again, this did not seem like "appropriate" training for our future ministry -- but God knew!

In early August I headed down to Northrop University School of Aviation Technology in Inglewood, California to study for my Airframe & Powerplant mechanic's licence. Willie was able to get a job in the Powell River Hospital back in BC until the end of the year, the same hospital in which she was born. That helped financially. I loved the lessons and the hands-on training and was able to stay pretty well at the top of my class. The plane remained in Canada where I was trying to sell it.

At the beginning of 1977 Willie and Hope were able to join me in Los Angeles and we found a little apartment not far from the school. A church in Westchester 'adopted' us and provided much encouragement. A member of the church, Gene Browne, was a Commercial, Instrument Flight Instructor and provided all the instruction I needed at a very reduced price. A precious couple, Ron and Suzi became dear friends and made sure we never lacked for a vehicle. We started a Bible study group, made up of students from my class and met alternately at our place and at Ron and Suzi's. Ron's father was a well known dentist in Beverly Hills and he provided us with limitless, free dental service.

In the mean time, AIM-AIR, the new "wing" of Africa Inland Mission had begun in Kenya. Shortly after that, we got a message that one of their pilots had been shot and killed in the crossfire in Sudan. We were told that the need for us to get out to the field was "desperate". I was still far from qualified.

The Clipper was not selling back in Canada, so I flew it down to California and did some overhaul work on it. A Christian Federal Aviation Administration Inspector supervised the work free. Tie-down space was hard to find and hangar space, about impossible. But one of my classmates gave me free hangar space for the work on my plane. As I write, I am rereading our old prayer letters from those days. I can hardly believe it! I can't take the time to tell of all the "miraculous" things that were going on.

About then we found out that Willie was expecting a little sibling for Hope. With the prohibitive cost of having a baby in the States we were considering having to send her and Hope back home to await the "arrival". A couple that we had just met offered to cover "all the cost" for prenatal preparation. So we began taking "birthing classes". Oh, you should have seen us doing our "breathing" together. And we both got certificates that declared we were trained and ready to have a baby. I have no idea how we ever managed to have Hopey without one of these certificates. As the time got closer, we felt it would be best that Willie and Hope go back to Canada near the end of the pregnancy. I planned to join them a week or so before the big day, which was expected to be very close to Hope's fifth birthday on December 9.

In the mean time I was finishing my A&P training at Northrop and preparing for the final exams. At the end of the course, I had to go through "practical tests", in which I was given several mechanical tasks, like making sheet metal repairs on a wing, inspecting turbine and piston engines, timing magnetos and filling out required paperwork. Then there was the "oral test", where I was questioned by an FAA examiner on all sorts of things. Finally, there were three written exams, each about four hours long. Normally, candidates would take a day for each exam and they did not have to be taken on sequential days. It was approaching late November and I was eager to prepare to leave California and join the family. So, I went to the FAA testing office to begin as soon as the place opened in the morning. The first test went well so I asked to write the second. That also went well. There were still two hours left so I asked if I could write the third. They said that there was likely not enough time to finish it. After some discussion they agreed and at the last minute I handed in my exam.

God had taken someone who, in the past, had failed repeatedly and who felt like he had no scholastic potential; someone whose teachers years ago, had encouraged him to seek a job that did not require any academic brilliance. He gave me a desire and the ability to accomplish what I never would have dreamed of accomplishing on my own. I passed all the exams with very good marks. God was still performing miracles!

CHAPTER 23

IT'S A BOY!

On November 27 I got a phone call informing me that "junior" was about to arrive. I caught a plane right away but could only make it to Seattle that day, where I had to overnight. I called home and was told that my new *son* had arrived! Wow! First a daughter and now a son! Life could not possibly be better! I arrived in Powell River the next morning and went straight to the hospital. As I walked by the nursery, there he was, in one of those clear plastic "laundry baskets" that they use. "Mitchell -- Boy" was printed on a blue sign. We had decided that if it was a boy, his name would be Andrew Lloyd Mitchell but for now he was just "boy". I couldn't see much of him as he was so bundled up but it was clear that the future Prime Minister of Canada was in that blanket. I hurried into Willie's room and while we were celebrating together, a doctor came into the room. She did not look as happy as us. She sat down on the edge of the bed and after a moment said, "I have some bad news for you. We think that your son is a Mongoloid. You don't have to let this ruin your life. We have places for people like that!" (This was the common term used for Down's Syndrome back then. In fact when speaking to another doctor later, he used the term "Mongol idiot.")

I vividly recall hearing what she said but I cannot recall my reaction. Confusion most likely. For so long we had been carried along with blessings that were unfathomable. Everything was going so "right". AIM was expecting us to return within a very few months to set up the program. We had been communicating with those back in the NFD about details of housing, and schedules for teaching. In some ways it felt a little like when I went through the explosion in Peseux. It seemed unreal. It could be a mistake, right? We were told that they were doing further tests. At the same time, we both had an indescribable sense of peace. That did not mean that we were not intensely eager to hear the results of the "further tests." But we were learning that no matter what it may look like to us, God does not make mistakes and He is never taken by surprise.

As the reality settled in, it was like going through a process of mourning and then renewed excitement and then discouragement and then.... Like any mourning, it was, in fact, a process. At times we felt buoyed by God's love, often expressed through other people. At other times we felt like we might sink in despair. The mourning involved acknowledging that Andrew would never be the child we had planned for or dreamed about. He would never be the Prime Minister of Canada, or a doctor, or a pastor, or a pilot, or a father. He would not be carrying on the Mitchell name through children of his own. What did this mean for our returning to Africa?

I cannot remember how it happened but somehow before leaving California, I had come in contact with the people at Mission Aviation Fellowship in Ramona. It may have been through AIM contacts. They had agreed to evaluate my readiness as a pilot/mechanic for field service and if ready, they would allow me to go through "Flight Orientation". Evaluation was to begin on January 3, 1978. Now we wondered how or if that could possibly happen.

On December 21, less than a month after Andrew's arrival, a pilot friend in Powell River, loaned me his Cessna 150 so I went flying. On the south end of Texada Island near Powell River was a short section of logging road where I used to practice landing and taking-off with my Clipper. It was a remote spot with tall trees all around. My little Piper had no flaps but it could "slip" very nicely. I would come very slowly, close over the trees on the approach, cut the power and push down the nose, which gave it just enough added speed to nicely flare and land. I had done it many times. "Why not go down there for a while?"

Without much forethought and probably being a little distracted by the things going on in our lives, I did not think about all the factors. The old Cessnas had 40 degrees of flaps that produced a lot of drag. I thought that if I could land my Clipper there, I should be able to get in even shorter with all these flaps. The approach was right on target. With full flaps and minimum speed I passed over the tree tops, chopped the power and pushed the nose over. "OOPS!" You know that pilots, hairdressers and surgeons are not allowed to say, "OOPS?" With all that drag from the flaps the plane did not pick up enough speed when I pushed the nose down. Without that needed velocity, there was not enough speed to allow the plane to flare. It stalled, slightly nose down and landed nose-wheel first, then flipped over on its back.

There I was, hanging up-side-down in the harness. I was not injured but I could not say the same for the poor little Cessna. Of course, when I undid the seatbelt I fell on my head and managed to get a door open and roll out. "Now what?" All I could think of was Willie and the kids waiting for me to return and worrying. The VHF communication antenna was broken off under the inverted plane. I was able to rig the radio to the Emergency Locator Transmitter antenna that I pulled off the tail and grounded to the inverted wing. That took quite a while, during which I heard several airplanes in the area. By the time I had the radio rigged, I couldn't hear anything.

I transmitted and eventually got a response from a student pilot who was on his solo cross-country flight. I asked him to call the Westview Flying Club in Powell River and let them know what had happened. I gave him the frequency but forgot that it had just been changed. That was the last I heard from him. About 30 minutes later, I heard an Air Force, Buffalo flying slowly overhead. It circled for a while and then a search and rescue helicopter came into sight over the mountain ridge. It seems that when the student pilot could not contact the flying club, he called Search and Rescue at CFB Comox, which was on Vancouver Island, just about 40 miles away.

The huge "chopper" landed on the logging road/landing strip. I was walking towards it when three or four men jumped out and came running. They did not even look at me. They just ran right past me to the airplane. For a moment the thought went through my head that I was dead and they were running to get my body out of the plane. Really! It was weird! Even the pilot, sitting in the helicopter was not looking at me but past me, at the wreck. It was as though they could not see me.

Eventually, they realized that I was the pilot and checked me over. On board, they took a brief report and started back to the base at Comox. I explained that I was from Powell River, across the strait from their base. They agreed to drop me off at the flying club. Several of the club members were gathered there. They were concerned that I was away for an unusually long time and suspected that there had been an accident. When the chopper departed it flew in a direction towards the hospital. Before this, Willie's sister, Jean had phoned the club to see if they had heard from me. Their evasive response left her nervous and when she saw the helicopter flying in that direction she assumed it was taking me to the hospital. None of us were in need of more excitement or surprises just about then.

CHAPTER 24

MISSION AVIATION FELLOWSHIP

After Christmas, I left the family and went back to California for the flight evaluation with MAF. Although I had flown several different taildraggers, I had never flown a Cessna 185. It literally had twice the horsepower of anything I had flown. All of my flight training was "here and there" with different private instructors in the States and Canada. All I had was a Canadian private licence with 330 hours total time. After the evaluation flight, Denny Hoekstra suggested that I finish my US instrument and commercial ratings, which were the basic requirements, and try again later. I also learned that the minimum that they accepted for their recruits was 400 hours.

Ramona, where MAF had its flight operations was not far from El Cajon, and not far from the Mexican border. The School Of Mission Aviation (SOMA) was at the El Cajon airport. Colonel Underwood owned several aircraft that the school was using at that time. He and his wife had had a daughter with mental disabilities and because of Andrew, we became friends. He was very generous to me. Over the next couple of months, with my SOMA instructor, Gary Rickman, I was able to work and get my American commercial license and also finish the instrument rating that I had started earlier.

I was living in El Cajon in the home of the Snowbargers. They were a wonderful, godly family who allowed me to stay in their home and eat their food free, while flying at SOMA. Whenever I could get away, I would fly up to Los Angeles to visit

Ron and Suzi Hanna. One evening I borrowed an old Cessna 170, registration N2629D, that we called "Two Niner Dog" and flew up the coast to LA. It was a great evening and the lights along the shore were beautiful. I decided to adjust my seat back a bit to relax. Bad move! The pin that locks the seat in position, came out in my hand. The seat was rolling back and forward on the rails and I could not stop it. In case you hadn't guessed, the seat needs to be firmly locked in place to operate the control yoke, the rudders and the brakes. Another bit of information: the 170 is a taildragger and you need to be able to 'dance' on the rudders and brakes or else you will ground loop.

Up until now, I had never attempted to land a plane from the right seat and I was not sure it would be a good time to give it a try. What to do? I trimmed the airplane so it would fly level, climbed over to the right seat and got down on my hands and knees with my flash light, that you are required to carry on a night flight. If I heard the engine speed up, I knew I was descending, so I would reach up and pull the yoke back a bit. If the engine slowed down, I knew the nose was going up so I would reach up and push the yoke forward. Yeah, I was scared! Eventually, I found a small bolt and jammed it into the rail to lock the seat in place. It's hard to fly a plane from under the panel.

Bob Johansen became one of my MAF heroes. He had flown in Indonesia and had "grounded" himself when he found the pressures, politically, emotionally, spiritually and physically were ganging up on him. When I met him he was returning to flight status and was working as a flight instructor in Ramona. I still was not ready for the level of flying that MAF required for a candidate. Bob spent many hours, grooming, coaching, and preparing me to qualify. What an incredible, patient man! He has a way of conveying a flight concept that I had never seen in anyone else. Without him, I know I would never have made it. He had a ton of little phrases that I adopted and used throughout my flying; like, "Reach for the ground with the back of the wings." Concerning the use of power on the approach to landing; "Give it a dollar and take back the change." It might not mean anything to anyone else but I can remember on some "hairy" approaches in the mountains, using both of those and many more of his wise sayings through my own career.

In March, I was back in Ramona going through MAF flight orientation. It was more than challenging but it was also exciting. I could see why we had to do the things that we did. The mountain strips that we landed on; the canyons that we "contoured"; the low and close "terrain sculpting"; the precision approaches; the cargo and message drops and the emergency procedures were all in preparation for the real thing. The pilot, aircraft and environment were all explored and stretched to the limit. Most of the other pilots-under-instruction, with me, were graduates of schools like Moody Aviation, SOMA or Le Tourneau. From the very beginning of their training they had a rigid curriculum and many of the instructors in those schools were experienced missionary pilots. They definitely had training more appropriate for this course than I did. Well that's my excuse anyway.

After about 50 hours of training, Elmer Reaser, the chief flight instructor called me in for final evaluation. That was almost 40 years ago but I remember it so well. Basically, he said, "Art, you are able to perform all of the required maneuvers and have passed all the tests but it is evident that you do not have the maturity as a pilot to be ready for field service. When I endorse a pilot for service with MAF I have to be ready to put my family in your plane and send you to the most difficult field and air strip and I'm afraid I could not do that with you right now." Elmer was a professional but I could see that it was not easy for him to give me this news.

If this was hard for him, it was terrible for me. I knew that I was not as competent as most of the others on the course but it still hurt. That did not reduce my respect for MAF but increased it. What now? What was God saying? As my dad would say, "I felt so low, I could walk under a snake's belly with a top hat." AIM was planning on me arriving in Kenya soon. I felt like a failure and did not look forward to seeing supporters or even family.

There has been more than once that the Lord saw pride in me that needed some correction. This was one of those times. Being trained by the flight organization that I considered to be the top in their field was pretty heady stuff. Being 'rejected' by them was humbling to say the least. In fact, although I felt rejected, Elmer was very encouraging and suggested a few things, including flying for some Canadian mission group for a while.

CHAPTER 25

THE SHANTYMEN AND JOE OTTOM

With my "tail between my legs", I went home to Powell River. Within a few weeks, I was offered an opportunity to fly a float plane for the Shantyman's Christian Association (SCA) out of Campbell River; the place where I had learned to fly. During my college days, I had worked a little with SCA on the mission boat, the "Messenger III". The mission now had a 1966 Found FBA2C aircraft on floats. That was the first year Found Brothers Aviation had produced this plane. I had serial number 13. It was registered CF-RXI. It was definitely not overpowered! On the ocean it worked okay because salt water is much more dense, so the floats don't sink so deep in the water. At sea level the engine develops its maximum power. The problem came when we tried to take off in the fresh water of some mountain lake.

Most of the time, I flew evangelist Joe Ottom up and down Vancouver Island and the coast of the BC mainland. We would go into logging camps, Indian villages or coastal towns and spend time sharing the Gospel with whoever we could find. In those days, we carried a 16 mm movie projector and we would show Christian movies, especially some of the old "Moody Science" films. What an education! Not just the flying, but working with Joe. Arthur Dixon, the director of SCA referred to Joe as "a reaper". To this day, I have never known anyone who could turn any conversation into an opportunity to present Jesus Christ. He was not at all offensive. He loved people and they could not help loving him. If someone asked him if he had any change, he would reach in his pocket, pull out some coins and say, "I need to tell you about change. I used to drink a bottle of Johnny Walker a day until I met Jesus and he changed me completely. Let me tell you about it." One time a young man asked Joe what time it was. He pulled up his sleeve, looked at his watch and exclaimed, "Look at that, there is almost no time left. Christ could come any time now. Let me tell you how you can be ready." I could go on for hours about how God used Joe to teach me. If you can get your hands on the book that he co-wrote with Martin J. Gouldthorpe just before he died, you should. It's called, "Not an Ordinary Joe: My Lifetime Adventure With My Extraordinary God."

Flying the Found was a bit like flying a Mack truck. Looking through my log book just now, so many memories come streaming back. Landing in the fjords was often "fun". There was normally an ocean swell coming in from behind, which could get higher as the fjord narrowed. The wind was likely from behind above 50 feet but would reverse and come off-shore as you descend. This was caused by cold air coming down the valley from glaciers at the top of the mountains. The waves could be coming from any direction. Fjords almost always have a fast flowing river emptying into them at their end. That causes an off-shore current. So as you approach, the wind and the water reverse while the swell gets bigger.

But it is worse if there is no wind or waves. Until you experience a "glassy water landing", it's hard to imagine just how dangerous it can be. There is no way of knowing when to flare for landing because you cannot judge where the surface is. One day, Joe and I were landing in a big bay, along the coast at a logging operation. When making a low turn onto 'final' in a high wing plane like the Found, the pilot has to lean way forward and look out the top of the windshield, past the leading edge of the wing. That is just what I was doing. I wanted to land far enough off shore to be safe but not so far that there would be a long "water taxi". I judged that we were about 50 feet off the water. The next thing I knew, we were bouncing back up into the air and the plane was banked in the opposite direction. The loggers on shore thought that my left wing hit the water but if it had, I would likely not be around to tell this story now. The left float actually ricocheted off the water, turning the plane and shooting us back up into the air. I had enough airspeed to recover. I can't remember now but I'm sure Joe used it with the loggers as an illustration of how imminent death can be and how we all need to be ready.

Snow on a tied-up float plane has special problems. The wings and the horizontal stabilizer can carry quite a load. The snow on the wing is right over the centre of lift and also the centre of gravity. The plane sits on the floats so the centre of gravity is in their middle. Have you ever noticed that floats stick out in front of the plane, beyond the propeller but they don't go all the way to the back of the airframe? So any amount of weight i.e. snow on the wing just pushes the plane straight downward. However, the snow load on the tail tips the plane, nose up. The floats are designed with several "chambers" so that if one floods the others should not. The cables that operate the water rudders normally run along the outside of the floats. Well, some clever person designed these particular floats with the cables running through the bulkheads. As a result, when the snow pushed the tail down, submerging the aft part of the floats, they flooded, one chamber after another.

One morning I arrived to find the plane aiming at the sky and the aft fuselage under water all the way to the back of the pilot seat. I can't explain it all now but the process of getting it out of the water caused a gash in the side of the right float. Working on an aluminum airplane outside, in winter, is no fun. It took a while but finally I had it repaired.

By this time the weather was beginning to warm up some so I took the "bird" for a little ride. I landed at a small uninhabited island called Mitlenach. It was beautiful. The sea was calm. So I pushed the floats up on shore a little and decided to stretch out on the shore and enjoy the moment. Above were the vapour trails from jets coming from and going to exotic lands. The many sea birds were soaring effortlessly over head. Life was finally peaceful. Not a thing to worry about. Then I happened to glance toward the plane!

While I was enjoying the moment, the tide was rising, which meant the plane was floating and with the ever so gentle breeze it was about 100 meters off shore. The ocean is very cold, even in the summer. Now, in early spring, it was horrible. I ran down the stony beach, throwing off my clothes as I ran. The weight of them would have drowned me. I found an old broken oar and grabbed it so I would have something to help me stay afloat. As I swam the plane continued to drift but I could not let God's airplane get away. Exhausted, I finally climbed up on the float. In nothing but my underwear, the cold air actually felt warm compared to the water. In my haste, while throwing off my clothes I left my pants behind with the airplane key in the pocket. The oar was broken and kind of useless but most float planes carry a canoe paddle on the side of the float. The breeze was getting stronger but I had to get back to the island. Airplanes are made to respond to moving air and this moving air was not going my way. I don't know how but eventually I made it back, gathered my belongings and flew home.

The Shantymen had a couple of other pilots. One was Orlo Davis, in the Yukon. I had the privilege of flying his Cessna 172 on wheels around the north country. Seldom did I plan to land at any airport when flying there. I would just land on a road or mining slag pile. No one was surprised by a plane sitting on the side of the road. There were adventures there too but I don't think I will get into that, other than to say I did have a surprise, while trying to cross a mountain ridge in very low visibility in a snowstorm and seeing the lights of a pick-up truck coming towards me. All of the people in those remote places were very friendly. Food and accommodation were freely shared with strangers.

During my time with SCA, I was able to get my Canadian commercial license, a multi-engine rating and an instructor rating.

I made some money by flying tourists over the glaciers and landing on some of the Pacific island beaches. I also taught students for Bill White, my old original instructor.

By this time, Willie, Hope, Andrew and I were living in Campbell River. Shortly after his birth, the doctors determined that Andrew had a "hole" in his heart. They were hoping that it would seal but it didn't and at 16 months of age he had open-heart surgery on his tiny little heart. Before that, he could not put on weight and he had very poor muscle tone. After the procedure, he developed so much better. He always seemed to be happy and he made those around him happy. We learned that God had very special purposes for Andrew. One was to give us many opportunities to share the goodness, wisdom and grace of God.

Doctors advised us to not have any more children since so little was known about Downs Syndrome back then. We began a process to adopt a child. Things were lining up and we were getting close to finding the right child. It would likely have been an Indian - Native - Aboriginal - First Nation (whatever was the appropriate name at the time). Then came the surprise! God had other plans and a few months later, on November 16, 1979 we welcomed Amy Florance (with an A) Mitchell into our happy little family. Note: *This same Amy, who as I write this, is editing my manuscript and who herself has written several books, thought it would be good for me to pause here and make special note of "how this event changed our lives and made them so much better." Yes Amy, without you life would be a lot less fun. Now back to the story.* Throughout this whole time we were still members of Africa Inland Mission and God was graciously providing for our needs through faithful supporters.

CHAPTER 26

TRINITY WESTERN

Somewhere along the way, I met Dave Olson, a veteran MAF pilot, who was teaching aviation at Trinity Western College in Langley, BC. He asked if I would consider instructing for them. We contacted AIM and asked if that would be okay. They agreed and we moved from Campbell River to Fort Langley, BC. What a privilege to teach all these young people, many of whom later became missionary pilots. Others went on into the airlines and the Air Force. Some have remained dear friends to this day. Not only did I have Dave Olson as a mentor, Ivan Pettigrew also joined the staff. He had flown in South America for many years with a mission there. The experience was great! We were feeling much more prepared for service in Northern Kenya. I had started instructing at Trinity in January of 1980.

I have had a few chances to teach aviation and I loved it. At Trinity and in cooperation with Transport Canada I was able to develop the Mountain Flying Course that was used at the college for years after. But my favourite part of instructing was with the brand new students. I believe that the first ten or so hours of flight instruction can "set" an attitude of safety and professionalism that can carry a pilot through their whole career. I learned lessons from Bill White in the beginning and men like Bob Johansson, both of whom modelled what I wanted to become.

At Trinity Western College there were some "adventures" that I cannot forget. One day I was flying with Dale. He was an eager student who came prepared each day. But he had a problem. Before the flight and after, he could explain everything about each maneuver. However, as soon as the propeller turned, he would clutch the controls in a "death grip" and his eyes would be locked straight ahead. After a while, I was able to get him to relax. An old military instructor gave me some advice, and as odd as it may sound, it was to fly low down the Fraser River and let the student get a sense of comparative motion that you can't get at altitude. The river is plenty wide where we went with no obstructions. It worked!

It was with this same young man that I had, what should have been my last flight. We were doing "circuits", landing and taking off. We had taken off, climbed straight out to about 500 feet, made a climbing left turn and continued to 1000 feet where we levelled off and began to turn left on the "down-wind". This student, who at that time was flying with eyes locked straight ahead, for some reason looked out and to the rear. His eyes got as big as plates and he suddenly rolled the plane farther left until the wing was almost vertical. My first impulse was to grab the yoke and level the wings but I happened to glance back to see another Cessna 150 descending onto us. An instructor and student were joining the down-wind leg at the same point where we were turning. You are only ever supposed to join down-wind while flying level, never descending. They could not see us under them but when Dale rolled left, our right wingtip popped up in front of them. The student in the other plane rolled hard right while we were rolling left. Our planes were now continuing to converge belly first. According to the tower, who by now had us in sight, the other plane's left wing passed between our right wing and horizontal stabilizer. I looked out my window and was able to read, "TSO-C620" on the tire of the other plane. It seemed like the longest time that we were almost locked together before we drifted apart. One second can seem like an hour at times like that.

I knew that we should not be alive and so did the tower. With my heart racing, as calmly as I could, I "suggested" that we land and review what had just happened. If somehow I appeared calm on the outside, I was pretty panicked on the inside. Some experiences get locked in one's memory, indelibly for many years after. I am not positive that the TSO number was exactly that but that is what I "remember".

CHAPTER 27

BACK TO WHERE? WITH WHOM?

In the middle of September I got a phone call from Mission Aviation Fellowship in California. They announced that a friend of ours back in Zaire, Jack Spurlock, had been killed in a crash. We were told that he was the fifth mission pilot who had been killed in the Bukavu area. The local missionaries were now requesting that MAF establish a flight program in the region. Because we had the languages (French and Swahili) necessary and were familiar with Zaire, MAF wanted to know if we would be willing to go "on loan" from AIM to MAF and start the program.

This was the country that we had fled earlier and where we determined never to go again. We had prepared to go to the NFD of Kenya where there were few mountains, almost no trees and fairly predictable weather. The Kivu province of Zaire was on the western edge of the Great Rift Valley and included much of the Ituri Forest (the second biggest jungle in the world) and very high mountains as well as several active volcanoes. The weather was anything but predictable. It had been the jungle, mountains and weather that had cost the lives of five mission pilots. Why would we ever want to go to such a place?

Then we realized that almost all of my preparation was on the west coast of Canada and the US. Much of that was mountainous forest with very challenging weather. At Trinity, I developed the mountain flying course. So much of the experience that I had really didn't make sense in preparation for service in the NFD but it seemed ideal for eastern Zaire. But Zaire? Really? After what we had been through? We felt like we were totally unprepared for this move. And yet, perhaps God had particularly prepared us for it.

Within a couple of weeks, I was back in California, redoing MAF Flight Orientation. This time I had about 1300 hours with commercial, float, instrument, multi-engine and instructor ratings. MAF was no longer based in Ramona but had moved north to Redlands, near San Bernardino. I think that it may have been the first orientation class conducted in that area. Having already been through the training, although unsuccessfully, it was a lot more "fun". Almost all of my flying was with Denny Hoekstra. Since much of this was review, we took the opportunity to explore the area for future training situations. At the end of the five weeks, Elmer Reaser appeared. He was no longer a member of MAF but was working for an airline. It was so great to see him again. Then he climbed into the plane that I was to be flying and announced that he was conducting this lesson/test. For some reason he had brought his father along, which was most unusual. We flew out to a little airstrip that had some special challenges, doing several air exercises along the way. At one point, on route Elmer fell asleep. Maybe he only pretended to fall asleep. After putting me through a thorough "workout", we flew back. Back on the ground, when we were doing the post-flight debriefing he said something that earlier may have caused some pride in me. Now it was very humbling. He said, "Art, after flying with you today, I would gladly put my family in your plane and send you to any region and airstrip where MAF serves." There is no way that I can describe what that meant to me. It was like God giving me a big hug. There was no other human whose words and approval could possibly be more encouraging.

I returned to Trinity Western and continued teaching until the end of November. Then Willie, Hope, Andrew, Amy and I moved back to Powell River to pack and prepare to go back to Zaire, the country we had fled four and a half years earlier. Willie and I spent a few weeks during December going through "non-technical" orientation with MAF in a place called Twenty Nine Palms, California. Then, back in BC, I instructed in a little flight school that one of my previous students was running in Powell River. We had now been members of Africa Inland Mission since May of 1972. It was becoming clear that our future ministry would be under MAF.

Here is the letter that we sent to Africa Inland Mission:

December 11, 1980
Dear Mr. Frew,
When Willie and I first met Peter Stam in April of 1972, he made it clear to us that A.I.M. was not in the business of building a mission, but that their chief concern was to help build the Church of Christ. Before we met Mr. Stam, other mission representatives seemed to be much more eager to have us join their mission. A.I.M. clearly sought to help us find God's will for our lives, wherever that might be. In our eight years with the mission, we have seen this attitude lived out.

You have stood with us through the long training session. You have allowed us to do God's will with the Shantyman's Christian Association and Trinity Western College, and never once put any pressure on us other than to encourage us to continue in His will. The term, "Servant to God's Servants" is becoming more and more the best description of the A.I.M. family.

It is therefore with a deep sense of sadness, yet also with the assurance of God's leading, that we submit this letter of resignation. We feel that the Lord is leading us to service with Mission Aviation Fellowship. At present, it would appear that we will be assigned to Nyankunde and Bukavu.

The thought of serving the people of A.I.M. as M.A.F. personnel is a really exciting one. The most important thing to us is that we always be found obedient to the Lord.

Thank you for your faithful prayers and labour for God on our behalf.
In His exciting service,
Art & Willie Mitchell

We formally became members of MAF USA after that. That's when we found out that there was a Canadian office of MAF in Guelph, Ontario. So by default, we became members of MAF Canada. It is sort of strange, now that I think about it, that we hadn't really applied for service with the Shantymen, Trinity Western College or MAF Canada but ended up as members of them all. God has His ways and they are not always the ways we plan. Again, we seemed to have had as much control over our lives as someone in a barrel at the top of Niagara Falls. What a ride!

CHAPTER 28

BACK 'HOME'

In July, 1981 we arrived in Kinshasa to begin MAF Field Orientation. It had been July of 1974 that we had first touched down in Africa, in this very city. No way could we have ever imagined the course of events that would come to pass in that time. The first time there were the three of us. Now there were five. The first time we had no one from our mission within one thousand miles to help. This time the MAF folks met us and provided for our every need. We got to meet the Kinshasa staff and over the few days that we were there, several of the pilots from some of the out-bases came to town and we met them. The MAF staff were used to serving missionaries from many missions and they were especially good to us during the time we were getting visas and other paperwork done.

By the end of the month we were settling in on the opposite side of the country. Nyankunde was the only base for MAF in eastern Zaire. Bob Schleicher and Don Tully were the pilots stationed there. I guess Bob was the senior pilot since my log book shows that I did most of my familiarization flying with him. After having "fled" that region years earlier with no intention of ever returning, we actually felt that we were "home". I couldn't help remembering my trip with the Land Rover from Linga to Beni that had taken a couple of days. On my first flight with Bob, we flew to Oicha and Beni in less than 35 minutes. On that same flight we continued on down to Bukavu and then on to Kama in the jungle.

That was the first time that I had seen the region that would become our home for the next few years.

Willie and the kids were enjoying setting up home, even though it would only be for about six months. Shortly after arriving back in Zaire, we had to send Hopey off to school at Rethy Academy. Years before, we had lived in Rethy when we did our Swahili language study so it was not totally unfamiliar. I learned later, from transporting many missionary kids (MKs) to and from school, that the separation is more often harder on the parents than on the kids. Fortunately, Hope settled in quite well. Andrew and Amy took to Zaire like they had lived there all their short lives. It didn't hurt that Nyankunde had a swimming pool. For the first several years, although Andrew and Amy were two years apart, they were about the same developmentally.

Nyankunde is about one and a half degrees north of the equator near the eastern border with Uganda. Bukavu is approximately two and a half degrees south of the equator on the border with Rwanda. The flight in a Cessna 206 or 185 is two hours. At that time any flying that was done for the people in Bukavu was done by the Nyankunde pilots. Since there were no MAF pilots checked out in the Bukavu area, for six months I flew from Nyankunde and Kinshasa to get familiar with Zaire. At that particular time the Zaire fleet consisted of one Cessna 404 Titan, one Partinavia 68V, one 207, eight 206s and two 185s. They were positioned on six bases across the country. One of the 185s was flying from Vanga in the west and one was sitting out back of the hangar in Nyankunde. It had been purchased earlier but had not seen much service. Unlike all the others it had not received its red and white paint job. It was several shades of green, with patches on the airframe and some broken windows.

9Q-CVJ was its registration (Victor Juliet). For your information, each nation has special designations for their aircraft registration. Canada has C-F_ _ _ . America has N and some numbers. Zaire (now Democratic Republic of Congo) has 9Q- _

__. Victor Juliet was not the "queen of the fleet". Not only the exterior but the interior too was pretty "ratty." Paul Rule was assigned to come out to Nyankunde and get it airworthy enough to fly back to Kinshasa. I needed to go there so I helped him put some barrels in with a hand pump rigged to the fuel feed line so we could refuel in the air. There was something about this "orphan" that I liked.

From September 17 to 25, I did the initial part of my formal field flight checkout in the Kinshasa region with John Kliewer. All of it was in a 206. We flew into almost all of the airstrips in western and central Zaire. It was so great to be at the controls, although I was 'under supervision.'

In October, I was back in Nyankunde flying with Bob and Don until a qualified check pilot could finish my training in that region. Finally, Dave Voetman, one of my MAF heroes, arrived. We did a few days of training and then flew off, over Uganda to Nairobi, Kenya. The last time I made that trip it was by car during our "evacuation'" and it took over 22 hours instead of four hours by air. This time I also had my family on board, except for Hope, who was in school. But this time I was eager to return. My first "solo" flight was from Nairobi back to Nyankunde. Like the first solo that I ever flew, back in Campbell River, this was forever memorable! I was now a missionary pilot! However did *that* happen?

The eastern and western parts of the country are very different. In the west there are lots more grasslands with some hills and scattered jungle. The weather, near the equator pretty well always comes from the east, which means that by the time it gets to the west, it has crossed lots of dry land and is not nearly so wet. In the east, where Nyankunde and especially Bukavu are situated, it is mountainous jungle and flat jungle, and by the time the weather gets there it has crossed Lake Victoria and the other Great Lakes of Africa, picking up moisture and it is looking for some place to dump its load.

For the last couple of months of 1981, I flew from Nyankunde to all the northern airstrips as well as serving the Bukavu area. So far, MAF did not have a plane for the Bukavu program. I remember the day my first "bird" arrived. Dave Voetman arrived with it from Nairobi; registered N346EA, a turbo 206. For some reason he had a "start up fire" in Nairobi and the side of the airplane was covered in black soot. What an arrival! It was American registered and had been purchased from AIM AIR. Can you believe it? The first airplane that I had was from Africa Inland Mission. It was painted in the AIM colours and was the only plane that we operated that did not have Zaire registration. A few months later it was repainted in MAF red and white and registered locally, becoming 9Q-CEI (Nine Quebec Charlie Echo India.)

Although much of what I am writing involves airplanes, MAF is not just about airplanes. It is all about people. Airplanes are what we use to serve people. When Willie and I served with Africa Inland Mission, we experienced the blessing of airplanes when she had to be flown to the medical centre for emergency surgery. Now serving with Mission Aviation Fellowship I had the tremendous privilege of using aircraft to bless many others. I have been writing about the different planes that I flew and places that I went but these flights were not so that I could have fun. They were so that lives could be saved and God's love displayed. I was always very much aware of that.

CHAPTER 29

BUKAVU

When Hope got out of school for the Christmas break, we moved to Bukavu. I should mention that the school at Rethy, like many mission schools, had three trimesters. School went from September through November with December off. Then January through March with April off and finally May through July with August off. So the boarding school kids were away for three months and home for one month, three times a year. Very few could go by road so most of them crammed into our planes for the trip. In the middle of each trimester there was a "long weekend" where parents could go to the school to see their little stars "perform". Usually there was a sports day or some special events. The flying for students and parents alone could keep us busy. There was also a very special privilege for the pilots. We could arrange to "pop in" whenever we were doing flights near the school.

The first house where we lived in Bukavu was on the "BAMS" compound. There were two semidetached houses that belonged to the Berian African Mission Society. We had one unit and Tom and Kathy Lindquist had the other. To get in and out of the walled grounds we had to drive by the gates of the regional prison. We were not actually right next to it since there was a house between us. It seems that some "ladies" carried on a "business" that served the needs or desires of some men of lower morals. Quite a neighbourhood! But then the reason we were in

Africa was to bring the Gospel to those who did not know Christ and this was a great location to do it.

The grounds were sort of built into the side of a hill. So the wall behind us was taller than the house but near the top of the back wall were gardens and "things" could fall into our compound. Often the things that fell were venomous snakes, escaping from the gardeners. I can't remember how many we found in different places where we walked and the children played. The Lord always revealed them before they could strike.

The airport was about 45 minutes out of town in Kavumu. There was no hangar so I had to keep all my barrels of fuel at home in the storage shed on the compound. I eventually got a little Isuzu diesel pickup and would pack everything back and forth to the plane. On a typical day I would get up at 4 a.m. so that I could load my fuel and freight and pick up passengers by five. Then I could be at the airport by six, to be ready for take-off as close to seven (daybreak) as possible. As the day went on the weather would normally continue to get worse, so the earlier we could get away the better. In the beginning I had almost no spare parts for the plane. I kept some tools in the pickup for basic maintenance. Once the plane was loaded, I would have to taxi over to the 'tower' and do all the "paperwork" and after the daily hassle, get airborne. The tower was a small, round, metal building with a dirt floor, a desk and a radio, operated by someone who likely "bought" his job, like many government officials and employees did. Oh, there are stories to tell about the "dealings" with the tower! Maybe later.

The six MAF bases in western Zaire made up what we called a Program. Nyankunde was considered an independent Program and because Bukavu was new and isolated from the others, it was also considered a separate Program. In MAF it is unusual for one pilot and one plane to be a Program. For the first three years I had no hangar. A few months after settling there, I was able to buy a 20 foot shipping container where I could keep some tools, parts, fuel and freight. I made a small cement pad, a little more than the size of the plane where I could do the aircraft inspections and maintenance without everything falling into the mud. The pad was also nice for keeping freight from getting dirty while I was loading.

Kavumu airport is at 5,633 feet above sea level, and at the base of the mountains that run north and south along the western edge of the Great Rift Valley. It is also near the shore of Lake Kivu, which at 4,780 feet is the highest major body of water in Africa. Across the lake to the east was Rwanda and across the mountains to the west was the Ituri Forest, a huge jungle with almost no sign of life from a pilot's perspective. About 75% of my flying was on the other side of those mountains.

On that jungle side of the mountains there were very few roads and in most areas there were no roads at all. Katshungu was typical of the mission stations that I flew into. There was a hospital there and a Bible school. Most of the time it was staffed by three or four single missionary ladies and several wonderful African teachers. The road to Katshungu had long since been swallowed up by the jungle so that there was no sign of it at all from the air or from the ground. The flight from Kavumu to Katshungu was about 43 minutes. The next fastest way to get there was by foot-courier which would take about 10 days. Families travelling down there would take about two weeks. If someone was dying of malaria or was wounded by rebels, they would be completely helpless without the plane. Mind you, God is not dependant on airplanes and has so often answered prayers without them. It is humbling to be used by Him to be the answer to some of those prayers. There were countless times when I had that privilege.

The Lindquists grew up out there and have more stories than any book could contain. Missionary kids most often call adult missionaries, "uncle" or "aunt". Tom Lindquist grew up with the older, single, missionary ladies at Katshungu and once told me that he would like to write a book called "My Life With The White Aunts."

Whatever they had on the station almost certainly came by plane: food, building supplies, books, medical supplies, clothing and fuel to mention a few things. Transporting fuel often had some "adventure" to it. I could carry three barrels at a time along with some other supplies. In MAF, we are sometimes accused of spending more time tying down our load than delivering it, and fuel was especially well secured. As much as I tried to remember, business, fatigue, official hassle and the heat would distract me so I would forget that barrels of fuel expand and contract a lot with the change of temperature and altitude. With the plane loaded, I would climb out and make my way over to the mountains. Even with a normally aspirated aircraft, at that altitude, I could normally catch some very strong up-drafts when I "nuzzled" in close to the terrain. Remember, the winds pretty well always come from the east and the mountains were west of the airport. That meant that when they confronted the ridge they had to go up. As warm, moist air is forced aloft it accelerates vertically. That gave me quite a 'kick in the pants'. While I was working the ridge as close as safely possible, which takes a lot of attention, I would forget the barrels. Then, just about at the top of the mountains, where you are committing to cross the ridge, **BANG!** (really loud!) The barrels would start going off like little explosions. That is not at all dangerous except with my mind totally occupied with everything that could go possibly go wrong, it seemed that my heart stopped and my mind flashed into super emergency mode.

I would normally cross the ridge at 11,000 to 12,000 feet. Since I pretty well owned the airspace, (it was very rare to ever see another airplane out there) I would set a long, slow decent so I would arrive at my destination a couple of thousand feet over the runway. As I descended, it got hotter and more humid and my nice clean uniform shirt would get wetter and wetter. Somewhere along the way, while giving position reports by radio to Willie and monitoring the engine and navigating-**BANG!** and the bulged fuel drums would take me by surprise and scare me half to death again.

There is no other flying that has given me more satisfaction or been more challenging than flying the Bukavu program. It commanded my full respect and attention. I was told that five missionary pilots had been killed flying from that base. I know of four and the last one was a friend of mine who I highly respected. Several commercial pilots had also been killed. I often wondered if MAF selected me for that program because they thought I was up to it or they were trying to get rid of me – not really! In any event, God had us there and I was depending on His grace more than my skill. There were several times when I was quite sure that I was going to be added to the list.

The very first official flight of the MAF Bukavu program occurred December 26, 1981. The Archbishop of the Anglican church of Zaire, Rwanda and Burundi died on Christmas day and I was transporting his body along with his widow from Bukavu to Boga almost two hours north, near Nyankunde. At the north end of Lake Kivu is the town of Goma, which is at the base of one of several large active volcanoes. From that place, the water of Africa flows in all directions to the Atlantic, the Indian ocean and the Mediterranean. There had been no report of any recent eruptions so I was somewhat unprepared for what happened next.

As I was passing just west of the volcanoes, visibility was decreasing but it looked like typical cloud "tendrils". Then suddenly my airplane was surrounded with a sort of crackling sparks. It still did not occur to me that I was flying through volcanic ash since I had never experienced anything like that. It took several seconds to realize what this was. You can see through the ash as well as mist but when you enter it, visibility drops much more quickly, maybe because of the static electricity generated by the plane flying through it. Turning around was a scary option since I was surrounded by terrain much higher than me without reasonable visibility. So I found myself flying on instruments and searching for some visual references. It seemed like a lot longer than it was but finally I was out the other side. It's a good thing the plane was going to be repainted soon because the ash really took the surface off the leading edges of all parts of the plane.

I can't tell you all the things that were going through my mind but I do remember wondering if I was really up to this. Was this first "official" Bukavu flight a sign of things to come? I did not think this was fun and I was plenty scared but not as scared as I would be in some future flights. I should say before I go too far that, while there were plenty of "challenging" flights, probably 90% of them were 'normal' and many times they were just boring. You may have heard it said that flying is 90% boring and 10% stark terror. From my experience it seemed about 30% boring, 50% fun, 15% exciting and 5% of the time I hated the Wright Brothers for ever coming up with such a crazy idea. Of course those were the times that were stamped most vividly in my mind.

The only navigation charts that we had were called Operational Navigation Charts, and they were not all that accurate in those days. On large sections of them could be found the words, "Topographical information unavailable." GPS did not exist and there were no radio navigation aids that worked over the jungle. "Clock and compass" was all there was. On some flights, there were no checkpoints at all for well over half an hour. In that time you could be off by several miles, even though we flew within one half of a degree normally on our Remote Magnetic Indicators. My chart was always on my lap and my finger was normally on the course line. We made corrections to the charts as we became familiar with the terrain. Most of the mission airstrips were penciled on. I did not have the advantage of experienced pilots who could give me some guidance or share navigation 'secrets' with me.

From the time that the engine started until it was shut down, someone back home had to be standing by on the radio. Willie had to take care of everything back home, which included caring for Andrew and Amy, especially before they started school, buying veggies at the gate, caring for the house, responding to minor medical problems that came up and a host of other things. At the same time, she could never be out of hearing range of the radio. Before take-off, I would call "Thirty Flight" (our Bukavu base call sign) and give Willie my location, fuel-on-board, number of souls-on-board, and destination. She would repeat the information and then wait…. Sometimes it seemed like a long time. Within five minutes, she would expect to hear me call back with my time off and estimated time of arrival. If she didn't hear within that time, she would try calling me back. Then if there still was no response, she would call the nearest MAF base and report.

Most of the airstrips that I used were not too bad but some required all my attention and skill. Before starting the engine we would pray and commit the flight into God's hands. Not only did we want to acknowledge our dependence on God but we also wanted to let the passengers know that this was God's airplane and we were serving them in God's name. Sometimes I would ask a passenger to pray. I only asked Pastor Kankisengi to pray once! It was clear that he was very nervous and felt a lot more comfortable praying than flying. Eventually, after reminding God of every possible thing that could go wrong with this 'machine that is only made by man's hands' he said "Amen" and we were off.

Sometimes, because of things that were going on in the plane, like the time the frightened Zairian young lady grabbed the control yoke as we were just barely clearing the trees at Katanti, I might forget to call Willie, while trying to wrestle the controls back. You can imagine all the thoughts that go through the mind of the one, waiting for that call and hearing nothing. The radios that we had were pretty good back then but not nearly as reliable as today's. This was several years before the invention of the cell phone. There were a couple of times when the radio failed. That made the pilot 'up tight' knowing that the flight follower would be trying desperately to contact the plane. Flight followers get very good at praying.

After the post take-off report, the pilot is expected to give a position report every twenty to thirty minutes, depending on the area. I had found several "markers" in the jungle that might not have been obvious to others but to me they were precious and eagerly sought. I discovered that if you see something on the ground that is identifiable and give it a ridiculous name, it becomes locked in your navigation mind. Here's a few that I remember. "The snake pit, the pope's nose, the grandstand, equatorial coliseum and Dagmar." They would all be marked on the map at home. Most of the time, I would just be able to give a co-ordinate on the map like, "delta echo three niner." Many times the co-ordinate was precluded with "estimated position—." If I ever included the word, "Xray" in the report, Willie knew that I was experiencing some special challenge, like being trapped in thunder storms over the jungle or mechanical issues or some sort of 'interference' by someone on board. Often it was not a good idea to state the problem because of who might be listening in. Willie had some prayer warriors among her friends who she would call on another frequency or on the CB radio. God was faithful in answering the prayers of those people.

Each mission station had an HF radio with their own mission frequency so they could communicate with each other. They also had the MAF frequency so they could call for supplies or in case of an emergency. There were lots of emergencies in that area. Often it was a medical call. Sometimes it was bullet or arrow wounds or someone who had broken bones or animal attacks, but very often it had to do with late pregnancy complications. There was no lack of malaria, cholera and even measles outbreaks. I remember one particular call I got from the Free Methodists down in Baraka on Lake Tanganyika. Someone had come there reporting that over two hundred people, mostly children, had died of cholera. I was able to load the plane with bags of IV solution and make some trips to the location. Hundreds more would likely have died without it.

Once, I was flying south from Rethy back to Bukavu with a missionary we called "Dusty Rhodes". We were just crossing the equator on the east side of the mountain ridge. Joyce Owens was frantically trying to contact me from Katshungu. Some rebels (unpaid local soldiers) while robbing some people, had shot a man. He needed to be evacuated but the soldiers where holding Maxine Gordon (the only other missionary on the station) with the wounded guy in her truck. The robbers didn't know that Joyce was on the radio and that I was coming. I set a course towards the station over unfamiliar terrain. Fortunately, I had extra fuel and only one passenger with me and the weather was acceptable. About an hour later, I was approaching a more familiar area and eventually I could see the ridge behind the mission station. I recognized some gardens, cut into the mountain side and was able to use that to aim for the opening in the jungle where Maxine was being held.

Although I do not like flying very close to the tops of the trees, I went down as low as I safely could. With the engine RPM reduced as much as I dared to be as quiet as possible, I approached the spot. When the little clearing came into sight, I pushed the RPM and power to "full" to make as much noise as possible, dove down into the opening in the forest and immediately pulled up and began circling upward. When I was able to see the place again, I could see that the soldiers had run off and that Max was driving fast along the trail to the airstrip. I landed and waited until she arrived with the wounded man. Meanwhile back at the station, Joyce radioed me to say that as far as she could tell the trouble makers had left and were likely still running. That group did not come back. Note: Every action was reported to Willie, who kept up to the minute records and contacted others for prayer.

It was always a special problem when I had to evacuate anyone with lung wounds. It is dangerous to go very high because their lungs might collapse, so instead of going directly home over the mountains, I had to fly a lot farther southwest to get through a lower pass. From what I heard, the wounded man survived. Medical evacuations were frequent. Most of those who flew out would likely have died without those flights. Even with the plane, some did not survive. Then there were those horrible times when someone was in urgent need and I could not fly because of weather, or perhaps I had the airplane apart for maintenance. It may seem like a lack of faith or courage to not fly off into unacceptable weather or to just "sort of" put the plane together, in the middle of maintenance and "take a chance".

Early on, I learned that it takes no more faith to trust God to keep the person alive until I can safely get there, than to dash off into conditions that are unacceptable. People in desperate need can sometimes give weather reports that are 'optimistic' so the pilot will come. Most missionaries are very understanding but I have encountered the odd one who will gladly risk my life for mail from home. One such time, I had a scheduled flight to Kasongo. It was 126 miles southwest of Bukavu. The missionary said that the weather was fine and from my end I had no reason to doubt him. I kept some barrels of fuel there, and I wanted to carry the maximum payload for them. So I planned to refuel at the turn-around. About two thirds of the way, I contacted the station and was told that it was okay. As I got closer storms were in all directions but I was still assured I could make it. After diverting several times and trying to find a place to descend through the clouds, it was clear that there was no safe way. With no GPS or any way of knowing just where I was, and having flown for close to an hour in the area, I had no choice but to turn back across the jungle and try to get home. Every indication was that I did not have enough fuel and there were no places to get any. Heading east, toward home meant increasing headwinds. To fly lower near the forest would give me less headwind but would give me less time to glide if or when I ran out of fuel. Flying higher would mean more headwind but also more time to pick a place to crash. No, there were no places to land and by this time, and with the strong winds and flight diversions, I really did not have a good idea of where I was.

Fortunately, I chose to go higher. MAF had just developed a device that could detect the heading of a VHF signal and I had one of the originals. VHF signals travel by line-of-sight. In other words, they don't go over, around or through obstacles, like mountains. About that time, I heard Bob Roberts, the Seventh Day Adventist pilot giving a report to the tower at Kavumu (the Bukavu airport). I had enough altitude to call him and asked him to give a long transmission so that I could calculate a heading to home. Without that, it would have likely taken much more time to get home. As it was, I should have not had enough fuel to make it. The closer I got to home, the higher the mountains. The forest, in the lower jungle or in the mountains provides virtually no place to land safely. I was waiting for the engine to go silent since the fuel gauges "pegged" at empty. Since I am writing this, it is evident that there was enough gas to make it but when I landed, there was no measurable or visible fuel on the dip stick.

Later, when I questioned the missionary about his weather report he told me that in fact the weather was bad but he expected it to improve by the time I got there! I told those giving weather reports to do so as if I had their children on board because my children's father was on board.

There was no such thing back then as GPS and any other radio navigation system was either ineffective or too expensive for our little airplanes. So "clock and compass" and checkpoints, when they could be found, were the only navigation we had and that was with charts that were not very accurate at all. The VHF direction finder mentioned earlier became a huge help. We gave some missionaries Emergency Locator Transmitters (ELT) tuned to 121.6 instead of the 121.5 that they normally used. They would put these units on a tall pole with cables running down to a car battery on the ground. If we had enough altitude for "line of sight" we could use the signal to find the station. This was particularly useful in the mornings when the jungle was often covered with mist that made finding any checkpoints impossible.

One of the jobs of a mission pilot is to make the missionary's job more effective and efficient. Being told by people that they could not be there or accomplish their ministry without the work of MAF can be kind of 'heady' stuff. But it can also encourage us to put efficiency above ministry. Knowing that the more we fly, the more others can work, I found myself booking my schedule tighter and tighter. One day, I landed at a remote station. I had the airplane turned, stopped and unloaded in what seemed like record time. I was sure that the missionary who had come out to the airstrip would be impressed. I really didn't have time to talk because I had to get away so I could "be a blessing" to someone else. As I pushed the power for take-off, I glanced out to see the missionary looking totally dejected. He was serving in a very difficult environment and I knew immediately that all the "stuff" that I had brought was not what he needed as much as he needed someone to stop and listen and pray with him. That was a painful lesson but one that reminded me that people were more important than production. Hopefully, lessons like this change us—it did me!

Booking your schedule very tight may not just be harmful to others; it can also be dangerous to the pilot. It is easy to blame fatigue on the weather and the continuous hassle from government officials. Sometimes there is just plain "too much work". In the early days of the Bukavu program, in the midst of a very busy schedule, I had a flight to Bomili. The mission station was one of the most remote jungle stations that I served. It was about 2.3 hours over totally unbroken jungle with no airstrips anywhere along my course and almost no checkpoints. Actually, there was one little village with about five huts and a clearing for a soccer field. Because it was right on the equator, I called it the "Equatorial Coliseum". When I landed at Bomili that day, it was the last landing of five in 5.2 hours. Fortunately, I was planning to remain overnight. In the evening and morning I could hear the "talking drums" in the jungle.

The next morning, I was to take the Baird family; parents Bob and Dawn and the three kids, back to Bukavu, south-south-east from our position. I was feeling quite tired but didn't think a lot of it. I had four hours of fuel on board, which was normally plenty. To get from Bomili to Bukavu I had to fly through five distinct weather areas. With no mission stations enroute, the only weather report that I had was from Willie at home and her observation only gave me weather for the last five minutes of the flight.

As I recall, rain started about twenty minutes after take-off. I made several diversions but could not go south. I normally kept tract of my course and diversions with a 'grease pencil' on the plastic covers of my charts. After flying for a couple of hours, with no reliable checkpoints, and unable to go south, east or back north because of storms, (there was nothing but jungle to the west) and being in desperate need of some reference on the ground, I realized that there was no way that we could get home. I knew there was a river with a recognizable bend and some rapids somewhere north east. I flew lower than I wanted to because of the clouds. It is much easier to spot navigation points on the ground from higher altitudes.

Finally, after quite a long time, I found the river and the rapids. From there I was able to take a heading to a spot where Victor Ngezayo was building an airstrip that I had seen in the past. I found the strip and although it had never been used, it was usable. After landing, I called Bob, the MAF pilot at Nyankunde. He, along with Willie, in Bukavu had been following me on the radio and knew that I was in trouble. On the ground, I checked my fuel with the dip-stick. Bob reported that the weather was pretty good there. I remember having to ask him advice because I was having a hard time thinking clearly. My body felt like it weighed double and I realize now that I was not really able to make clear decisions. Nyankunde was almost due east and the mountains between me and that destination were not a huge challenge.

When I finally landed, Bob and some others met me. I had been airborne longer than the estimated fuel-on-board. I was too weak to get out of the plane. The others carried me to a vehicle. Fortunately, Nyankunde is the main mission medical centre (at that time, the only medical centre) in that region. The doctors were all away at a conference but there were some mission nurses there. My temperature was going way high and way low and when it was up, I was feeling no pain. I don't remember losing consciousness but I was definitely not able to think clearly. God had guided that little plane to the only place where I could have survived.

They decided that I had dengue fever and started treating me. For days, I was getting worse and had gone from 145 pounds to less than 120. The medicine that I was getting was doing nothing. Don Tully the second Nyankunde pilot, was sent to bring Willie, Amy and Andrew up to be with me. There is a little cemetery on the station where other missionaries had been buried and they were now selecting my "spot". Willie and the kids were there to be with me "at the end". After a few days, Drs. Ruth Dix and Phil Woods arrived back from conference. They checked me over and found a sight on my ankle where a tick had made his home. They immediately started treating me for typhus.

I had landed on March 3 and on the 19th I was released to fly home. The conditions of my release was that I would fly only emergency flights. After having been grounded for over two weeks, there were many "emergency" flights that needed to be done. Stations were now out of supplies. Missionaries had been unable to get in or out of the jungle and there were medical cases stacked up. By April 12, I was exhausted. I was able to load up my family and fly to Nairobi, where they found that I had pneumonia. We caught the train to Mombasa and I just lay on the beach and did nothing for a week. Being on a "one plane, one pilot/mechanic" program has serious problems; one of those problems is that there is no one to monitor the pilot and ground him when things get "marginal".

After I had been flying on the Bukavu program for six months, John Kliewer, our check pilot at that time, came out to fly with me for a few days. We flew to some of my regular airstrips and some of the more challenging ones. One day, after landing at Katshungu, Katanti and Shabunda I took him to one of my favourite mountain strips; Ikozi. The threshold was a fairly flat area, about 80 feet long, at the top of a cliff that dropped about 400 feet. After touch-down on the level spot, the strip turned a few degrees to the right and went up a slop of 12 degrees to another fairly flat spot and turned left. It was one of those approaches that required a decision to land about one quarter mile from touch-down. If you tried to "go around" after that, the plane would not be able to out climb the terrain and there was no room for a turn. So if someone or something suddenly appeared on the runway, there was no choice but to land anyway.

We were flying 9Q-CMR, a normally aspirated 206. I like 206s, which are nose-wheel planes with electric flaps, but I much prefer the 185s with the tailwheel and manual flaps. There are lots of reasons but there is not the time to go into all of that. In our landings and emergency procedures practice, I mentioned my preference to John. With the electric flaps on the 206, you just set the position and wait, what seems to be a long time for them to get into position. The pilot had to trust that the mechanism would do what it was supposed to. The 185 manual flaps give the pilot immediate control. John did not agree. He said that he had never heard of a failure on the electrical system.

We finished our exercises and headed back to Bukavu. I don't blame anyone for not believing this but it is true. We made our final approach and landed on that big flat runway with 40 degrees of flaps, like normal. After turning off the runway, I selected "flaps up". They just stayed down. Circuit breakers were good but the flaps were locked in the down position. If that had happened one landing earlier, I would certainly not be around to tell about it. The flap actuator has a "jack-screw" that turns and makes a control rod go in and out. There are electric "limit switches" on each end of the jack-screw to stop it from going too far. Would you believe the "down" limit switch, set screw had come loose? I had never heard of such a thing. By the way, although I was operating that plane for some time, I had never made any adjustments to that control.

Willie and I have often – very often, remarked that God has brought me through what I had no right to expect Him to bring me through. Despite the fact that much of the flying that I did was just plain hard work and sometimes boring, there were times when I fully expected to join the five missionary pilots who had been killed in Bukavu area. One time, after a very long and challenging day I was approaching the west side of the mountains in preparation of crossing and landing at home. As it normally was at this time, there were clouds down on the tops of the higher mountains and cloud "tendrils" hanging down along the ridge. Our normal practice is to never cross a ridge at less than 45 degrees. That allows time to peek over the ridge and turn back if things are not acceptable. On this particular day, like "normal" I approached the ridge and through the tendrils I could see Lake Kivu on the other side. I gave Willie my regular call, "Over the ridge-descending for landing Kavumu." Suddenly, I realized that what had looked like the big flat lake was really a bamboo plateau and I was totally surrounded by rocky mountain slopes that went into the clouds. At over 11,000 feet, the 185 does not have much power but I pushed in full throttle and full RPM and started a left "sort-of-climbing" turn. Immediately, I was in the clouds. Somewhere in my past I had determined that if anything like this ever happened, I should not do a 180 degree turn but a 190. That way I stood a better chance of coming out where I went in. Throughout the turn I was certain that I would not survive but when they found the wreckage, they would find the "needle" on the turn-and-bank indicator, right in the centre. I remember waiting for the noise of the crash and knowing that there was no chance of survival after that. By God's good grace, after what seemed like a very long time, I broke out of the clouds over the jungle on the side of the ridge where I started. I called Willie to tell her that I had changed my mind and would call again before attempting to cross. I flew back and forth along the edge of the mountains for about 15 minutes before my knees stopped knocking and I felt ready to try it again.

About now I should mention that, while at home in Canada, after this I had different people approach me and ask what was happening to us in Africa on such and such a day. As I recall, it was always women who asked that question. I am sure that those were the very days when one of these 'events' had occurred. These ladies, and there were more than one, would tell me that they could not sleep but for some reason the Lord got them up to pray for me. I know, that may sound so 'hokey' and unreal but God answers prayer. If He didn't there is no way that I would have survived.

Early on, in my flight training I had imagined and even looked forward to exciting adventures. Not long after beginning to fly in Zaire, I longed for boredom. I did not go looking for trouble. I wanted to serve but I also wanted to come home at the end of the day. There have been books and stories written about courageous mission pilots. Some had died in service. I did not want to be one of them. Some of the missionaries said that I was perhaps too conservative. When I would decline to fly in certain conditions or carry certain loads, I sometimes heard people say, "Well Jack would have done it." I had a very great respect for Jack. My response was normally, "Well perhaps Jack was a better pilot than me."

I began to have an appreciation for, what some called, spiritual warfare. While there were dear folks back home praying for my safety, it was evident that there were others praying for my demise.

After landing at Shabunda one day, a young man was brought to the plane. He was accompanied by some others who were assigned to bring him to justice. I have no idea what he was accused of or who the others were; they were just passengers. There was quite an argument going on with some people that I think were his parents, who where evidently witch doctors. They told me that if I took this young man, they would curse the plane and we would all die in a crash. They danced around the plane and threatened and shouted. Others standing by were certain that the plane was doomed and tried to warn me. The Bible verse, "Greater is He that is in you than he that is in the world." kept going through my mind. If I ever had a fear of disaster it was not now. It seemed that the louder they chanted and the more furiously they threatened, the safer I felt. The flight went without evident problems. I don't know what was going on in the "spiritual" realm. That was not evident to me.

I did enjoy flying and I wanted my passengers to enjoy it too. I have no use for pilots who try to impress people by demonstrating their "great skill" and poor judgement. If you are ever in a plane and the pilot says, "Watch this!" Look out! I tried to make the trips comfortable and fun. One time I picked up a young missionary lady at Boga to take to Bukavu. There was no other passenger. I pulled out the Pilot's Operating Handbook; flipped to the page on how to start the engine and acted like I had never done this before. Before each; start-up, run-up, taxi and take-off, I carefully read the appropriate page. The passenger just politely sat there, trying to act "normal". After establishing cruise at altitude, I opened the book to the page on landing and gave her the book to hold for me. For the rest of the almost two hour flight, she carefully held it up at just the right angle so that I could see the information. She was staying at our home that night and at supper she told Willie how that she had helped me get the plane safely on the ground. Of course Willie clued her in to the fact that I had pretty well memorized the book and never referred to it for those procedures.

You have to be careful who you kid around with! There was the doctor that I had to take from Rutshuru to Nyankunde. As I was on my knees, loading the belly-pod, I asked him if he thought that my heart medication might conflict with my nerve and anti-depression drugs. Of course I was kidding! He didn't respond so I guessed he hadn't heard me and it was too silly to repeat so I finished loading and we took off. He had heard me and had taken me seriously. By the time we landed he had written out a long list of possible interactions between the different drugs. He actually thought I was flying with all those medications!

Although you may not want to read it, I could almost write a book about the "Barf Bag" adventures. It seemed that the missionary kids (MKs) were the worst at getting "air-sick". One guy hardly got to the airport before he started feeling woozy. I called him "Barfalo Bill". He even got the back of my helmet one time. Another time, upon landing at Baraka, along the shore of Lake Tanganyika, with a load of MKs, while they were hugging their parents, I was down under the plane unloading the pod. On the floor of the plane, right in front of me were two, still warm, plastic bags full of someone's – well you know. Baraka had the worse behaved African kids. They would actually throw stones at the soldiers and would steal anything they could. I saw two little guys crawling through the grass on the other side of the plane. They were very evidently looking for something to steal. Without skipping a beat, I took the two bags and set them down near the edge of all the baggage that I was putting on the ground. Sure enough, they slithered, commando-like, through the tall grass and grabbed their prizes and took off running. At least I didn't have to worry about how to get rid of that "treasure".

Everything cost much more out there than it would back home, and barf bags were no exception. I had previously bought the nice ones that you sometimes see on airliners; with the plastic bag in the nice blue envelope. To keep costs down I saved the blue envelopes and once, while in Nairobi, I found a place where I could buy a roll of small bags. What a deal! I folded them up neatly and slipped them into the envelopes and nobody knew the difference – for awhile. I got the roll of bags at a great price but I got what I paid for. It seems that not all of them had the bottoms sealed. In fact they had no bottoms at all and were no more than a hollow tube that delivered the 'goods' right onto the passengers shoes and my floor. Okay! Enough of the barf bag adventures.

After about a year living at the BAMS mission compound, we moved across the town of Bukavu to a home that belonged to the Grace Mission. It was a lovely, two story brick house, shaped a bit like a chalet. We had fewer poisonous shakes but there were still some. It is very important to keep your grass short to discourage them. Our grass was cut by men who we would hire. They would use a sort of extra long machete that curved at the end, called a "coupe-coupe". It was while living at that house that snakes killed our dog and parrot.

I had built a "play ground" for Andrew and Amy, around a big tree in the centre of our lawn. There was a circular ladder made from pipes driven into the tree with a tree house and 'monkey bars'. These really were monkey bars. Neighbourhood monkeys would come through the trees and play with the kids—real monkeys! MAF recruited an American teacher to teach our kids and some of the other MKs in the town. We called him FPMJ. Quite a character! He raised guinea pigs to eat, which was fine with the Africans but not so much with our kids.

All three of the kids were busy. Hope was having a great time in Rethy Academy and Andrew and Amy were doing well at home. We had wondered when Andrew was born just how this would affect our lives in Africa. If anything, because of him, doors were opened that would not have been otherwise. I can think of no particular case where his condition was a problem to our ministry. In fact, because of him we were more popular with the people.

The birth order of a child is a very important thing in one of the tribes with whom we worked. When you first meet them they want to know how many brothers and sisters you have and what is your birth order among them? How many children do your siblings have and what gender? When they found out that Willie was the youngest of three sisters and that each of her sisters had two daughters and that we also had two daughters, with Andrew in the middle, they were really excited. They exclaimed that Andrew was the "Chief". I don't understand it exactly but because of this specific order, he and his offspring would form a new 'dynasty' in our 'tribe'. In their villages if this occurred, the family that may have been the chief's family would no longer be chief and the new chief would take over until this birth sequence occurred again. I agree – strange!

When we drove through town with our kids in the back of the pickup, children along the road would see Andrew and shout, "Chef, chef." He learned to give them the 'Royal Wave'. They had given him the name, "Kabutso". I think it actually means "little eyes". He was of such importance that rather than me being recognized as being the pilot and Willie the nurse, we became "Baba Kabutso" and "Nya Kabutso" which translated, "father of little eyes" and "mother of little eyes." That became our status in that tribe.

There was no lack of characters. Adrian de Schryver was a Belgian from the colonial days. He was married to a Zairian woman, who we got to know quite well. If you Google his name, you will likely see YouTube videos of him being charged by Gorillas. Adrian knew the "system" better than anyone I knew. He had purchased an airplane; a twin engine airplane and a book and taught himself to fly. His second plane was a tail-dragger. He boasted that he flew several hours before his first crash. He was hated by the poachers because he was in charge of the national parks in the area and would fly over the parks and shoot poachers.

They had killed his brother. He was always armed and probably could not remember how many people he had shot.

In the beginning of the Bukavu program, he became a good friend and although I had a lot of hassle from officials, I probably had a lot less than if he was not my friend. He kept an Uzi under the seat of his plane and tried to give me a Colt 45 for my plane – "just in case". He assured me that I would likely not have to kill anyone. "Just fire a few shots in the air to get their attention." I don't think he really understood that I was there to serve the locals. He ran an air-taxi operation and as long as he had fuel, I never went without. If he needed fuel, he could always depend on borrowing some of mine. I don't know if that was a normal MAF procedure but it worked.

"Normal" in Zaire would be totally bizarre in most other places. It was "normal" that I had been arrested for several things, including; espionage, attempted murder, attempting to assassinate President Mobutu, riding past an official on a motorcycle and other things that I can't remember now. The way it worked was, you would get stopped by the military, who would ask you for your ID, then your license, then your vehicle safety card, then your log book…. This would go on until they asked for something that you didn't have, like a certificate of baptism – really! Or they would determine that the vehicle you were driving did not have enough water in the windshield washer system for your proposed trip – no kidding! In any event, they would then declare that this was a "very serious crime" but because you were a good person, they would try to find a way to not take you to jail. Instead, they would be willing to settle for some "monetary consideration".

After a while you learn to play the same game with them. I got to know the "top cop" in town. There were no civilian police; just some military who had a red band painted around their helmets. They were supposed to be in charge of traffic etc. This guy's name was Mboizani. Over some time, I had "loaned" him a can of gas for his "picki-picki (motorcycle) and had taken his daughter on a flight to Bunia so she could attend school. I was promised payment for both but knew it would never happen. However, now I was his "friend" and with that came certain privileges. When one of his soldiers would pull me over for an inspection or infraction, they would go through the procedure until they determined what my "crime" was. Then they would announce that this was very serious and they feared taking me to the police station. I insisted that since I had committed such an offence, as a missionary, I should have to face the consequence. They had no vehicles of their own, so I would have to drive them to the station. Fortunately, the two times that I did this, Mboizani was there. The first time we arrived he beat up the soldier who arrested me. The second time he just told him off and tore up the "charge". After that, when the gendarme saw me coming at a "checkpoint" they just looked disgusted and waved me through.

The last place you would want to end up is in a Zairian prison. Having lived just a few feet from the main one for our region, we saw things that were horrible. People who were killed, for whatever reason were left where ever they died for three days. Many, perhaps most, prisoners were there because they could not afford to pay the judge more than their accusers could. No food, clothing or medical aid was provided. Family members had to find accommodation nearby so that they could bring them whatever they needed. To execute someone they would just imprison him or her far enough away from family that they would actually starve.

At different times, local missionaries would go into the prison to do what little they could. Carolyn Butler had a vision to help provide for these locked-up men in the local prison. Willie joined her and eventually headed up a 'feeding' program. There were nine different mission groups in Bukavu, with ministry all over the region. Up until this time, they really had no cooperative ministry that they did together. We even had three different mission printing presses that struggled to keep operating independently rather than working together. For the first time, as far as I know, almost all of the missions joined in this work. They would provide money and I would pick up 100 kilo sacks of beans and some palm oil, out in the forest and fly them to town. Others would provide onions and salt or other seasoning. I cut some of my gas barrels in half and the Zairian ladies used them as giant pots in which to cook the beans overnight. Once a week at first and then twice a week, the ladies would carry big "sufarias" (a plastic or aluminum basin) full of the cooked beans on their heads, about a kilometre through the town and into the prison. It was wonderful to see them in a long row, in their colourful "kikwembes", parading down the streets, often singing as they went.

Of course, they had to first provide some to the abusive guards. In the early days, almost none of the prisoners had anything to receive the food. They would use the corner of their shirt or some cloth or an old tin can. The ministry grew and eventually, when a new governor came to the region, his wife offered to buy a bunch of plastic bowls and cups. Eventually a church, made up of prisoners, including prisoner-pastors grew within those walls. There is so much more to this story that Willie has written and I may include it in an appendix at the end of this book, along with some of the letters from the inmates that are unbelievable. God knew way back when I was seventeen, when I accepted Christ through the testimony of an "ex-con" and later worked as a Correctional Officer in the BC Penitentiary that He was preparing me to show His love to these very special men.

I mentioned earlier that I served nine different mission associations from Bukavu. There were the Berian African Mission Society, Conservative Baptists, Grace Mission, Africa Christian Mission, Anglican Mission, Norwegian Pentecostal Mission, Swedish Pentecostal Mission, Free Methodist Mission and Wycliffe Bible Translators. I also served Africa Inland Mission, Unevangelized Foreign Mission and the Brethren Mission although they were not based in Bukavu, along with other groups like Samaritan's Purse, Peace Corps, and various United Nations groups. Although they could not really afford the service, I found creative ways to serve the local national churches as well.

There was potential for some commercial flying but Adrian de Schryver did most of that. One time, the owners of a gold mine asked to charter my plane to carry about eighteen pounds of gold. The deal was that they would charter the plane for three times the normal missionary price; I would not sign for the gold but carried it on my lap in a plastic bag and give it to the first person who asked for it, with or without identification, when I landed at Kavumu. If they wanted to put a passenger on board, they had to also pay for the seat, on top of the cost of the charter. They were in total agreement. So I loaded the plane with local church people and supplies and was able to deliver it down into the forest for free.

With all the missions that I flew for, they really did not have much to do with any cooperative ministry. They were generally friendly and we normally got together for fellowship on Sunday evening, where we took turns preaching. We also met together on Friday for 'video night'. Most Thursdays there was a MAF flight from Nairobi to Goma and Bukavu. Someone in Nairobi would rent a couple of videos from one of the local "pirate" shops in town. Some of them were actually shot in theatres on camera. You could see people in the theatre walking in front of the cameras at times. They were generally old, "safe" movies like John Wayne or Elvis Presley. We would all gather over at one of the houses with "munchies". It was a time to relax and be a little silly. If it was a "chick flick" the ladies would sit up front with their Kleenex and try to ignore the comments of the guys in the back. One of the ladies usually previewed the movies to make sure they were "safe" for us to watch. There was this one time where there was a scene with a 'scantily clad' lady. It was very brief but our 'censor' was at the ready with the remote so she could stop and fast forward past the scene. Sure enough, she paused right at the moment when we all got to see what we were not supposed to see. The flustered lady with the remote kept pushing buttons and as I recall, it reversed and went forward and paused a couple of times; each time stopping where it wasn't supposed to.

Hardship, persecution and uncertainty were common and at times discouraging. But to face them together with the other missionaries and also with many national Christians creates a special bond. Lately, whenever there is a chance to sit and talk with old friends, or anyone who lived there in those days, there is an immediate closeness. We might remember how God "came through" with something very special, when we were about "finished". Recalling some great sorrow or great joy, talking about the time we banded together to pray through some event, that stirs up precious memories! These are things that those who have not been through it with you, just could not understand. There are many things that I dare not share with those who haven't been there. Whatever credibility that I might have would be lost if I was to tell of some of the things that happened, like the time some older visiting Americans were looking into Lake Kivu and were arrested by soldiers for signalling "enemy submarines" – really! For your information that lake, in which this underwater attack was supposed to occur is the highest major body of water in Africa and is in the middle of the continent.

Then there was my alleged attempt at doing away with President Mobutu Sese Seko. I better stop! Well okay, since you insist. I was driving home from the airport, back when we lived in Kinshasa. I drove past the "Palace of the People" and came to the end of that street where there was a stop sign. As I looked to my right I saw a military motorcade with several motorcycles and limousines approaching. I assumed that they were going to turn left and go to the "palace" with the President. So, since there was plenty of time, I proceeded to turn left to "get out of their way."

Whenever the President goes anywhere, armed soldiers are stationed every 30 metres along both sides of the road. Suddenly, about a dozen of these men, each determined to be the one to save the President's life, surrounded my car and forced me off the road.

They were all yelling and pointing their weapons into the windows of my little car and accusing me of trying to assassinate their leader. After the motorcade passed by, a fairly high ranking officer came over. I tried to explain my case. He looked a bit tired and disgusted. I'm not sure if he was angry with me or his men. He shouted something at them and they quickly dispersed. I tried to thank him but he then shouted something at me, turned around and walked away.

Jon Lewis joined the Nyankunde team as a pilot. Since there were really no other pilots who knew the Bukavu program and I had no one to cover for me during sickness or holidays, it was decided that he would come and spend some time with me. Later, Jon became the director for MAF Zaire. He was a great pilot and became a wonderful friend. He had developed a system whereby he could record messages as he flew. These messages were then sent to his hometown in the States and played over the local radio station. They were called, "Tall Tales From Zaire."

Well, he had plenty to report during one of the flights that he took with me. We flew from Bukavu, south to Kalemi, on the shore of Lake Tanganyika. The runway was a nice, level, paved strip, parallel to the shore and surrounded by sand dunes. Just off the approach end were a couple of old "Ferrets" a sort of light tank with rubber tires. I guess they are really armoured cars but they have a turret like a tank. Anyway, some had been destroyed during some fighting in the past and the "remains" were strewn around. There were also six anti-aircraft guns in "bunkers" along the sides of the runway. Rarely were they manned but I have made several landings with all six guns being trained on my little airplane. Sort of makes it tough to pull off a nice smooth landing, wondering how many fingers are on the triggers of those things.

The airport is a few miles north of the town of Kalemi so the standard procedure is to overfly the airport and then circle over the town above 1,000 feet, return, land and wait for the missionaries to come and meet us. We did the "fly-over" and landed. While waiting, Jon just had to go have a "look" at the Ferrets. We ended up climbing into the blown up machines and "playing" army like a couple of kids. There was no one around, so what could go wrong? Jon collected several empty bullet cartridges and a shell casing. We started walking over the sand dunes between the airstrip and shoreline. Suddenly, we were surrounded by a bunch of soldiers who had popped up with their rifles aimed at us. After a lot of shouting, questioning and accusing, we were "arrested" for espionage, attempted murder and dangerous flying, among other things. I never enjoyed having a group of angry people pointing loaded guns at me and yelling. This was not the first time nor the last time that it happened. It was getting late, and in the tropics, it goes from full daylight to dark in about twenty minutes. Our accusers/arresters/jury decided to release us into the custody of the local missionaries for the night but insisted that the "trial" would continue first thing in the morning, at the airport. Before daybreak, we headed back to the plane, loaded up and took off, as soon as there was enough daylight to make it legal. It was a while before I had to go there again, but when I did, the "officials" just smiled and laughed as if to say, "You got away with that one." So what's new? In Ontario, there used to be a TV commercial, years ago for Red Rose Tea. The punch line in it was, "Only in Canada you say. Pity!" We changed that a bit and would very often say, "Only in Zaire you say. Pity!"

Okay, enough of that. Well since you insist…but just one more. Adrian de Schryver, mentioned earlier, once got stopped at a "checkpoint" in the mountains. As per "normal" the guards accused him of all sorts of "evil" and demanded a "fee" to let him pass. I rarely saw him upset. In this case, he calmly told them to open the gate or he would shoot them. They continued to argue and threaten, so Adrian took out one of his guns and shot the main guy in the knee and calmly carried on with his trip. A little over a year later, he was driving across the Rwanda-Zaire border, where there was a legitimate inspection station. As he was going through the process, he noticed a man limping out of the guard shack on a crutch. The man recognized Adrian and with a big smile on his face, waved at him and shouted, "Hey, Bwana de Schryver. I'm the one you shot in the knee. Remember me?" It was like they were old buddies. Only in Zaire you say…!!

In May of 1984, Dick and his family were assigned to Bukavu to help with the flying and take over the program while we went back to Canada for our furlough. It was great having help with the flying and maintenance and Dick was great at making things work. At the end of July when Hope got out of school, we left. We were home for a year and in that year I went through some of the most rewarding, confusing, affirming, horrible, humbling experiences of my life. It is hard to express the pleasure, and at the same time, horrible pain of that period.

After having returned to Zaire, the land that we never wanted to see again, we felt like we totally belonged. Just surviving Bukavu, where others before me had been killed in crashes, was an answer to the prayers of many supporters and friends. It had been challenging in many ways but perhaps it did leave me with a false sense of pride that God needed to knock out of me. Mission pilots are looked at as some sort of heroes. Many of the missionary kids want to grow up to be pilots. And several of the kids that I carried around on the field became pilots when they grew up. As we traveled around Canada, visiting churches and reporting to supporters, we sometimes would share in mission conferences with other missionaries. It was not uncommon for these missionaries to praise the work of MAF and tell stories of how they would have had a much harder time doing their work without our ministry. For some reason, many people look up (literally and figuratively) to pilots. It is easy to begin to believe that you are somehow "special". God is not in need of servants who feel they are "special" in that way.

On furlough (today called Home Ministry) we made Powell River, B.C. our home base. Hope was in 7th grade, Andrew was able to receive some "special education" and Amy spent much of her kindergarten year under the table in her class. It's hard to believe today, but Amy was the definition of the word "shy". Hope did very well and was a bit of a celebrity in her class, having lived in Africa. We met and were encouraged by other parents of Down Syndrome children.

While we were back in Canada, the MAF leadership in Zaire decided that I should become the new Chief Pilot for the country. I was sent to MAF headquarters in Redlands, California for, what was then called, the Safety Officer/Check Pilot (SOCP) course. I learned a lot and came away very impressed with the seriousness and privilege of the position. It's kind of funny that while I was humbled, at the same time it added a little pride and that was something I didn't need.

Also during that furlough, Dave Voetman, who was now based in Washington State, had heard of an almost new, turbo Partinavia that had been severely damaged in a landing accident in the mountains. The fuselage was beyond repair but the rest was in good shape. As only Dave could do, he inspired a group of aircraft mechanics and others to purchase the "wreckage", order a new fuselage from Italy and rebuild the airplane. When it was completely rebuilt he called me to Seattle and presented it to me for service in Bukavu. The plane was registered in the US and my American Commercial licence did not have a multi-engine endorsement although my Canadian one did. The Partinavia is a high-wing, twin-engine, seven passenger airplane. Dave had to fly it to Bellingham, Washington and I took it home from there. For a couple of months, I flew it around western BC and had several "dedication services" with different church groups.

I had flown a normally aspirated Partinavia a little in Zaire but was not impressed with its performance on a single engine. This turbo had amazing performance and was a delight to fly. It was decided that I should go back again to MAF Redlands and do a full check-out with the plane there. From there it was supposed to be ferried to Zaire. Unfortunately, as it was being flown through Mali, West Africa, there was an urgent need for it because of a famine. I never saw the plane again. At the same time, MAF Zaire was wrestling with the use of twin-engine aircraft in the jungle, on very limited length runways. To operate safely in a twin, you really need enough runway length to be able to accelerate well over take-off speed, and then be able to cut the power and stop safely. That, in most cases, required more than double the runway length of a single engine airplane. Without going into too much detail, it was determined that since there were two engines, there was twice the possibility of an engine failure on take-off. The safety of two engines in cruise was not worth the risk on take-off. All that to say, I didn't get my pretty bird in Bukavu. I agreed completely with the decision of the leadership.

CHAPTER 30

PRIDE COMETH BEFORE A FALL

It was July of 1985 and we were ready to return to Bukavu from Canada. At that time, I was still expecting that the Partinavia would be waiting for me. I was returning to Zaire as the new Chief Pilot, responsible for safety and training of the current staff and any new ones that came. Then it happened! Everything changed! We had been waiting for our tickets back to Africa and the time was getting close for our departure. About the same time, a new President/CEO was appointed for Mission Aviation Fellowship in the States. We were called down to California for a "meeting". We had no idea what the meeting was for but were not too concerned. On arriving at headquarters in Redlands, Willie and I were ushered into the main boardroom where many of our friends sat around the table with the new CEO at the head. As I recall, everyone seemed quiet and not at all friendly. There was Bob, John, Gene and some others that I can't remember now.

The things that I am about to share are based on our very limited perspective and if they did not have such a profound, and eventually positive effect on my life, I would not bring it up. However, much of what I am today is because of this difficult time. No organization is perfect but I hold no group in higher regard than MAF. Bear with me!

The CEO asked one of the others to speak first. He said something about how expectations were not final decisions. Then our new leader spoke. To this day I really don't know what it was all about but he began. I definitely cannot recall all that he said but I was told that I was an incompetent pilot and a very poor example of MAF staff. If I insisted on remaining in the mission I would have to return to Zaire and fly for one year under the supervision of any other pilot and I was not permitted to return to Bukavu for that year but was to fly out of Kinshasa so that I could be "observed".

After awhile, we were dismissed while the meeting continued. Willie and I sat in silence, not knowing what to say, even to each other. We were totally unprepared. Later the others in the room took us out to lunch at a Mexican restaurant. They were all quite friendly now and were even joking with us. We were stunned! Willie went to the restroom and completely broke down in tears. She remembers being comforted by a stranger who saw her there. It was like a weird nightmare but we knew we were awake. Some of them commented that we had taken this very well. Apparently, there had been another couple who had been in the same boardroom with the same people, going through a similar "disgracing" who had argued back. Nothing made sense. I couldn't recall any instance or example of my incompetence being mentioned in the meeting or any support for the verdict. After the meeting, I went to my instructors from the SOCP course and offered to surrender my certificate. They told me that I had accomplished all the requirements and performed well and that I was qualified to be a Chief Pilot.

I was told, later, by a friend that our new leader had become the new CEO just a few weeks earlier and that there had been two accidents since then in our worldwide fleet. That was a *most* unusual thing. MAF has an outstanding safety record that is recognized and admired in every area where we operate. We were informed that as a result of these accidents and some other factors, the new leader was making a statement that he was in charge and "things" were going to change. I have no idea what was going through his mind or what was the real cause for this "shake-up".

Confused! Ashamed! Humiliated! Unworthy! Crushed! Those were some of the feelings that we both experienced. What now? We asked to be sent back to Zaire anyway, under whatever conditions were to be imposed. We returned to Canada in preparation for our trip to Kinshasa. Fortunately, there were no other churches to visit and not many friends or family to face.

Back in Africa, other feelings began to surface. Hatred and bitterness towards this man and a distrust of our fellow staff. "Someone must have said something, 'behind our backs' to someone, that caused this." Some time after arriving in Kinshasa, there was the Zaire MAF Family Conference. I don't recall ever being so uncomfortable around my peers. "Who said what about us? How many are aware of my incompetence and shame? Was I really a danger to myself and my passengers? Could I ever be accepted by the 'team'?"

During the family conference, there was a psychologist available. I tried to share with him my increasing fear of flight. He told me that whenever I began to feel afraid, I was to imagine that there was a "fear gauge" on the post between the windscreen and the door, with "high fear" on the top and "no fear" on the bottom and that I was to take my hand and push the indicator from the top to the bottom. Well, maybe that worked for some guys but it just made me feel that there was no one who could help me.

Spiritually, I felt that God Himself was ashamed of me. In the past, we had several faithful praying friends with whom we could share just about anything. Now, when we needed prayer most, we felt that we could not let people know the failure or the shame we were experiencing. Some of the staff, perhaps all of them, knew that we were "on trial". Most were very supportive and tried to encourage us. My fear of flying increased. The constant fear was that I must be incompetent and unsafe and that an accident was inevitable. Adrenaline, fuelled by coffee kept me hyper alert in the plane but when I was not flying I felt totally exhausted. I don't believe any of my passengers were at all aware of my state. I always loved caring for the people that I served and that sustained me through the tough times.

During our year in Kinshasa, Hope went to The American School of Kinshasa (TASOK). Amy went to the British school and Andrew was home schooled. Besides teaching Andrew, Willie did a lot of shopping for missionaries in the out-bases. She would be in contact with folks all over Western Zaire on the "crackly" old HF radio, taking their orders for flights and supplies. One time, when it was particularly difficult to hear clearly, she got a flight request for a couple named Schmidt. You know how your tongue and brain can somehow get a brief "disconnect". Wanting to get the spelling correct, instead of saying, "How do you spell Schmidt?" She shouted over the entire radio network, "How do you smell spit?" A little humour kept us alive in those days.

Despite my 'ban on training pilots" I was asked to do some check-out on some new guys. They were very encouraging. The people that I served were also so supportive. I think that, to those around me, I was just another "safe" pilot. I rarely felt like that. We did grow to love so many of the people in Kinshasa and on the out-bases. There were few airstrips that were very challenging and some of them had great names, like Popokabaka, Kasongo Lunda, Matamba Solo or Wamba Luadi. They were fun to just say. The main airport in Kinshasa was Njili and the runway was 15,000 feet long. MAF was based on a smaller but very adequate airport called Ndolo where there was a military presence.

One strip that was a bit challenging was Panzi. It was down in the Mennonite country near the medical work at Kajiji. There was quite a slope, and frequently deep water ruts. I normally would fly in the valley past the lower end of the runway to get an altitude reading so I could then go out a mile or so on final and know what my approach angle was. If I had 500 feet above the touch-down spot at one half mile with 19 inches of manifold pressure, things were "go". The approach was over a deep valley so there was no way of judging height without ground proximity. It had a "dogleg" and was also short enough that we could only take off with about half a load.

One day I had a full load of passengers out of Kajiji, including the mission Director for Mennonite Central Committee (MCC). Normally, we don't do mail drops with passengers on board but I decided that since I had not landed at Panzi for some time and they were without mail, that I would use my passenger, the Director to help. The mail was in a flour sack tied with a big knot at the top. I told George to hold the sack out the window, against the side of the plane and to drop it when I hit him on the knee. We were a little higher than I would have done it alone but I wanted a good safety buffer, since this was unusual and things could go wrong. Well you know what Murphy says...! I gave him the signal at the right time and kept flying the plane but he just continued looking out the window. Then he turned around to me with this sad look on his face and said, "It's stuck on the landing gear."

The contents of the bag formed a bulge on one end about equal to the big knot on the other and the two were flowing back in the wind. I flew over the station again and tried to yaw the plane back and forth to make it slip off. That just forced it down the gear leg to the wheel. There was another airstrip with plenty of length just about twenty minutes away over the jungle. We would be able to land safely and retrieve the bag. I don't know just where it happened, but somewhere between Panzi and Kazembe the mail got "delivered" likely to some surprised chimpanzee. George wrote up the whole event for their mission magazine and the missionaries at Panzi got more mail than they had ever received; each writer thinking that their letter had been in the wayward bag.

Near the end of our "trial" year, Denny came out to the field to do some annual flight evaluations with all of us. I guess he was satisfied with my performance because it was recommended that we return to Bukavu. When the kids finished that year of school, we moved "home". Dick had been flying the program now for about 18 months and headquarters said that he was to remain as manager. It was a bit hard to take since I had started the program and gone through all the challenges of putting up with local officialdom and establishing safe practices in an environment where there was little or no information. Dick was great with the missionaries, especially in Bukavu but those who chartered the plane preferred me. It was not that I was a better pilot, just that I weighed at least 65 pounds less than him and that meant they got 65 pounds more in the plane for the same price.

He and his family were living in a house that MAF had bought and we moved to our third home in Bukavu. It was on a hill just above the Ruzizi River, which was the border between Zaire and Rwanda. There were 12 bedrooms. Eight were down one hallway that had its own living room, dining room and kitchen. The Allen family lived in that part and we had four bedrooms a kitchen and a huge living/dining room. And I mean huge! Four full living room suites of furniture would not fill it. There was a big fireplace in the middle. It was all on one floor with several out buildings. I don't remember the cost of rent but it was not much.

In those days, the currency, called the "Zaire" was depreciating rapidly. When we first arrived in the country, back in 1973, one Zaire was worth two dollars US. When we finally left in 1987 one dollar was worth several million Zaires. We would trade fifty Zaire bills for meat – one kilo of meat for one kilo of 50 Z bills. I remember taking an airplane loaded with big bags of money down to the teachers in the jungle. It cost about the same amount of money to charter the plane as the value of the money on board and that was at our subsidized rate. It made no sense to try to save any money because its value dropped so rapidly. So, those with money would build houses and rent them out; the price going up continually to keep pace with devaluation.

Occasionally, the government would declare that all currency in circulation would be void within a few days. They would put out new bills and give people such a limited time to exchange them that most of the money out there would become worthless. One time President Mobutu Sese Seko ordered the printing of all new money from the British American Banknote Company. When they found out he could not pay for the printing, he told them to print some more and keep it. "Only in Zaire you say…Pity."

I loved serving and being part of the ministry of the missionaries and national Christian leaders. I was also teaching a couple of half days a week at a small pastor's school out near the airport. The prison ministry was going well but my fear of flying continued and if anything, was getting worse. Again, I am fairly sure that none of my passengers were aware. I continued to joke with them and life "on the ground" seemed okay. But it only "seemed" okay. In my heart, my bitterness towards our CEO was eating me up. My heart had no love for my leader. I only wished him harm and can you believe, I actually prayed for that harm to overtake him?

At one point, he came out to Bukavu and visited us. He said that he wanted to apologize to us. He said he was sorry, for the way we had received it. One of the comments that he had made back at the Redlands meeting was that he had seen the Bukavu program and it was not as difficult as its reputation. If Bukavu was such a simple program to fly, then I really was a poor pilot because it required every bit of energy, devotion and skill that I had and there were times, even before the "meeting" that I felt I should let MAF know that I was in over my head.

While my local "clients" may not have been aware of the pressure and tension that I was experiencing, my African hangar workers definitely were. As I mentioned before, as long as I was flying, adrenaline kept me hyper-focused. But I can remember, at the end of some long days and after emptying my load at the "tower" and taxiing back to my hangar, I would shut off the engine and immediately fall asleep with my helmet and harness still on. The workers would stay away and let me sleep for some time and then wake me up to put the plane away.

Then one day, I was returning from a flight in 'Victor Juliet' when I got a call from Connie Turning saying that her husband, Dick had an incident with 'Alpha Romeo' on take-off from our highest runway (about 8,400 ft). He was airborne but had 'clipped' something on the runway and was coming home with six souls on board and some serious damage to the right wing. I was waiting for him when he landed. Dick was upset, to say the least. He was as skilled a pilot as anyone on the field. The circumstances were quite confusing to us all. Policy requires that a pilot be taken off flight duty after such an event, for his sake as much as anything. But now our two-man, two-airplane program was back down to one and that "one" was carrying too much emotional baggage to be able to perform safely.

As you read this, are you becoming a little fed up with all the negativism, doom and gloom and just plain bitterness? You should! What I am sharing is not meant to justify me or make anyone feel sorry for me. My attitude and behaviour was immature, selfish and definitely ungodly. However, today as I look back, I realize that all that had happened and was happening, was likely the *most significant experience* that I have lived through, to teach me what God had planned for my future ministry. But permit me to continue....

As part of the SOCP course that I had taken back in Redlands, we had a brief but intensive course on accident investigation through the University of California, San Diego and the NTSB. The local Zairian transportation authorities were aware of this and so I was asked to accompany them, in fact to fly them to the accident site. Let me explain that the local aviation transportation authority knew very little about aircraft accident investigation or aviation or transportation. Most "officials" purchased their job from people with whom they had to share some of the profit of their appointed office. Many customs, immigration, transportation or other officials had no training or knowledge concerning their job. There seemed to be some regulation somewhere of some sort, but normally rules were made up according to the whim of the one in power. For instance, pilots were required to have an annual medical exam, performed by some doctor. The medical report was then given to an "official" who kept a record and signed the pilot licence for renewal. Of course, it was just fine if you went directly to the "official" and paid him, without visiting any medical examiner.

"ET" was the name that Dick had given to our official. I won't try to describe his physical characteristics, but if you saw the movie, "ET" you would have an idea. I had to fly "ET" to the accident site for his "investigation". After walking over the scene he concluded that there had been an accident, and that was "not good." Brilliant! When I flew him down to the site I could have flown most of the way over Lake Tanganyika, which would have been relatively smooth but for some devious reason I chose to fly along the ridge of the mountains just east of the lake. That was anything but smooth and going both ways he held on with all his strength to the seat in stark fear. Forgive me Lord!

An aside to this is that after the flight, "ET" was so impressed with "my ability" to control the plane in such turbulence that he appointed me as the Flight Test Examiner for the region. Go figure! He boasted to others of my wonderful skill and judgement. Really?! Reminds me of the guy who had his knee shot out and that made him a friend of the one who shot him. Zaire!

It was a little while later that Paul Rule, the Chief Pilot, was sent from Kinshasa with a letter from the MAF Zaire Director, Jon Lewis. This was the same Jon Lewis with whom I had committed those "terrible crimes" in Kalemi earlier. I had been requesting that I be released from flight duty since I felt it was only a matter of time before something very bad happened. Jon was a friend and did not want to be the one to ground me. When I received the letter saying that I was relieved from flight status, it was a huge relief but at the same time sad. My respect for Jon and those who had been so supportive only increased. Paul did some flying for me and eventually Joe Hartt was sent to Bukavu to have me check him out on the program. He did the flying so my main job was to make him as familiar with the jungle region and airstrips as I could.

I wasn't going to write this but here goes. When Paul arrived with the letter, it did not immediately ground me and since I had not had a "six month" flight review on the Bukavu program for a few years, Paul, who was then the Chief Pilot agreed to give me one. We flew for about an hour and a half and I was preparing for the final landing. Paul wanted to see my best short field landing. Somehow, I had a reputation for very short field landings. My approach was quite low, with extra power. I flew very slowly along the runway to the predetermined spot, cut the power, touched down and was stopped almost right away. That is a good way to land short but not realistic. He said, "Okay, that was good but let's do *'one more'*, this time with a steep approach angle."

Why is it that it is always that, "one more" that has the problems? We climbed out, did the circuit (pattern) and lined up again on final. This time I set up a very steep descent. The plane was light, so I knew that I could flare at a fairly low speed. From about 150 feet above touch-down, I established 55 knots, full flaps and 19 inches of manifold pressure, which was perfect. At about 50 feet, since we were right on the edge, Paul said, "Are you sure you have enough speed to flare." I said, "Yes." and gave the control yoke a little tug to show him. Wrong move! That tiny change in pitch reduced my airspeed to below what I required to flare. We were now losing altitude too fast. I applied power to give me some more airspeed and reduce the descent but the 206 that we were using was turbo charged and they do not "spin up" as fast as a normally aspirated engine.

My landings were normally pretty smooth but this one was anything but. If you were on board, you would not have had to wonder if we had landed. It was painfully evident. We touched down – I am deliberately not calling it a crash – so hard on all three wheels and the main gear spread so much that the belly pod hit the ground. The pressure on the nose gear sheared the drag-link bolt and the gear folded forward, causing the propeller to strike the ground. Really! I had flown in and out of some of Zaire's most challenging strips and over our worst terrain without causing any serious damage to plane or passenger. According to plan, this was to be my last landing in the country. Why now? What a way to go out! This did not add to my confidence but if anything made me feel greater disgrace.

CHAPTER 31

TANZANIA

A good friend from the MAF Europe program came to Bukavu and met with me. MAF Europe or British MAF as it was known, operated the programs in Kenya, Uganda, Tanzania, Ethiopia and Sudan at that time. He had flown in and out of Zaire from Nairobi. His name was Max Gove. He was then the director of the East Africa programs (oops! "programmes" as the British spelled it). He knew my situation and that I was not interested in flying. He told me that they were in need of an Operations Manager for Tanzania and asked if I would consider it. A short time later, I connected with a MAF flight from Bukavu to Dodoma, TZ and spent a week there. I could hardly believe the difference between the Zairian and Tanzanian aviation officials. These people were, trained, competent, efficient and (shockingly) courteous. No bribes were demanded or even suggested. The MAF team was great, not to mention that almost half of them were Canadians. We still had several months of our term to serve before our next furlough but arrangements were made between MAF US, who ran the Zaire program and BMAF, who ran the Tanzanian programme and we moved.

Hope was at school in Rift Valley Academy, one hour from Nairobi so the move did not affect her at all. Well, not scholastically but it was hard in some ways because we had moved to a new country while she was at school and she had never been there. "Where do I live?" Andrew and Amy were able to attend a local, British Christian school called Andrea Mwaka and they both did very well there. There was none of the oppressive atmosphere of Zaire. I later realized that if we had left Africa without experiencing some other country, our view of the whole continent would have been distorted and depressing.

We enjoyed our time there. The Swahili that we spoke in Zaire, was sort of a "hillbilly" type of Swahili compared to what they spoke. We had no trouble speaking with the people and after providing them with some chuckles, became fairly competent with the local dialect. I was able to help out some by teaching at a local Bible school and had plenty of opportunity to preach. We became involved in a Bible distribution program and would go out with John Hall and spend weekends in remote villages, 'selling' Bibles to Christians, Muslims and anyone who would buy them. The price they paid was very highly subsidized, less than 10%. Later Willie and I were able to start a puppet ministry using largemouth puppets to share the Gospel. Missionaries and nationals joined us to produce plays that we would take into the villages and schools. After our previous experience, this was such a breath of fresh air.

That was during the days when the "Cold War" was cooling down. The USSR was beginning to dissolve. There were lots of Russian Military Advisors at a base nearby. Our pilots were not permitted to fly over the installation where they had missiles and other visible weapons. One of our missionary ladies, Maureen found out that the Russian officers' wives brought their children into town once a week to go to the swimming pool. She planned to be there at the same time, and after a while she and her own little girls got to be somewhat friendly with the Russians. After a while she asked the women to ask their men if they would like to have a volleyball game with our missionary staff. Little by little we got to know one another quite well and played once a week at their compound. Most of them spoke English and as "Glasnost" became more acceptable, we formed some close friendships.

We asked them about their lives and were given opportunity to share our lives and our faith. Then, late at night, one by one, they started arriving at our homes because they heard that we had some Russian Bibles. We were not to tell any of their comrades that they had them. Little did they know that some of those comrades had come earlier to get their own Bibles. First there was one of the Russian wives that prayed to accept Jesus Christ as her Lord and Saviour. Then there were some children. Then other women and eventually some men. They told us about the terrible treatment some Christians had received in Russia and yet those "true believers" as they called them, stayed faithful and even loving to their abusers. Some of our MAF staff even visited their newfound friends in Russia and Ukraine when they went from Tanzania to Canada on furlough.

A funny sideline from all of this occurred when our pilots offered to take these guys for airplane rides. The first thing that they wanted to see was the area that had always been restricted to us, where the military installation was. They would fly over and take pictures to send home. Months before, our planes may have been shot out of the air.

I was responsible for eleven aircraft and their crew on six outbases and the main base of Dodoma, in the centre of the country. Often, Tom, our Programme Manager was out of the country and I became the Acting Programme Manager. A dear friend, Leo Degner, who had come out to Bukavu to build a hangar for us, came to Dodoma and helped me build a 100 feet by 100 feet hangar and office building. I had a great staff in Operations and that gave me time to do a lot of the actual building. I needed to be able to do something that made a visible and acceptable difference. This was a healing time but there was still a lot that the Lord had to do to my bitter old heart.

At the end of that term, we had a six month furlough in Canada, after which we happily returned to Tanzania. I did not have to fly although I set up an aviation safety training programme for our pilots that the Civil Aviation Authority checked out and recommended to others including Air Tanzania. The only time I actually flew was when a team from MAF US, MAF Europe and Mission Safety International were sent out to do a safety audit. I was able to do a flight review which re-established my flying status with the mission. Even with that accomplished, I was happy to leave the flying to the great young pilots that we had. God allowed us to feel "good" about ourselves and our ministry again and I found myself laughing once more.

Then after another three years in Tanzania, Hope graduated from high school at Kijabe in July of 1990. Amy spent that last year with her big sister at boarding school. Andrew continued at Andrea Mwaka. The puppet ministry was being passed on to others, who were expanding and improving it. The hangar was finished and it seemed clear that it was time to 'come home' to Canada. Had we left just three years earlier, the mental burden of failure would have been the most prevalent thought. Although to just leave Bukavu alive after flying there for that amount of time was "unique".

But something much more important than any of that was occurring. Through all my "bad attitude" God was dealing with me. I was driven to His Word like never before. Seeing how Christ had suffered unjustly and gave forgiveness and love in return was a powerful challenge. I knew that I needed to forgive those who I felt had treated me wrongly but I argued that they didn't deserve forgiveness. It was as if God smacked me over the head and showed me that no one "deserves" forgiveness, especially me. My horrible bitterness against my leader didn't hurt him at all. It only poisoned me. Someone has said that refusing to forgive is like drinking poison and hoping that the other person dies. Dumb eh?

I began to realize that he was not the bad guy at all. In fact, he was thrust into a situation that was very difficult and he was trying as best as he could to bring things under control, and he did. He didn't have all the information, but who does? I'm definitely not saying that I was the good guy. There was so much pride and ungodliness that had to be exposed and dealt with and sometimes the deeper and more toxic the infection, the more radical and painful the treatment has to be. What God was graciously teaching me was of more value than anything I could learn in any seminary or school of counselling. Understanding what God did through Jesus, in forgiving me made this whole process wonderfully enriching. I began to understand that to really forgive meant to desire and pray for God to bless the one I had wished cursed.

Several years after all of this, I met this man in Colorado. I realized that God had taken every bit of bitterness out of this old heart of mine. We hugged, and reminisced and even laughed together. I highly respect and admire him today. I consider him to be one of my heroes and a major part of making MAF into the godly mission that it is today. I pray that all the bitterness that I had towards him will not have caused him any of the pain that I once wished on him. The whole experience was crushing, confusing, life changing and humbling. It taught me more about the character of my healing, affirming, forgiving, wonderful God than anything I had ever known. In later years, at my ordination, someone asked me, "What was the most significant event in your life, that God used to make you the man you are today?" Besides the day that I declared Jesus as my Lord and Saviour, this was it. I would not have missed it for the world! I thank God for taking the time and effort to chisel off so much of my old nature and shaping me more into the person that He intended me to be. That's love! Thank you, God.

CHAPTER 32

GOODBYE AFRICA

After leaving Dodoma, Willie, Andrew and I travelled to Nairobi and on to Kijabe for Hope's graduation. She was one of 90 graduates in the class of 1990 at Rift Valley Academy. The ceremonies were great but for Hope, and us too, it meant leaving Africa, which by now had become "home". It meant saying, "Good bye." to dear friends that she would likely never see again. Well who knew about Facebook in those days? Everyone was hugging everyone. We likely hugged people that we had never even seen before. Then we drove the one hour trip back to Nairobi for the night.

Because MAF is considered an international air carrier, several airlines gave us the privilege of traveling 'ID-75' or 'ID-90'. That meant that we only had to pay 25% or 10% of the normal ticket price. However, that also meant that we had to travel "stand-by". When traveling stand-by, you often wait until the very last minute and then your bags are thrown on and you scurry to whatever seats are left. Actually, as often as not, when we finally got on board, we found ourselves in First Class because they were the seats most likely not filled. Most of the time, it worked very well – most of the time.

We were waiting to see if we could get on our planned flight with Air Kenya to London. Our bags were sitting on the ground outside that aircraft when we got the word that they were able to get us on. The agent said, "We have seats for you. Just take your passports through that door." When she heard the word, "passport", Hope froze. I still remember the horror on her face. We all knew what that meant. She didn't have her passport. It was back at Kijabe, over an hour away. What now?

I ran outside onto the ramp, where our bags were sitting and grabbed a couple of them. Then I hurried Willie, Andrew and Amy down the gangway and told them that we would try to catch up with them in England the next day. There was no time to do anything else. The door to the plane closed as soon as they went on board and within minutes they were on their way. At this time I didn't have access to a vehicle and had no idea how we could return to RVA, find the passport and get back to the airport to catch another plane. Cell phones were still in the distant future. We found a phone and called the school. Seppo, an old friend of mine from MAF was still there and getting ready to leave for Nairobi. He was able to find the missing document and meet us in the city that night. The next day Hope and I were able to get standby seats on a British Airways flight.

I can't remember how we got to the hotel near Heathrow. It must have been someone from the British MAF office. But before we even saw Willie, we were told that she had been seen by a doctor and was being cared for by someone from our office in Folkestone, who had been with her through the night. Max Gove had taken Amy and Andrew for a tour of London and Windsor Castle. I had no idea that she was sick but it was much more than some sort of cold. The hotel was not happy that they had a person from Africa with some unknown sickness. They wanted to see us leave as soon as possible.

Most of the time our cheap, standby ticket was a real blessing but not this time. For about six days, we would pack up all our baggage and head to the airport and wait. Each evening, we would return to the hotel. Willie was not getting worse but she was not getting any better. The kids were great, sitting for those long hours in one of the busiest airports in the world. It was early July and the only seats available to us for that entire time were to Atlanta, Georgia, which was of no value to us. At least in London, we had MAF people who knew where we were. Eventually, the MAF Canada office sent full-fare tickets for us to Toronto but because of the busy season, even they were standby.

There was a time, a few years earlier when we experienced something similar. It was during our time in Bukavu when Willie began having severe headaches. After a while the doctors in Zaire recommended that we return to Canada to find out what the problem was. They feared that she had a brain tumour and there was nothing they could do for her there. That time, we flew from Nairobi to Frankfurt, Germany. We had ID-90 tickets with Air Canada but there was no room on any flights from Germany to Canada. More than that, it was during a heightened terrorist alert and there were armed soldiers and equipment all over the airport. While trying to sleep in a lounge, some drunken man tried to molest Andrew. With armed military people everywhere, I ended up fighting with this guy. The soldiers just looked on as we wrestled around and under the lounge seats.

With a lot of begging, after a couple of days, we were finally able to get seats to Toronto. There, the doctors from the Missionary Health Institute determined that she had nerve damage from an accident that she had a few months earlier in Bukavu when she hit her head on a staircase that went up to our attic.

Now, after arriving in Toronto from London we went to the same Missionary Health Institute where Willie and all of us went through a thorough "post-field" medical and psychological testing. It wasn't until two weeks later, after driving from Ontario to BC, and while visiting friends and supporters, that we learned that Willie had hepatitis.

CHAPTER 33

ESPERANZA

Before leaving Tanzania, we had decided that we would likely not be returning to Africa and therefore likely not continuing to work with MAF. I was much more interested in being involved in some sort of ministry to provide care for burned-out, discouraged and "fallen" missionaries and Christian workers. Although I had a lot to learn, God had taught me, through my own burn-out, discouragement, fall and growth that there was a desperate need for some place of healing. Arthur Dixon, the director of the Shantyman's Christian Association (SCA) and a man I had admired for his wisdom and godliness, had been encouraging me to join his mission to establish such a place of healing at Esperanza on Vancouver Island. I was quite familiar with SCA, having worked on the *Messenger III* mission boat during my college days and also having flown with Joe Ottom, up and down the west coast for over a year. During that time I had flown into Esperanza with Arthur, Joe and others, so I knew the location.

When we first arrived back on the west coast, we stayed for a few weeks with Willie's family in Powell River before settling in to the new "work". In the meantime Hope moved to Nanaimo, on the east side of the island where she went to college and, at the same time, got her Private Pilot Licence. Andrew and Amy did correspondence classes at home with Willie.

Esperanza had been the location of a medical mission many years ago, serving what was then thriving fishing and logging industries. Just a couple of kilometres south, along the shore had been a fish-canning plant called Ceepeecee. Mining, fishing and logging drew men to the area. The mission had an old, three storey, wooden hospital building that still stood on the shore at the base of the mountains. Most of the cottages were previously "float houses" (cabins that were built on a raft of large logs) and had been sold or donated to the mission by people who no longer needed them. The missionaries had used winches to drag them ashore and place them on foundations. Two large docks were built by the Canadian government, where fishing trawlers, tourists, small government ships and transport vessels would tie up. We operated an ESSO marine fuel depot for those sailing up and down the coast. There was a lovely stream coming down from the mountains that provided the station with pure, clear water and many of the boats would fill their holds when they came for fuel. Salmon spawned in the lower section of the stream.

In fact, we were amply supplied with sea food. We could catch cod, three types of salmon and halibut. We had scallops, clams, oysters, prawns and if you liked them, sea cucumbers. From our kitchen window we would watch seals, sea lions and killer whales along with all sorts of water fowl and bald eagles. Cougars and black bears came down from the mountains too. Although in our time we never actually saw cougars, we saw plenty of bears, some of which I had to get rid of because they had no fear of the children.

There was also an old schoolhouse where staff families' children, in the past, had attended. The main building, besides the hospital, housed the dining hall, chapel, kitchen, library, prayer room and a small gym. All building supplies, in fact all supplies of any kind came by boat or aircraft. The nearest roads were about 25 minutes away by speed boat. There were gravel roads that came from the Vancouver Island Highway on the east side of the island, to the little towns of Zeballos and Tahsis. An old Navy minesweeper that had been converted to carry freight and passengers would come by each week and we could order whatever food or items that we needed from the store in Gold River. It would be slung onto our dock on a pallet from the deck of the "Uchuck", which was its name. Most passengers called it the "Upchuck."

By the time we settled there in the Autumn of 1990, there was less than 10% of the fishing of the "old days". The canneries had long since closed down and the logging was just a small part of what it had been. Scenery-wise, it was as beautiful as any place we had ever seen.

People communicated by marine radio mostly. There was an old telephone system that ran between the houses on the station. Three other missionary families lived there with us. There were not really any roads except the trails between the buildings, so the only vehicles on the station were an old pickup truck and a tractor. A couple of diesel generators provided power at that time. Later, there was a team from the Vancouver area that installed a hydro generator. Down at the North Dock was a building holding all the shop equipment and weighs that could pull a 40 foot trawler up out of the water for maintenance. It's hard to describe the peaceful atmosphere, standing out on the end of the dock, when the fog descends so that you cannot even see the shore behind you. Most of the time, it is clear and you look upward in every direction to the snow capped, forested mountains. But there are times when the weather is so violent that it would be crazy to take a boat out into it.

For all the harrowing experiences that I experienced flying in different countries, I never felt closer to death than during one short trip in one of our speed boats. The owner of a fish farm, that was out in the channel about two miles away, was visiting and I offered to take him home. When we rounded the point and turned toward his fish farm, the seas, which had already been pretty rough, turned violent. I didn't dare get too far away from the shore in case we sank. The jagged rocky shore with the crashing sea would be impossible to land on. The boat would be instantly smashed to pieces if we got too close and it was impossible to turn around with the huge swells and wild wind. The boat, called "The Westerly" had a cabin roof with a hatch that was partly open. As we advanced, she would rise up on the swell and then "dive" down the windward side into the trough. At the bottom of the trough, one time, the bow went so far underwater that the sea actually came in through the hatch, which was above and behind where we were sitting. Have you ever thrown a stick, spear-like, into the water and watched how it springs right back out? That is what happened to us. We were thrust backward with the outboard engine coming completely out of the water. I am writing this story now, so it is evident that we finally made it to his floating home. Here was a "west coaster" with more experience than I could imagine but when he described the event to his waiting wife, he said that he had never experienced such a scare in his life.

Since I wasn't flying and didn't own an airplane, the only way in or out of the station was by one of the mission's two boats, the *Westerly* and the *School Boy*. I eventually bought a 19 foot Double Eagle with a sturdy cabin that slept about six people. It had belonged to someone from the local tribe who had killed his brother-in-law and owed money to the local Indian band. I was able to get it from them at a good price since most people wanted nothing to do with it. I don't remember what it was called before but I re-registered it as the *Hope*. I spent much more time fixing it than cruising but when it was running, it was wonderful.

We would sail across the sound to Nootka Island and catch cod. Most of those fish were not really big; about eight to ten inches. But they were perfect for attracting the magnificent bald eagles that nested high up in the trees along the shore. We would knock the fish on the side of the boat and then throw them 30 or 40 feet away, in the water. The eagles were able to see them clearly from over 500 feet away. When they became familiar with the *Hope* they would watch us and wait. Then, when they spotted the floating fish, they would glide, circling closer and closer and finally make a beautiful swoop, stretching their talons forward, grasping the fish and without hardly a splash, soar back up to their nests to their waiting, hungry brood. I was able to video many of these events.

We also videoed seals, sea lions and especially killer whales, who would swim for miles along side our boat in pods. They seemed as curious about us as we were about them and never produced a threat, other than the times that they would surface so close to us that it would rock the boat. You have to think that they must have a sense of humour.

Esperanza is also where I learned about "JJ". I would often hear staff talk about "JJ". It took a while to realize that this was not the initials of some person but a description of much of the "goodies" that people sent to the mission. It stood for "Junk for Jesus". There are some well intentioned folk who, when they have some old washing machine or TV or something and don't know what to do with it, come up with the idea of sending it to the missionaries. To get anything to Esperanza involved some time, effort and expense. But we had one whole cabin full of old washers, dryers, refrigerators…. Things that were not good enough to keep but "too good to throw away". It's sort of like the old story about saving used tea bags to send to the missionaries.

There were three other families who were serving there with us. Like many missions, a lot of time was spent keeping the aging facilities from being reclaimed by nature. If a rainforest is anything, it is wet, causing the old wood-frame buildings to rot unless they were constantly cared for. We had a limitless supply of wood, not only from the forest all around us but from the many logs that had escaped log booms that were often being towed past Esperanza to some mill. Most of them were one to four feet in diameter and about fifty feet long. I had been very impressed with a portable sawmill made by a Christian company, called 'Woodmizer'. It cost about $15,000. Normally, I would not even consider spending that kind of money. However, some time before, we had received an unexpected amount of money that we knew was to be spent for the Lord's work and this looked like a great use for that money.

We were able to cut all the lumber that we needed for building, siding and even shakes for roofing the cottages on the station. However, no amount of "fixing" could save the old hospital. It had been condemned. Rotted staircases lay crumpled on the floors. Many main beams were sagging and some were broken. In places, you could reach six inches into a ten inch beam and pull rot out with your hand. It had been a monument to God's love and faithfulness and many of the local people did not want to see it destroyed, but at this time it was downright dangerous. To some, I became infamous for being the one who tore it down and burned it. I don't know, but I imagine that if you were to mention my name around there, some would remember me most for being the "outsider" who came in and destroyed a "sacred" site.

The reason that we were there was to try to establish a place where burned out Christian leaders could come and be ministered to. Through my study and the experiences that we had gone through and were still going through, I became very aware of "Spiritual Warfare" in a personal, powerful way. Not that I had the answers but I was perhaps learning that Jesus is the "Wonderful Counsellor" and I was not. Pastors began sending people whom they thought I could help. That drew me into a state of dependence on God and acknowledgement of my own limitation. I think that it was about that time, while reading several authors and searching Scripture for answers, I came upon the work of Neil Anderson and Freedom In Christ Ministry (FICM). Most of the books I read before this seemed to be either Christian counsellors using secular methods with some Bible verses to validate their teaching, or those who seemed eager to beat up Satan with special, "Spiritual Power." This is not the best place to go into details but I saw that FICM promoted, what could best be called, "truth" or reality encounters rather than "power" encounters. Since we started using this "method" (although that is not a good definition of it) I have seen many people, who were struggling with painful issues, find lasting freedom without all of the shouting, naming, claiming intimidation or the clinical philosophy that required the highly trained, credentialed specialists.

It was evident, even among the little team we had at Esperanza that we were not exempt from "attacks". One of many events that got our attention happened one day when the youngest son of our camp cook, just stopped breathing in his crib. His mother, April, came running to get Willie. We headed over toward their cabin and met Tim who was carrying little Matthew in his arms. He took him into his house and kept applying CPR. I got the boat ready. April and Tim jumped in while still trying to revive Matthew. With the boat going as fast as it could it took about 25 minutes to reach the dock in Tahsis. Dave, one of the other workers from Esperanza was with us, and called ahead by radio. For a few brief minutes, at the hospital, the baby seemed to be reviving but in the end we lost him. They determined that he had died of a very fast acting pneumonia.

Some people would argue that if we are busy serving the Lord, only "good" things will happen to us. Some will even use events like this to accuse people of being irresponsible or just plain mean. After all, if they had lived in town, where there was good medical care available, this likely would not have happened. I don't have all the answers but I am convinced that the safest place in the world for our loved ones is in the centre of God's will and this dear family was obediently serving God. As painful as this was and as confused as we are when these things happen, God lovingly uses everything that happens to us for our good. I have seen it many times.

Esperanza was such a beautiful place, ideal for drawing away from the world and getting in touch with God in many ways. The main advantage was also its great drawback. It was remote. To get there from somewhere like Vancouver could take the better part of a day. Driving from the city to the ferry, the ferry crossing to Vancouver Island, driving up to Campbell River, then across the island to Gold River on paved roads, gravel logging roads from there to Tahsis and finally a 25 to 35 minute motor boat ride. That could take over twelve hours. It was hardly a place to go for a weekend.

CHAPTER 34

BACK TO MAF

The Shantymen were having a conference in Ontario and while I was there, I took the time to pop in on the Mission Aviation Fellowship Canadian headquarters in Guelph. I had the privilege of going to the dedication of a Beechcraft King Air aircraft that was going to Angola. While I was there, Gene Parkins, the President of MAFC spoke to me. He had a burden for the staff who were going through emotional, cultural and spiritual challenges and asked me if I would consider coming back into MAF to help. He was aware of the things we had gone through. He also knew that I was much more interested in serving in a more "pastoral" role, like what we were trying to do on the west coast. He challenged me by saying that I could wait until Christian workers burned out and then work with them or be a part of helping to equip them to be successful and avoid the "crash". I promised to pray about it.

Back on the island, it was becoming clear that the vision for a Christian worker's retreat/recovery centre was likely not so realistic. At the same time, we were able to use the facilities more effectively for local people who needed a place to 'dry out' from alcohol and drug abuse. A few months later, we found ourselves driving back to Ontario. I had the U-Haul with my mother, and Willie had our Blazer with Andrew, Amy and Houdini, the psychotic cat. Hope would be coming across the country later in her little Chevette. We were back to MAF: "Move Again Friend." After a couple of weeks, we found a house in Guelph and for the first time in our lives, bought a home. My mother had been living in a small room in a hotel in Pemberton, B.C., where she worked. We created an apartment downstairs with a ground level entrance for her to live.

One thing that still amazes me is the fact that almost every person who was supporting us financially from our early days in 1972, continued to support us through the moves from Africa Inland Mission, Shantymen, Trinity Western College, Mission Aviation Fellowship Zaire, MAF Tanzania, Shantymen and now back to MAF Canada. We cannot fully express our gratitude to the many dear folks who gave month after month. Many of them were not giving from their surplus but were sacrificing other things to keep us on the field. We were always acutely aware of that. But more than anything, we thank God for His provision, through those many people. We realize that God has always provided all we need – perhaps not all we wanted. Now that I am retired, we do not have those supporters. We do not have a retirement plan. I suppose we never expected to still be alive at this age. God was our provider back then and the last I heard, He has not retired. I'm told that retirement for a missionary is "Out of this world."

Gene, our MAFC President, gave me my new job description. I was called the Overseas Staff Facilitator and was responsible to do "whatever it takes to make the missionary staff's ministry successful." From their initial application to their repatriation at the end of their service, I was to be there for them. We didn't have an HR department. We didn't have a Recruiting department, or a Ministry Partnership department or a Member Care department. They were my jobs. In fact there was no need for recruiting. We always had more applicants than we could process.

This was the early days of computer use. I had a big spreadsheet, not electronic but an actual big piece of graft paper, about 18" by 36" with the name of each family down one side and the monthly income and expenses for each along the top. As support came in I would record it under income. As expenses, like transport, education, medical, passports, housing, etc. came in I would write in the amount under the expense categories. There was lots of correspondence and most of it was still by letter. But we were not without technology. In the hall entrance was our

Telex machine. Fax was a wonderful tool. Gene was eager to get everyone onto the computers as they were being introduced. Those were the days of "DOS" and understanding the code on those two-tone green monitors. He would work late into the night, pulling wires through the ceilings and walls so we could "talk" to each other. Although I had to call in the "programmer" very often, the new electronic spreadsheet did make life a lot easier.

CHAPTER 35

FLYPASS Ltd.

By this time Hope had her Private Pilot Licence and mine was still valid but it was just too expensive to rent airplanes. I had heard of people who built their own planes but that just seemed silly. To me, homebuilt aircraft were flimsy machines made from bits and pieces of junk and built by people who had a lot more courage than good sense. My brother-in-law had purchased a kit for an RV-3 but the parts just hung around in the ceiling of his basement. As a "professional" (and I guess, a rather arrogant one) this all seemed so "amateur". But I heard about an outfit, a couple of hours north of Guelph that produced kits for two seat, all aluminum sports planes. It wouldn't hurt to go have a look, right? I could not have imagined all that would come out of that innocent little visit.

My first visit to Zenair in Midland was on a Saturday and there were only two workers there. They allowed me to look through the manufacturing facilities, where several aircraft were being assembled and many aircraft kit parts were being manufactured. I was impressed with the quality of the equipment and the organization of the raw materials and finished parts. But, when I looked at the planes I had a lot of questions. They were doing things and using materials that were very different from what I knew of "certificated" aircraft. I was worried that this was unconventional, unprofessional and unsafe. After all, this was different from the way we did things for the last 60 years. The look on the face of Vern Boker, one of the workers who was there that day, sort of said, "I know you think you know everything there is to know about airplanes but if you like I am willing to explain why these planes are different." For years after this, I had reason to say that very thing to many aviation "professionals".

These "amateur" planes were built with, what appeared to me as, Pop rivets – totally unacceptable in 'real' airplanes. He explained that these "Avdel" blind rivets, were not only certified for aircraft but in some ways were much safer than the "bucked" rivets that the industry had been using for many years. I saw one thing that was definitely just plain silly. There was no aileron hinge! The skin of the aileron just tucked under the skin of the wing and bent up and down. Everyone knows that after bending up and down for a while, it would get brittle and just break off. Well, it would break off if it was the same aluminum that we traditionally used on airplanes but this was not that old aluminum.

If this is boring, just skip down a paragraph or so. For the last 60 or so years we had used 2024 T3 aluminum, which is very corrosive and brittle. While it has good tensile strength, it needs to be very well protected from the environment and not allowed to flex. Zenair and other kit builders were using 6061 T6, which could tolerate almost limitless flexing, which is different from "bending". Many "amateur" aircraft built with this alloy have flown for thousands of hours and many years without even being painted and have not suffered significant corrosion.

Allow me to continue just a little more and explain the engine that they recommended. Sorry for the techie stuff! Most of these Zenair aircraft were fitted with a four-stroke, water-cooled, electronic-ignition, Rotax aircraft engine. They were very unlike the engines that I had worked on. Of course, the gas engines that I was trained on, and that are on almost all certificated aircraft today, were designed in the 1930s and 40s and have not changed significantly in all those years. Strange! In the years that followed, I learned that these "amateur" engines were generations ahead of the old "certificated" stuff. They were at least as safe and much more efficient.

After some consideration and with a little fear, I finally bought an airframe kit for the model CH 601 AUL 'Zodiac'. Then it occurred to me that I didn't really have a good place to build it. Oh, I could have laid out the wings on my mom's bed down stairs, but somehow I think she might have found some excuse to complain. My next door neighbour came over and said if I helped him clean out his single-car garage, he would let me build it in there. I can't remember just when I bought the kit but the first flight occurred on May 7, 1994. It was built in about nine months, in my spare time while still working full-time with MAF.

During the build, I got to know and really appreciate Chris Heintz, the owner of Zenair and designer of many models of aircraft. He was a professional Aeronautical Engineer, had worked on the design of the supersonic transport, Concord and had designed several certified aircraft for Avion Robin in France. By the time that I had finished that first plane, I had also created a company, called Flypass Ltd. and became a dealer for Zenair. My intention was to do this part-time and continue with MAF. My company became federally incorporated on January 11 of 1993.

The name was sort of an accident. I had given my lawyer, who was processing the incorporation, a few proposed names for the company. After each "search" she would call me to tell me that that name was not available. The last name I tried was Skypass. Again, after checking she reported that some insurance company out west had that name. At that moment, I was very busy with a missionary candidate in my office, so without thinking much, the name "Flypass" came to mind, so I asked her to try that one. Within a couple of hours, she called me to announce that my company was called Flypass Ltd. For a moment, I wondered where she came up with a name like that, until I remembered giving it to her. That was the start of something much bigger than we could have ever dreamed.

To start out, I rented a little, open "T" hanger at the airpark in Guelph. Officially, I was not permitted to conduct business there because the flight school, based there had exclusive rights to any profitable activity, including flight training, sales and aircraft maintenance. My flight instructor's license was no longer valid so all I could do was to "check-out" pilots in my aircraft. Several other "amateur" aircraft builders began coming to me to be checked out on my plane and in many cases, I would test-fly theirs and then check them out in their own planes. That didn't seem to conflict with the local flight school, which was owned by people who had become my friends, but eventually it became clear that I needed to be somewhere else.

For a while, I rented a 45 by 50 foot hangar at the Waterloo Regional Airport near Kitchener. By this time I had sold some Zenair kits and was busy building planes for customers. Susan Hutchinson, came on board as my bookkeeper. I had known her from when she was first born, since her parents were friends of my parents. She understood business and had worked for some big-time, well-known companies, like 3M. She would spend a dollar to find a penny but the books were always kept perfectly. Willie worked alongside of her and between the two of them they kept the office humming like a well oiled aircraft engine.

There was never a time when we had to worry about what to do with the "huge profit." For the next ten years, Flypass crawled, scraped and at times flew along. In the early days, God sent different people to be part of the company and in most cases, the people He sent were just exactly what was needed. One of those people was Jack Vanderveen. Jack had been trained as a missionary pilot/mechanic at Moody Bible Institute in Chicago and Tennessee. In speaking to his instructors and the director of the flight school, the most common remark was, "I wish every one of our students was like Jack Vanderveen." While I was working as Overseas Staff Facilitator in the MAF Canada office, Jack and his dear wife Janice, along with their three little boys had applied and had been accepted. I have had the wonderful privilege of interviewing, accepting and preparing many pilots for MAF service and met some of the most amazing, professional, godly people but none stood higher in my estimation than Jack. After a short and very difficult field assignment, the Vanderveens came back to settle in Sarnia, Ontario. I had maintained close contact with them and was aware that they were exhausted, confused and searching for God's place for their lives.

There was a little air show in St Thomas, not awfully far from Sarnia that I was attending on behalf of Flypass and I arranged to meet with Jack. We were not growing very fast and financially we were still struggling but I asked him if he would consider moving to Guelph and coming to work for me. It was a risk for him and Janice as much as it was for me. Looking back, I can't imagine how Flypass could have accomplished what it finally did if Jack had not come on board.

By this time, I had renewed my Flight Instructor license, although it was only for the new Ultra Light permit. Most of the planes that we built could be flown with a UL permit. Soon Jack had his instructor permit, and we had a busy little flying school going at the Waterloo airport. I had other instructors working for me as well. The only problem with Jack was that any student who flew with him always wanted him as their instructor. I don't blame them.

CHAPTER 36

FLYPASS' CONNECTION WITH THE MOON

I can't remember if it was before Jack came to Flypass or after that I met Owen. At some time, a reporter from the Kitchener news paper came to interview me and write an article about Flypass Ltd. A few days after the paper came out, I got a call from some old guy, who asked if he could come by and visit me at the hangar. I was busy building a plane but invited him anyway. He showed up and wandered around the place, talking something about airplanes and some experience that he had. He made a comment about the design of the nose gear on the plane I was working on; how that is was a bit like the one he designed for some plane called an Arrow.

It was not unusual for people to drop by to look at planes and do some 'hangar flying' and this guy seemed to be just like many. I didn't want to throw him out but at that moment, I needed to close up the place and go to Canadian Tire (an auto parts place) to try to find an "O" ring for my project. To not be rude, I asked him if he would like to go along with me. At the store I asked the man at the parts counter for the part I needed. The problem was, I knew the part size in metric but they only sold standard. When I told him the metric size of the ring, he went to figure out the comparable size in what they had. A couple of seconds later, Owen had figured it out in his head and told us what we needed. We were both impressed. "Who was this guy anyway?" That was my introduction to one of the most influential people to ever 'pop' into my life.

As we talked, I finally began to realize that he was one of the Aeronautical Engineers who designed the famous Avro Arrow along with the CF 100. Born and raised in Sarnia, Ontario, Owen joined the Royal Canadian Air Force during WWII. He trained, like most young pilots those days on everything from old Tiger Moths through Harvards (T-6s). But unlike most, he went directly into the twin-engine "Mosquito" fighter-bombers. Owen went on to become the youngest pilot to fly, not just one of the models but all three models of this airplane.

After the war he studied at the University of Toronto and became an Aeronautical Engineer. Then he was hired by Avro to work on the CF 100. His talent got the attention of the leaders of the CF 105, *Arrow* team where he was given the job of designing the landing gear system. The plane was many years ahead of anything like it but politics won over technology and after the successful flight of several Arrows, the project was cancelled. When the Arrow plant was suddenly and tragically closed and all plans, planes and parts were supposedly destroyed, Owen was one of several who were approached by recruiters from what was to become NASA in the States.

Among other things, he worked on the Gemini and Mercury Manned-Space Projects and when Apollo was first conceived he was made the Chief of Project Engineering. I later learned that when he was called in, they announced to him that they were starting a new program called Apollo and that he was in charge of all the engineers and one of the main people to determine the objectives of the project. In the early days, there was as much talk of Mars as there was of the Moon. I have seen and handled models that he had made of a Mars vehicle. It had "arms" that spread out from a centre and that would turn, while traveling. This was to allow high G forces at the outward parts and low G forces near the hub. Other models that he showed me were of the earliest concepts of modular space travel.

While Dr. Owen E. Maynard became one my greatest heroes, he also became a very close friend and mentor. When he would have a speaking engagement, he would bring me along to be a "plant". My job, in the audience was to ask him certain questions that would lead him to areas that he wanted to talk about. When I went to speak to groups, he would come along and do the same thing for me. He called it "our mutual admiration society." It would be easy to write chapters about him but I guess that is not the objective of this book.

But I cannot resist telling about the time he was granted an Honorary Doctorate from the University of Toronto, the school where he had graduated back in the 40s. A special banquet was arranged by the Dean of the Engineering School. Eighteen of Owen's closest friends and associates were invited to this very "posh" affair. There were directors from NASA, the President of the Canadian Space Agency and from the old Avro team, and Art Mitchell! I kept my mouth shut most of the time and they probably thought that I was somebody else. One of the things that Owen discussed most with the guests was the aircraft that I was developing that would eventually be called the CH 801. He went around giving out my brochures to his old buddies at the table. After the dinner, when no one was looking, I went around the table and took all the name place markers. Somewhere among my mementos are those cards with the names of all those famous guys – and me!

I know his name will appear again in these pages but please permit one more comment before I move along. After his funeral, where Willie and I were with just his family and maybe twenty others, the family created a special, memorial award, called the "Dr. Owen E. Maynard Friends of Aviation Society" award, to be granted annually for "Outstanding contribution to the field of aviation." The first one awarded hangs on my office wall with Willie's and my name on it. Okay! Back to Earth.

CHAPTER 37

FLYPASS GROWS

Two or three times a year we would conduct a weekend workshop to teach prospective builders how to build an all-metal aircraft. On Friday people would arrive from many places. We would sell them all the parts and some tools to build an actual aircraft rudder for whichever model of Zenair aircraft they were thinking of building. While the people came away with a rudder of their own, the most important thing that they acquired was the skill and confidence to tackle their own project. Often it would be a husband and wife team, two friends, a father and son pair or just one person alone. In the early days, they would find accommodation nearby but in the last few years, when we owned the Breslau Country Manor, a bed & breakfast, they would stay with us. We made a profit on the parts and planes that we sold but not on the service we provided. At any time, a customer could come for advice or bring in some part, like a wing to get assistance and advice. That was free to them but could be costly to us since it did consume a lot of time. I have been asked how many planes I have built. I don't know. Many times it was actually one of our employees like Jack who did the work. Sometimes, I (we) would do a wing or some other part(s). Putting them all together, I suppose there would be maybe 12 or more.

Our little flight school was fairly successful. I had several instructors. At least one moved on to become the Chief Flight Instructor of the main flying school on the airport. There were three other schools, with from two to fifteen aircraft but many times our little "fleet" did more air hours than any of them. One reason was the cost. With the old Cessna fleet and a few newer Katanas, that the others used, rental alone was well over $100 per hour. At $40 per hour, with our Zodiacs we could make more profit than the others and ours out-performed any of the competition's two-place planes. Like I said before, we could not use our equipment to teach private or commercial permits but for those who wanted a recreational permit, they were great.

After a year or two of renting, I bought the hanger and later a second one of the same size, that was joined to it. The first hanger was mostly for offices and planes under construction or development. The second had flight-line planes, mostly for the flying school. There were generally three or four CH 601s; two that we owned and others that belonged to customers, who leased them back to us. Some people would come with planes that they had built, for lessons or a check-out. When builders were getting close to completing their project, they would often come for lessons so they would be ready to fly. During the period of building, although the plans and parts were pretty straight forward, we normally had plenty of calls from customers. As often as not, they needed encouragement and confidence as much as instruction.

I visited many projects under construction, at the request of the owners. When a plane was finished and if it was within a couple hundred miles, I often did a final inspection and the initial test flight. It was not nearly as frightening as you might think, since the design was quite easy to inspect very thoroughly before flying it. But, as you can imagine, there were some that were poorly (terribly) built and were fit to be used as a wind indicator, on the top of a pole. Sometimes, the problems could be remedied and sometimes not.

One man called me from Bethlehem, Georgia, who was having a real struggle. He paid for Willie and me to fly down to his place and spend a couple of weeks on his 601 HDS. The home was very much like the house in the movie, "Gone With The Wind". We were treated royally but we did put in a lot of hours, repairing the damage and getting it ready for inspection. I heard that the FAA Designated Inspector was very pleased with it.

ROYAL CANADIAN AIR FARCE

As we look back, it seems that there were very few people that we assisted, that didn't become good friends. I would say that we had the great privilege of helping most of them technically and encouraging many emotionally and especially spiritually. One character was "Mike from Canmore", John Morgan. Some people might remember the Royal Canadian Air Farce that was on radio for years and on TV many years after that. One of the creators and main actors on the show was John. Besides Mike from Canmore and many other characters, he was famous as "Jock MacBile." So many celebrities are artificial – not John. What you see is what you get. We found him to be very genuine and he became a great friend.

He showed up at Flypass one day to ask about getting training on the 601s. He was an experienced glider pilot at a nearby club but wanted "power plane" training. After flying for a while, he decided that he wanted to buy one of these 601s for himself. Some time before, I had sold a kit to a high school in Quebec. They had finished the airframe and were looking to sell it, so they could start another one. Overall, it was quite well built, especially for having had many hands working on it over a couple of years. We brought it in and finished it. John wanted it painted like a 'Yellow Taxi' with the black and white checkerboard pattern down each side. Along the side of the fuselage we had large black letters that said, "Air Farce One". That was one of the "lease-back" planes that we used in the flight school.

Our son Andrew and John became good friends. Often, on Mondays, John would come to our home and Andrew would tell him what he thought of the show, which was broadcast on Friday evening. In the earlier days of the show, the humour was brilliant. A lot of it was political or social satire. As the years rolled on, humour, including the stuff that John and the other show's writers produced become more and more vulgar. I remember Willie going after John at our table, about the declining moral material. He actually agreed and commented that the public were getting lower and lower in intellect and morals and less able to grasp good, clean humour, which was discouraging to him as well. He often invited us to his cottage in Bala, on the Moon River. He loved to cook and we got to be the very willing recipients of his creations. He had some serious health issues and the last time we left him, Willie commented, on the way home, that she didn't think we would see him again. A week or so later, we got word from his son Christopher that while just sitting in his chair, he suddenly just stopped breathing and died.

We were invited to his memorial which was at a pub in Toronto where we met several of the members of the crew and cast of the show. We had spoken to John many times about Christ and he was very open and not at all rejecting. In his Welsh past, he had heard the Gospel and never argued or rejected our conversations. Despite the characters that he played, he was a very intelligent and informed man. When we spoke to his son at the memorial, he made the comment that his dad had told him that he had known several "Christians" but that if he ever became one he would want to "be like Art and Willie." That was humbling but also hurting, to know that he understood and appreciated the Truth of the Gospel but had likely not accepted it before he died.

CHAPTER 38

HALF-TON 100 MPH AIRBORN PICKUP

The most popular aircraft that we built and sold was the CH 601 Zodiac in its various models. With the right engines, it was, as Owen Maynard used to say, "The simplest, safest, sweetest, light airplane" that he had seen. It was fun to fly and to instruct in. But we also built some CH 701 STOL (Short Take Off and Landing) planes. They were not nearly as "pretty" as the 601s. In fact, they were kind of ugly but it was that ugliness that made it perform so well. We used to joke that they looked just about as pretty as the crate that they came in. With two people on board they could take off in just about 100 feet. It was the sort of plane that people would use to just get up off any field and cruise, "low & slow". Owners were using them in Africa and other undeveloped areas for visiting places where there were no runways, or where they wanted to patrol game parks, hunting for poachers. One of my customers, an American police officer from Michigan, built his to patrol his area for drug "grow-ops" with his K-9 partner on board.

I enjoyed building and flying both models for different reasons. As I looked at the 701s, my mind went back to the jungle in Zaire. In that vast tropical rainforest, I had seen remote villages and had occasionally seen a soccer field carved out of the jungle. In my mind I felt that I could likely land my MAF plane and fairly surely survive, although the plane would probably be damaged. I wondered if we could create an airplane that could actually land safely and even take off on such a field and unlike the 701, carry four passengers or half a ton. It was a wild idea but 'what if....'

I spoke to Chris Heintz, who told me that they had thought of such a plane, that would be called a CH 801, but determined that there was "no market for a four-place homebuilt airplane." None of the other major kit manufacturers had more than two-place models. Chris had sketched some notes on plans of a 701 and there was a man in BC that was trying to build, what was basically a larger 701. Two of Chris' sons had even started putting some wings together but they felt it was not worth attempting and quickly abandoned it.

For over two years, I talked to him about it and finally he agreed to provide me with any flat-stock (sheet aluminum and tube steel) that I needed. I could also use some of their brakes and presses when they were not busy. He would also provide some of the 701 drawings with suggested figures. Owen Maynard took a special interest in it whenever he would come by the hanger.

Along with our other work at Flypass we spent the next two years on the project. There were some things on the 701 that we made simpler, which also made the build easier and even made the plane a bit prettier. I took a marker pen and drew out the full size image on the floor of the hangar. We laid out the many parts on the floor sketch as they were developed. There was no lack of challenges. I found that if I thought all day about some issue and still did not come up with a solution, it would often come to mind in the middle of the night. The problem was, that by morning, I had forgotten it. I began keeping blank paper and pencils beside the bed and would often get up and scribble about 3:30 am.

As the airframe was coming to a finish our search for the "right" engine got serious. A local company had developed, what looked like a very professionally modified Subaru auto engine. When it ran, it ran beautifully but we began to discover that there were several issues that had not been worked out. Most of the initial problems of the 801 had to do with the engine. Along with the developers of this engine, we created the engine mounting system and cowling, installed the instruments and began "run-up" testing.

In the meantime, I had trailered the project, in different stages of development, to the air shows, particularly, AirVenture in Oshkosh, Wisconsin and Sun-N-Fun in Florida. Remember, this was the plane for which there was "no market". Long before our prototype took to the sky and before there was any kit being produced, people who had heard about it and seen it were making orders. I had attended Oshkosh and other air shows for several years and even when Mission Aviation Fellowship had no official representation, I spoke to groups and individuals on behalf of the mission. When MAF did start attending, it seemed that they stayed away from me in droves. After all, now I had "gone over to the other side". I was now advocating "amateur" aviation, which by its very name was not considered "professional". In the years to come, after the first one was flying, Mission Safety International (MSI), Jungle Aviation And Radio Service (JAARS) and finally MAF came on board and not only acknowledged that the 801 had a place in missionary aviation but offered very helpful suggestions.

Anyway, back to the development of the first model. The plane flew at least as well as we had hoped. In fact, it performed better in some ways – that is when the engine worked. In the early days, we became fairly good at emergency and precautionary landings due to engine failures. Then came that fateful day! Jack Vanderveen and I were both doing the early flight testing. One thing that we were trying to determine was the best angle for the flaperons (a combination of ailerons and flaps). We would fly with the power set at a specific setting and measure the performance. Then we would land, adjust the angle and fly again. Each time we adjusted the flaperons, we had to loosen and then retighten a "jam nut".

We had flown about seven hours and things were going very well. Since we were required to do 40 hours of testing before going beyond 50 nautical miles or carry passengers, I decided to fill the tanks with seven hours fuel. I planned to do one circuit and depart to just "make holes in the sky" for a few hours. It was early on Saturday morning, April 18, 1998. Ed, one of my friends, was the controller in the tower.

I was cleared to taxi out to the threshold of runway "Two-Five". I announced my intentions to the tower and after all the pre-take-off checks, he cleared me for take-off. Even with all that fuel on board, the plane was off the ground in less than 200 feet and climbed like a home-sick angel. Before reaching the length of half of the airstrip, I was at 1,000 feet and levelled off. It was an amazing, exhilarating feeling. Too bad it was early in the morning and there were very few people to witness the performance. Every take-off requires some degree of tension and an awareness of potential problems. My mind is always prepared for an "abort" if things aren't just right. Only a fool assumes there will be no problem and I was scanning the instruments, listening to the engine and gently testing the controls throughout the climb. Everything appeared to be perfect. Until...!

Until I moved the control stick to the left to initiate the cross-wind turn. Suddenly, the stick fell free against my leg. The flapperons were evidently no longer connected to it. The elevator and rudder were still working but I could move the stick from side to side with no response. I had no way of banking the plane. That wonderful feeling I was enjoying moments before was replaced by a sudden combination of fear, confusion and a bit of anger. My mind was racing through the control system. I had built it. What could this possibly be?

The plane wanted to continue to roll hard to the right and I had no aileron control to stop it. I found that by applying full left rudder, I could reduce the right roll. By pushing the stick forward, I could increase the airspeed which made the rudder more effective and gave me less of a right roll tendency. This was happening over a matter of seconds and was not the result of careful, preplanned logic but "whatever works". I called the tower and told Ed that I had a control failure. If he was watching I'm sure he would have wondered why the plane was turning, yawing, and pitching so erratically. He cleared me to land on runway "Three-Two". I remember thinking that there was no way I would be able to make it to the runway. I just wanted to come down somewhere on or near the airport. As I write this, about 15 years after the event, I can vividly recall everything that was happening and the feelings I had then still make my heart race today. I did not think about dying or have my life "flash before my eyes", although I might well have been living through the last few seconds of my life. I was way too busy trying to balance power, rudder and elevators to keep the plane from flipping over and getting to the ground with some sort of control. From the time of the control failure to impact could not have been much more than a minute. So there was no time to learn how to make this anything less than a "controlled crash."

By increasing power from the engine I could yaw the plane slightly right and also give the rudder and elevator more airstream. This engine turned opposite to regular aircraft engines which would have yawed the plane to the left. With my hands and feet busy, my eyes as big as saucers and my brain working to make sense of it all, I found myself actually lining up on runway, "Three-Two". To keep the right wing up I still had full left rudder (I don't think that I had that rudder pedal off the floor from the time the problem started.) To keep the rudder effective I had to have the nose down at a very steep angle. I knew that near the ground I could not use power and I could not maintain such a nose-down attitude or I would not survive the impact. Just before 'touch-down' I had to pull back on the stick to reduce the angle of contact. That, of course, reduced the airflow over the rudder, which in turn allowed the plane to roll sharply to the right.

During the entire "adventure" I kept thinking about the seven hours of fuel that I had in the wings over my head. There was no doubt at all that this machine was not going to look like an airplane after touch-down and among other things I was very concerned that I would be unconscious in the burning wreckage. I remember actually reaching for my seat belt to undo it before impact. Of course I didn't but I was so aware of that fuel and I wanted to be able to get away from the plane as quickly as possible.

It struck the ground, right wing down, tearing it off. I was about 100 feet to the right of the runway in soft, grass-covered dirt. Immediately, it was upside-down facing back towards the approach path. The pilot's door had been torn open and there was enough space for me to squirm through an opening between the leading edge of the wing and the side of the windshield. It seemed like one motion of undoing the seatbelt, going through the opening and just continuing to run until I was about 50 feet from it. In the mean time Ed, the controller, had begun to dial 911. He held his finger on the last "1" and waited. When he saw me running from the wreckage, he hung up. What a blessing that was. I didn't need emergency vehicles, police and news people around.

When you build an airplane, especially a new, untried model, there are always those who are eager to tell you how foolish you are. I did not want to be on the 6 O'clock News proving them right. I could hear them all now. "What an idiot! Who do you think you are? You should have quit when you couldn't get Bobby Lazelle's plane off the ground." I was alive and a little surprised to be. Other than a little scrape on my right knee, there was no injury. I couldn't say that for the sad looking mess that lay on the ground, wheels pointing at the sky, one wing torn off and the rest twisted and spread around.

I walked back to the hangar. Jack was preparing for a flight with a student and was unaware of the crash. When he saw me walking back between the hangars he looked totally confused. I told him that the plane was destroyed, out on the field. He grabbed me and hugged me so hard. I'm sure there were a thousand thoughts racing through his mind. We walked into the building and called Willie, who was at home in Guelph. She came out immediately. I called Transport Canada and after making the initial report, they gave me permission to move the plane from the crash site after taking photos. Then the three of us walked out to the wreck. The cause of the failure was very obvious. The actuator that attached to the flapperon, the one that I already mentioned had a "jam nut" to keep it from coming undone, had evidently not been tightened after the last time it was adjusted. The normal vibration from the engine had caused it to slowly unscrew and it had finally separated at that moment when I tried to turn onto the crosswind leg at 1,000 feet.

One of the airport service workers arrived with a pickup truck as we were trying to disassemble it. We made several loads back to the hangar until it was all safely locked away. The mangled main fuselage sat there, upright and on its wheels. Willie, Jack and I climbed into it and just sat there, thankful to God but confused. What now?

Willie called Owen Maynard and he was there within minutes. He had been such an encouragement during the development of the plane. After checking the degree of damage of each part, he began telling us how excited he was about how the cabin had almost no distortion although the rest was pretty messed up. One of his greatest concerns, in the design of the Lunar Lander was the integrity of the "living space". He always talked about the principle of "frangibility". That's where you design parts of a vehicle to distort, crush and collapse so that the force is dissipated before the people inside are injured. He was all excited with how the cabin remained intact. Then he said, "Do you remember when the NASA Mercury crashed when a door flew off? I did that and later they made me the Chief Engineer for Apollo." Of course, he had not destroyed the Mercury but he was responsible for the people who designed the part that failed. He was trying to tell us that this project was not over and we were now able to learn so much more about the structural integrity of the plane than if this had never happened. God had sent Owen to us, knowing that he would become a huge encouragement when things seemed most hopeless.

I remember that one of my main concerns was insurance. Some time earlier, I had phoned the company that we used for our flight school planes, asking them to insure this 801 but until that moment we had only a verbal acknowledgement—no paperwork had yet arrived in the mail. I called them with fear, knowing that everything we had was invested in this project and there was nothing left to rebuild it or perhaps even carry on with Flypass. To our great delight, they sent an adjuster who declared it a total write-off and announced that it would be covered. I had requested a value of $50,000 when I phoned in for insurance. The company paid the full amount minus one month's premium and the deductible, which I think was $1,000. Then they allowed me to buy back the wreckage for $5,000. Is God good or what?

It had taken us two years to build the first CH801. During that time we had learned much and there were times when I thought, "If I ever do that again, I will do it differently." The second plane took just about three months to build. Well, actually, officially, it was a "repair" of the first plane. You see, the most significant part of an airplane, to Transport Canada, is the data plate. That is just a piece of fireproof metal about the size of a business card with the Make, Model, Serial number, Builder's name, Date and Location of build. There are many old, worn-out planes that are purchased for their data plate. So we were able to build a new plane around the old plate and, if we liked, we could have flown it with no inspection – strange! All of the forms and templates that we used to create the first one made building the second one much easier and even some of the parts from the original, like seats, instrument panel etc. were put into the "repair".

Again we used the modified Subaru engine because we had no money for anything else. The theory behind the engine was great and I hear that several people, later installed it on 801s, but again, ours failed in flight and Jack had to land in a field. I called the folks at Zenair, who were wanting to have the plane for testing and as a demonstrator. They came and got it from the field, took it to the factory and mounted a regular Lycoming O-360, 180 horsepower, aircraft engine onto it. Some of the people who flew that particular plane claimed that it handled better than any 801 since.

One could not possibly have a better team of people to work with than Chris Heintz, his sons and the others at Zenair. FYI, their company was called "Zenair Ltd" in Canada and "Zenith Aircraft Company" in the States. Whenever I was at any air show, I was accommodated, fed and entertained as one of the family. When Flypass was made the exclusive dealer of Zenair kits in Canada, they were very generous, charging me almost no exchange difference in all of the kits that I imported from their factory in Missouri. That was a saving of about 15% even before the 'dealer's' price. Chris and his sons were always available for any questions and accepted several changes and suggestions that I had, many of which were employed in their later products.

With my prototype down in their American facility, they developed the kit that was by now in demand. Before my first prototype ever flew, there were a lot of kits being ordered. This, despite the report earlier, that there was no interest or market for the CH801. As parts were developed in both of Chris' facilities, they were sent to me where we assembled the first of two 'proofs-of-concept' planes. The other was assembled at the same time, at Zenair factory in Huronia, Ontario. In the years that followed, several hundred kits were sold. It is always fun to show up at an airport and see one, or several, on the flight line. What is much more exciting is to know that some have ended up being used to serve missionaries in remote countries.

Zenair built their first 801, while developing the kit and at the same time I was building my second, using kit parts made from the factory. After researching several engines and determining what I could afford, I chose an aircraft engine from the Czech Republic, called the Walter LOM. It was an in-line, inverted, six cylinder, 235 horse-power, supercharged engine. That means that all six cylinders are in a single row with the crankshaft on top. While it was a common configuration years ago, it is not so popular today. At the same time, the technology was generations ahead of the Continental and Lycoming engines that are still being used in our archaic "modern" aircraft. I spent two weeks of training at the factory in Prague to get my certification to maintain their engines and propellers.

It was a delight to fly and possibly the safest engine that the 801 ever had. The one problem was that it was a very long engine, which made the plane "nose-heavy" and required about fifteen pounds of lead at the rudder hinge. Needless to say, it was a whole lot more fun to fly than the Subaru powered one. I also developed a belly-pod that incorporated a lot of the features that our MAF Cessnas lacked. It could carry 300 pounds, which was handy since there was not much baggage space in the cabin.

CHAPTER 39

VENEZUELA ADVENTURES

Way back before my first 801 even flew, I would "trailer" it to air shows like Oshkosh or Sun-N-Fun. One time, in the early development stages, I had the fuselage on display at Air Venture in Oshkosh. My planes were always part of the Zenair display, in the Home-Built section of the show. There was the normal crowd of 'tire kickers' and questioners standing around the plane, asking questions, making comments and suggestions. Most of these people just want to "talk airplanes" and some of them were there to impress everyone with their enormous amount of "aviation expertise". It is hard to talk with serious enquirers sometimes. Often the serious ones are standing at the back of the group trying to learn.

That happened with Michael Dawson. Mike was born in Venezuela into a family of American missionaries. Let me quote from one of several books written about him and his family. *"Michael Dawson was born in the middle of the Amazon jungle, the fifth child of 10, born to missionaries Joe and Mildred Dawson who settled their family in Coshilowateli, Venezuela. Here he has spent his life living and working among the Yanomamo and continues to serve God with his wife Keila, their three boys and two daughters."* It wasn't until he began school that Michael really learned to speak English. I won't say more but you can read about him and his family in the books, *Spirit Of The Rainforest*,

All The Day Long, *Growing Up Yanomamo* and *I Can See The Shore*.

As I explained the features of the 801 and answered questions from the Air Venture group that had gathered around my, soon-to-be-finished prototype, Mike stood listening at the back of the crowd. He had come to Oshkosh to try to find an airplane that he could use to reach out to the villages that were so difficult to get to on foot and by river. Mission Aviation Fellowship had served his family for many years but their service was being withdrawn. The other missionary aviation service, New Tribes Mission Aviation, was leaving since the government was kicking out all their jungle missionaries. Michael and most of his siblings, however, were born there, which made them Venezuelan citizens and able to remain.

Anyway, Mike needed a plane. He had a commercial pilot's license and he came to the air show to check out another plane but when he saw the 801 he was hooked. We became good friends and when Zenair began producing the kit, he and his family moved to Canada long enough to participate in building the airframe for his own CH801 in our Flypass hangar. A church in Kitchener sent several volunteers who did everything from sweeping the hangar floor to actually helping to build the first missionary 801. My own 801 was flying very well with the Walter LOM from the Czech Republic, so Mike decided to go with that engine.

When the airframe was almost finished, it and the engine were crated separately and sent to Venezuela. It finally arrived in country and was transported to Puerto Ayacucho, on the Orinoco River bordering Columbia. In November of 2000, I flew down with two friends and spent a couple of weeks finishing the airframe and mounting the engine. I remember the morning that we towed it, tail first, from the apartment where we assembled it, through the streets, to the airport. The wings were not mounted and it really looked "weird". We finished it enough to get the engine running and to actually do some "high-speed taxi testing". Someone once told me that if the plane does not go more than 50 feet above the ground, it can be called high-speed taxing. To do the test, we required a person on board with a Venezuela radio operator's license to communicate with the tower. Then I needed someone who could translate his Spanish to English. It is more than unusual to have more than one person on board for this test but since it was only "high-speed taxiing"....

While all this was going on, I contracted some type of sickness that caused my blood pressure to drop so low that they were concerned that they would have to contact Willie to see if it would be OK to bury me there in Venezuela. Along with the incapacitating fatigue and delirium from whatever I had contracted, I developed tropical ulcers in my skin that caused a horrible odour. I had lived for years in the tropics but never experienced anything quite like this. When I recovered enough to make it back home to Canada, I slept a lot until I finally got back on my feet.

Michael and some of the other pilots from New Tribes Mission and Mission Aviation Fellowship got the plane painted and sorted out some "squawks" so it was almost ready. In early June, I went back to Puerto Ayacucho to help finish the project. To have the plane registered in Venezuela and since there seemed to be no provision for "amateur-built" aircraft, I was required to train a group of national aircraft mechanics on the airframe and engine and present them with certificates. We worked with two government officials, who flew in from Caracas for several days, producing loads of paper-work. I had brought copies of the Canadian and American regulations that we used to create what was accepted by local airworthiness officials. After jumping through all the hoops, we received what I suppose was the first Venezuelan, amateur-aircraft registration. "Yankee Victor Three Three Xray" (YV-33X). I was then issued with a temporary Venezuelan pilot license, for the purpose of doing the initial hours of test flying and to train a local flight instructor, who then would train Mike.

The instructor that I had to train was a "bush pilot" who had been a DC 10 captain. Although I showed him several times that the CH801 lands more like an elevator than a traditional airplane, he insisted on doing long, low approaches like in an airliner. He later officially trained Mike but Mike had flown with me and was able to handle the plane the way it was designed to be handled.

Like the first trip to Venezuela, this one had some non-aviation challenges of its own. Before I even got to Puerto Ayacucho, on landing at the Caracas airport, Mike had arranged for a person to meet me. Andreas was his name and I had met him on the first trip. My plane landed quite late and as I was going through customs and immigration, I kept looking for Andreas. That should be easy. He had dark hair, dark skin and dark eyes – just like almost everyone else there! As I came through the gate, a fellow came up and called me Mister Mitchell. I didn't realize that he could read my baggage tag. Wouldn't you know it, he had dark hair, dark skin and dark eyes. Must be him. Big mistake! I said, "Andreas?" He just nodded and grabbed my bags. He led me out into the night, to a taxi.

On the way to the hotel he told me that he needed $120 to buy my ticket for the next day. When we arrived he carried my bags in. This was not the same place that I had stayed the last time and it was definitely not in the same area. The airport is right at sea level, very near the shoreline, so going anywhere from there meant going uphill. This hotel was definitely farther uphill and farther from the airport and it was totally dark, so I had no idea where I was. "Andreas" said several times that he would be back at 7 am to get me. As he left with the taxi driver I heard a crash, which turned out to be the taxi. Now what? I paid $50 and got my key to room number 2. It was nowhere near like the last place but there was a bed and that's what I needed. I was beginning to feel quite vulnerable and had a strong feeling that things were just not right.

It seems that I had just gotten to sleep when the desk clerk called to say that the taxi was waiting. My watch showed 4:15 am. By 4:30 I was at the door where two men met me with an old, unmarked car that had no indication of being a taxi. The clerk explained that the other taxi had had an accident and Andreas had sent these people for me. One of the guys, who said he was Andreas' brother put my bag into the trunk and me into the back seat. He climbed in the front seat with the driver. It might have been good if I had noticed that there were no door or window controls on the inside, in the back. As we travelled, he said he needed me to pay the money *"now"* for the taxi. He was scribbling on some piece of paper that he said was the receipt. I told him that when we got to the airport I would pay him.

About that time I realized that while I could see nothing in the dark, I knew that we had been driving uphill and the airport was definitely downhill. The driver kept driving as the other guy began to get more and more angry. He turned around, kneeling on his seat while grabbing at me. He tore my wallet out of my hands and reached back and pulled my belt pack from my waist. He told me that they were going to kill me if I didn't give them the rest of my money. I had nothing left but he refused to believe me. He had my passport, wallet, licenses, credit card – everything. He demanded the 'gun' from the driver. I could not actually see a gun in that darkness but something like one wrapped in a white rag. By now things were totally out of control and there was no pretence that they intended to let me go. I realized that, without door handles, I could not get out and if I could, where was I and would I be safer out there?

I found myself shouting back at them, "In the name of Jesus Christ, I demand that you release me." I don't really know what I was expecting to happen but things did not get better. As he shouted for me to shut up and lay down on the seat, I continued to shout back, "In Jesus name...." The driver was now driving very fast and erratically. In the meantime he had torn my socks and was trying to rip my clothes, insisting that I had money hidden on me. I don't know how long this went on but 'suddenly' I realized that we were approaching the airport. The driver jammed on the brakes, ran around and opened my door, pulled me out onto the sidewalk, pulled my bag out of the trunk and threw it on the ground beside me. I could not tell what the other guy and the driver were saying in Spanish but as they sped off the one with my stuff tossed it out the window. As they left he said that if I reported anything the "MAFIA" would get me. I don't think they had any such lofty connections.

When I gathered up my things, I found everything except the American money, about $260. There were 7,000 Bolivars (Venezuelan money), which was about enough to buy a cheap hamburger. I checked an airport clock, since he had my watch, and found that it was just about 5 a.m. There were some military or police around. I don't know if they had observed what just happened in the darkness but I didn't bother reporting anything to them, not because of the threats of the bad guys but from my experience with "police" in Zaire and from what I had heard, I figured it would cause more trouble than it was worth. With my credit card I was able to get a ticket for the flight to Puerto Ayacucho.

In the waiting room in the terminal there were several young Americans, who were planning on boarding the same plane. I recognized their leader from my previous visit. When he spotted me he came over and asked how my night had been. When I gave him my story, he was shocked. Apparently, Michael Dawson had asked him to meet me and take care of me. He had been in the airport waiting for me when I arrived but when he saw me connecting with 'Andreas' he thought that Mike must have made some other arrangements and left me with the team of desperadoes.

After that, flight testing the plane over the jungle was not all that 'exciting'. What was exciting was to look out over the Amazon towards Yanomamo country, where this plane was destined to serve those needy, wonderful people. Now I could say that I had flown over the two largest jungles in the world; the Amazon and the Ituri. For this test flying there was an English speaking controller in the tower. I was restricted to a range of 25 miles from the airport but it was still the Amazon. In the other direction was Columbia. With the airport being right on the border, most of my landing approaches were in Columbian airspace.

.

CHAPTER 40

BRESLAU COUNTRY MANOR

Meantime, back in Canada, Flypass was doing well and we continued some involvement with MAF. We had purchased a house that was built in 1850. It was a stately old place with nine bedrooms, two kitchens, some sitting rooms and four bathrooms. Our purpose was to establish a place where we could care for retired folk. We called it "The Breslau Country Manor." The nearest neighbour was a couple of fields away. The next nearest was a couple of kilometres away. There were two acres of grass and apple trees and an equipment shed that could hold at least six vehicles. The idea of caring for seniors never really took off so for a while we ran a Bed & Breakfast. That was fairly successful. By this time, Hope was married, Andrew and Amy were still with us as well as my mother. That still left lots of room.

When MAF conducted "Candidate Orientation" the missionary candidates would stay with us in the B&B and most of the classes were held in one of the sitting rooms. Willie and I both taught, along with other staff from the MAF office. The Waterloo Regional Airport, where Flypass was located, was just two miles away. I could sit outside the house and watch overhead to see if my student pilots were off course as they practiced take-offs and landings. With the large shed, which I insulated, I was able to do aircraft building. So I was able to sell one of my hangars. We began holding the builder training weekends there as well and housed the customers in the B&B. People from several countries stayed with us. Some of them were international students, who were training at the airport.

At one point, a group called, "Parents For Community Living" (PFCL) asked us if we would consider using the house to provide "respite" care for the families of autistic children with severe behavioural issues. It provided a much more stable income so we agreed to let them use the second floor, while we continued to provide B&B service on the main floor. One evening, while entertaining some guest in the center sitting area, a young lad, totally unclad, went screaming through the room where we were sitting. That and a few other events made us realize that we could not run both the respite centre and the B&B. For most of the rest of our time there (five years) we dedicated our attention to the children.

We did not have to deal with them that much because there were trained staff day and night from PFCL. We provided food and lodging and frequent repairs to the building due to the nature of our young guests. Pretty well all of the windows on the second floor had to be replaced once or twice. It was not a treatment centre so no therapy was involved and "no consequences" were allowed for their behaviour. We were bitten, pinched, scratched and kicked. Some children would be there just overnight and some for up to six months. The purpose was to provide a break for parents who contended with this for years. Looking back, we would both say that it was a privilege to be able to minister in this way. God also gave us many openings to get to know and share with the staff. Near the end of our time at Breslau Country Manor PFCL was able to purchase a suitable home in Waterloo.

CHAPTER 41

BACK TO MAF (AGAIN)

Ron Epp, the new interim CEO of MAF Canada along with Jeff Plett, a good friend from our days in Tanzania, came by to ask if I would consider coming back into MAF to assist with new candidates and take over Ministry Partnership. A major part of Ministry Partnership involves making people aware of the financial needs of MAF and training and coaching new and veteran missionaries as they raise their prayer and financial support. I enjoyed the technical work of Flypass but I always preferred the personal contact that I had with customers. Aviation and Flypass were great for meeting, getting to know and serving people.

For about ten years I had been serving as a Deacon at Crestwicke Baptist Church, in Guelph. Before this visit, I hadn't thought much about doing anything but Flypass. As I thought about it, I realized that working with, equipping and encouraging people, especially Christian workers, was much more 'my calling'. Shortly after coming home from Africa I became involved with Freedom In Christ Ministry, counselling people who were experiencing some of the "failure and trauma" that I had experienced in Zaire. Most of my studying, in those days, had to do with Christian counselling. More and more people were coming to me and God was blessing them.

After praying with Willie and asking others for their advice, I accepted the MAF offer and for a third time, I joined Mission

Aviation Fellowship. Unlike the previous times, I did not have to raise financial support but was salaried as a home staff member. That was a little odd, since one of my main responsibilities was to teach and encourage candidates on "support raising", but our family had lived for over 20 years on the prayers and dollars that faithful friends and churches had sent in on our behalf. We continued with Breslau Country Manor and Parents For Community Living and for a while we kept Flypass going. Then I sold the company to a couple of men who didn't seem to realize that the business involved much more than sitting by the phone, waiting for orders. I had the newest model of the CH 601 called the "XL". It was a wonderful flying airplane but I found that there was less and less time to fly and my interest in flying was not as rewarding as my interest in serving people.

I decided to sell the CH 801 with the Czech engine. A lawyer from California came out to Breslau and stayed with us for several days with the intention of buying the plane and that was the beginning of a not-so-great adventure. He was a "character"! I sent one of my young pilots, Ed Schwartzenberger, to help him fly the plane home. Ed had plenty of experience but it seems that the new owner paid no attention to him. It wasn't very long before we heard that this new owner had torn the airplane apart at a great altitude and parts were found over a two mile stretch in north-central California. Every sort of thought goes through your mind when an airplane that you built fails catastrophically. Many people including aircraft magazine test-pilots, a Royal Navy test-pilot and Jungle Aviation And Radio mission had put it through their testing. There were times when I had put it through well over three "Gs". It was designed for six Gs positive and three Gs negative. What could have gone wrong?

In a short time I was contacted by a lawyer in California who was suing me and Zenair for 5 million dollars. One of my first thoughts was how flattering that was to think that I was worth that sort of money. Letters and threats continued to arrive and although

I had insurance for legal assistance, it was useless outside of Ontario. For a full year this went on until Willie, checking the American National Transportation Safety Board web site, noticed that a "toxicology" report, which had finally arrived, revealed that the pilot and his passenger both had very heavy amounts of a couple of different recreational drugs in their blood, urine and liver. It was determined that they had to have been over 13,000 feet above sea level when they managed to disassemble the plane while putting it through *"stresses greater that the design limits."* At that altitude, even without the drugs, they would be high enough to experience hypoxia but with the drugs they would have been "high" in more than one way.

We never heard again from the California lawyer, who was trying to sue us. That was one of the most unpleasant experiences of my life; not just that we were under the legal pressure but even more, that someone had died while flying an airplane that I had built. Aviation was becoming less "fun" but having the privilege of coaching and encouraging young men and women who were preparing for God's service was so much more fulfilling.

We sold the Breslau Country Manor and moved to nearby Kitchener. As I calculate, this was at least my 50th address. We were now attending and serving at Benton Street Baptist Church. The pastoral staff and members there made us feel so welcome and useful. I thought that I would never want to leave. Surely we could put down roots.

I very much enjoyed my work at MAF. A couple of times I attended the MAF US Ministry Partnership training and adapted our training to closely follow theirs. When I began, the average missionary couple were taking almost two years to raise the required support. Within about four years, while the required amount continued to increase, the average time to raise full support was nine months. Most of those serving overseas now, as I write this, are those with whom I worked. They are among the finest, most technically and spiritually qualified, people that I have ever known.

Think about the type of people that you would want in a mission like this. As pilots, aircraft mechanics and other professionals, we expect them to be "control freaks". Aviation is exciting, demanding and totally unforgiving. There is no place in MAF for those with an easy going, "whatever" attitude. They take their role most seriously and leave nothing to chance. Would you like to fly over wild, mountainous jungle with a pilot who thought that "*maybe* there is enough fuel and *maybe* he will be able to find the runway and *perhaps* the maintenance on the plane is done properly?" In the end, every one of them (us) realizes that after doing everything in our power to reduce all the risks, "Safety is of the Lord." However, not having control is a very uncomfortable feeling for these professionals.

There are few experiences where you can feel less "in control" than going from place to place, person to person, sharing your burden and ministry with those whom you hope will promise to pray and send in regular financial support. While teaching our Ministry Partnership philosophy and methods, I have had some of these highly professional, emotionally mature men (and it was mostly the men) break down and even get angry. When I showed them that, unlike the world's economy, which is based on 'buying and selling' and 'getting the best deal whatever the cost'; God's economy is based on giving and receiving and providing the best service whatever the cost, they agreed. But every time I asked them if they would rather be a giver or receiver, they all answered, "giver". I came to realize that the main reason is that the receiver is not in control but the giver is and it is very difficult to come to terms with the idea of ever being, out of control. We readily quote the Scripture, "It is more blessed to give than to receive." When we think of receivers, we may have the image of some slick TV minister, conning the masses into sacrificially digging into their pockets and sending money to their "ministry". The thought of receiving somehow makes them feel, not only out of control but sleazy.

In fact, it often makes them feel humiliated. Now, there is a huge difference between humility and humiliation. Humiliation is toxic to our being and too often is associated with some sinful attitude that needs to be repented of. On the other hand humility is what God requires of us and desires in us and without it, He cannot work out His perfect plan for our lives. Rather than being toxic, humility is therapeutic to the being. If anything, Ministry Partnership (support raising) is at least humbling. Every pilot can use a healthy dose of humility. Several times, God lovingly humbled me. Then there were times when He allowed me to humiliate myself.

There was one candidate couple, who I now count as precious friends, who on the first day of training, argued that they would never "stoop to taking money from poor people at home to pay for their ministry." They had both left successful, professional careers. The second day was painful as well. On the third day they were fairly silent. Then on the fourth day, they came to class with a totally different attitude of beautiful humility. Raising funds for them, like so many others was anything but simple but God used the process to prepare them to go into one of the most challenging fields of MAF service in the world. I am very humbled to say that they are friends. They are also among my heroes.

Over the years, I would work with the new MAF families through the months of support raising and emotional and spiritual preparation. I loved it! I would have a weekly telephone call with each of them that lasted for about an hour. We would discuss the report that they would have sent in a day or two ahead of the call. We shared great victories and traumatic disappointments. I would share Scripture, coach and help keep them on track. Then we always ended our phone time with prayer. There were so many times when it seemed like there was no chance of success but then

God would do something amazing. I have learned that God desires *faith* in us more than anything else. It seems that the only way to get great faith is to experience great challenges.

Okay, I did not intend to preach but if I am to share anything about my own life, I suppose I need to share what is closest to my heart. Having lived through these challenges alongside these dear people has stamped them on my heart like they were my own family. It may seem like it was just an earthly, monetary, unspiritual type of work but I can't remember any ministry in my life that was more profoundly spiritual.

I had attended courses with Wycliffe Bible Translators in North Carolina on, what was then called, Pastors to Missionaries. Later it became known as Member Care. After returning to MAF, I attended the Link Care, Member Care training in Fresno, California for six years and developed a wonderful friendship with many of the staff. I can't think of anything that I enjoyed more than working with missionaries as they experience the challenges that come as they grow in their "calling" as servants of God. Flying, no matter where, is not as exciting or rewarding.

CHAPTER 42

MAPLE HILL BAPTIST CHURCH

Our oldest daughter Hope, with her husband Richard and their three children, Isaac, Keirsten and Aaron moved to Keswick, about 40 minutes north of Toronto. Richard's electrical business was growing and they were very involved in the ministry of Maple Hill Baptist Church. Andrew, our son was now living in Elmira, in an apartment sponsored by the Community Living Association. He and another "developmentally challenged" young man, also named Andrew, shared the "digs" and worked in the community. Our Andrew worked at a grocery store nearby. Between them, they had approximately 10 hours of "assisted living". Amy, our youngest, was now married to Alain who was studying Bible at Tyndale College. Amy worked as a Veterinarian Assistant and they were living in Toronto.

Okay, I just can't go past this point without explaining something about Amy and Alain. I always get in trouble for this but.... You see, when they were married, at the wedding, each of them publicly promised to be Virgins for the rest of their lives. (Pause for effect.) Since his name is Alain Virgin, she became Amy Virgin, which of course makes them both A. Virgin. Do you see now why I just couldn't resist it?

Willie and I would often visit Hope and the family in Keswick and several times I was asked to preach at the church. One time, while we were camping not far from their home, their pastor, Chad Houghton came to visit Willie and me at the campsite. He asked if we would consider a "call" to go on staff at the church. I was not eager to leave the ministry I had with the missionaries at MAF but we prayed to see what God might want. My assistant at the MAF office was at the end of the hall and much of our communication was by email or even phone. Most of the contact that I had with the missionaries was also by email or phone. We realized that if I lived a couple of hours away from Guelph, in Keswick I could communicate and carry on most of my work as easily from the church office as from my MAF office. I passed the idea on to the MAF Canada CEO, Mark Outerbridge. We agreed that if the church did, in fact, call me that I could spend half of my time serving the mission and half with the church. By this time, there were two other mission staff members, who were trained and capable of doing the Ministry Partnership work as well as I, and they could cover the part of the work that I would not be able to. I remained the Director of Ministry Partnership.

After quite a bit of prayer, not just by us but by many others, we notified Maple Hill Baptist Church that we would be open to a call to the position that they were offering of Mentoring Pastor. We went through all of the paperwork, interviews and presentation to the church. Then, while we were back in Guelph, a meeting was held where the church was to vote to approve the call.

Keswick and the area around have had a reputation of being a spiritually "dark" place. Pastors and their families have often suffered spiritually and their marriages have frequently failed. I was told that it is not "normal" for pastors to "leave well" when finishing their ministry. Besides satanic covens that pray against Christian leaders there are other "forces" that stand against them. The day that the church was to vote on the call, I left the MAF office, but at the end of the driveway I could not figure out whether I should turn left or right. I remember driving around confused, not knowing just how to get home. Somehow, after a while I made it home but, according to Willie, as I talked to her, I was not making any sense and kept repeating myself. She called Florance, my sister and between them they figured that I was experiencing a stroke. Willie called Hope to ask her to pray and to ask the people at the meeting to pray. As I was travelling to hospital in the ambulance, the church was voting.

While in emergency and going through all the tests, Hope called to say that the church had voted in favour of calling me. When she finally spoke to me with the news, I remember her saying, "Daddy, do you really want to come here?" My ministry hadn't even started and there was already an attack on me. I knew that if I went in my own strength and wisdom, I was bound to fail but if God was truly calling me, I could depend on Him to enable me to do whatever He had for me to do. The Senior Pastor, who had left some months before I arrived had had a moral failure. The ripples were felt not only in the church but throughout the community and beyond. The one who had been Youth Pastor assumed the role of Lead Pastor and I joined him as Mentoring Pastor. My job was to provide some guidance and encouragement to the hurting church and staff; to care for the seniors by visiting them at home, in nursing homes and hospital and to do a share of counselling, to teach, occasionally preach and take leadership in prayer.

At the same time, I continued as Director of Ministry Partnership for MAF. We jokingly said that I divided my time equally, 80% for Maple Hill and 80% for MAF. But I loved it. Both the church and the mission cooperated wonderfully. Most of my telephone, Skype and email time was spent with the mission and the missionaries and my face-to-face time with the church. About once every two or three months I would spend a day or two at the Guelph office and twice a year, I would spend two weeks teaching new missionaries. I was also responsible for recruiting, interviewing and receiving candidates from eastern and central Canada. Three or four times a year I would represent MAF at mission conferences in Halifax, Montreal, Toronto, Edmonton and Vancouver. Through all but the last year or so I represented MAF at Air Venture in Oshkosh plus many other air shows and flying clubs.

In January of 2012, the load was getting to be a bit too much and my own energy level was starting to "sag". That's when I retired from Mission Aviation Fellowship. Six months later, on July 1, the day before my 70th birthday, I retired from Maple Hill Baptist Church. A major concern from the day I started at the church, came from the knowledge that, according to all that I had been told, pastors here are almost expected to end their ministry in failure. That is not actually true but it was a serious concern. It appears that I was able to escape that since most of the members of the church are still some of my closest friends. Also, at our departure, the church gave Willie and me an all expense paid, ten day tour of Israel. That was a powerful experience that I wish I had had much earlier in my ministry. I am so very grateful to the people of Maple Hill for their love and that wonderful gift.

Today, three years later, Willie and I are enjoying wonderful health and wondering just how much longer the Lord intends to use us. We have so many friends, who have been a huge part of who we are today. Since you are reading this, you likely are among them. I enjoy teaching Bible, ministering to some hurting folk and encouraging some people who are on the battle lines in ministry. Willie is always involved in Bible teaching and prayer groups. If you know her at all you will not be surprised to hear that she continues to bless seniors and shut-ins. She is more beautiful and precious to me than I can possibly tell.

One of my favourite Bible verses is in 3 John, verse 4 and it expresses the great joy that I have right now. It says, *"I have no greater joy than to hear that my children [and grandchildren] are walking in the truth."* Each one of them are walking in God's truth and love. I am blessed beyond anything I could have ever imagined.

Now, I think back to those days, when I would lie and try to convince others and myself that I was "someone" or had experienced "something" so that I would be accepted. I could never have dreamed that God had so much more for me than anything that I could have "created".

CHAPTER 43

WRAPPING UP

A lot of people have been mentioned in this book. Others who have also been a huge part of my life were not included. I have taken up a lot of your time and dare not impose any longer on your patience. To include everyone who is really significant would more than double this tome. I hope that those mentioned as well as those omitted will not be offended. This has been the story of my past and please let me reiterate that it is told from *my very limited perspective*. Some people might justifiably say, "That's not the way I remember it at all." No doubt, some dear folks have been misrepresented because of my ignorance. Some who have read bits of this as I have worked on it, have reminded me of other events or details, some of which I don't remember at all or remember quite differently. Even now, I think of many things and life lessons that I could include but if you are still reading this, you deserve a little mercy.

Today people dwell on the past. The past may become our reason, often our excuse, for our present condition. That may at times be helpful but it may also be pathetic. Our past then becomes an anchor. That can have a good effect to keep us from falling for every silly, evil thing that is presented to us. It can also keep us from experiencing and enjoying life today.

But enough with the *past* already! I think I can safely say that most of those whom I have counselled suffer because of their past. We have no way of changing that but we can live victoriously and fruitfully by acknowledging the past and looking to the future that God has made available to those who trust in Him through Jesus Christ.

My life is so much more influenced and empowered by my *future*. Not just my future on this tiny piece of "space dust" but my eternal future with the God who has proven, through my past, that He is my loving, all knowing, providing, protecting, long-suffering, transcendent yet imminent Father.

As I live today, my mind goes back to those days *In His Exciting Service* and my heart wants to burst with thanksgiving. However, the things I do and think and work towards and long for; the things that occupy my mind and control my motives are influenced profoundly by the amazing, unending, glorious *future* waiting for me. I ain't seen nothin' yet!

My precious son Andrew may be considered by many as disabled, perhaps 'handicapped' or worse, but he is often my inspiration. It is not at all uncommon to be driving with him when he will suddenly look up and say, "Look at that cloud Dad, or that one. Do you think that Jesus could come from one of them?" He seems to always be eagerly looking to see Jesus returning for him like the Bible says.

The slaves in the South had horrible *past* lives but they survived by focusing on the *future*. Listen to the songs that they sang. "Way Over Jordan," "Swing Low Sweet Chariot," "Ain't Gonna Tarry Here," "Down By The Riverside" and "This World Is Not My Home." They were "heading for the promised land" and looking forward to "laying their heavy burden down by the riverside" and that is how they survived. Sometimes the more we look back, the less able we are to focus on where we are going and the more hopeless the future may seem. For those who have found Jesus, God's wonderful Son and made Him the Lord, Director and Master of their lives, nothing from the past counts for us or against us.

As I reread the things that I have written, I think that there may be things that I should not have written and there are likely things not recorded that should be. But as my youngest granddaughter, Vesper used to like to say, "There ya go." The real question that I ask is, "What does God have written about me in His book? How does that compare with what I have written in mine? What does He think?" I pray that He is pleased and you are blessed.

A SPECIAL REWARD FOR THOSE WHO HAVE READ THIS WHOLE BOOK.

A couple of related articles written by Willie, to inspire and entertain you.

ATTACK OF THE KILLER BEES

This story happened in Moshi, Tanzania. We were attending a weekend conference for missionaries in January 1990. The summer of that year was also the summer of our final return to Canada following about thirteen years of service, in Zaire and Tanzania.

There were three things of significance which preceded this event. First, I had been asked to speak to the children during the conference. While preparing at home, I picked up a magazine called 'Evangelizing Today's Child'. In the centerfold was an article called 'Is Islam in your neighborhood?' I felt compelled to teach the children about some of the false doctrine of Islam, especially the tyrant nature of their god whom they call Allah. Many of my closest Tanzanian women friends were Sikh and Muslim. I saw up close their experience with their religion. I learned that Islam is based on fear. I am a Christian and a believer in Jesus Christ whom I believe is truly the Son of the only true God. My God does not rule over his children in fear. When we trust Him and through belief in His Son, become his children, we are treated with love.

I do believe in the person of Satan and that God allows him sometimes to sift us through afflictions, in order to test and build up our faith. An untried faith will not carry us in this world. Satan means our testing for evil, but God allows it for our good. He says "when we are tested we will come forth as gold." I believe what transpired in the days following were times of affliction allowed for our sifting and for the building of our faith as the Lord carried us and was gracious in sparing us.

I had a dream documented in my journal on January 5, just two days prior to the event. I dreamed that I was looking at the face of Christ on the cross. He was suffering intensely and I watched him for what seemed a long time. The verse came to me and repeated through the dream "they looked on him whom they had pierced."
The phrase comes from Zechariah 12:10 and appears as well in John 19:37. The Bible has many references to Christ being the one who was pierced. At the time of the crucifixion a soldier pierced his side with a sword.

Looking back, I think I was being prepared for a time of suffering, not like anything Christ went through, but something bigger than I had ever experienced. He has gone before us, having felt all of our afflictions. Through the event with the bees, He surely carried all of us who were afflicted.

The missionary speaker in the morning service, that weekend, spoke on Psalm 23:1 'The Lord is my Shepherd'. He was teaching the children by holding up the fingers of one hand and attaching one word to each finger. The only finger I now remember was the fifth finger, and the word 'shepherd,' because the word became very important during the attack of the killer bees.

We chose to picnic that day along the steep cliffs above the rapid filled river below. To get down to the river we shimmied down the cliffs on our backsides. There were about thirty of us who went down. The children among us began to throw rocks in the water. We wondered if somehow the splashing may have excited the bees. Bees are agitated by vibration. They are also attracted to bold colours. Can you believe that was the day I wore bright purple capris?

<u>My diary entry of January 9, 1990.</u>

I am writing this entry on Tuesday about what happened this past Sunday afternoon while we were still at the Mission Conference at Moshi, Tanzania.

There is a steep cliff at the picnic grounds. The river below is a beautiful sight. It is a rushing river, shallow at the edges but filled with rapids in the midst of it.

Art, Andrew and I made our way down the cliff, at times resorting to sliding on our backsides, other times climbing around massive rocks and scrambling over smaller ones which threatened to make us stumble and fall.

Many other missionaries and children were with us. The sun was hot and the children's laughter rang out across the river. We only splashed around for a short while when Andrew suddenly let out a whoop of pain. He had been stung! Looking up the river we saw a great, yellow, cloud advancing toward us. There were thousands of bees coming our way! There were more yells, screams and chaos from all those around us as the bees descended.

Art, who was in the river, called out to Jane Green on shore to throw Andrew toward him into the water, so as to rescue him from the bees. Art and Andrew headed into the midst of the river which soon swirled and churned them out of sight.

I looked down to see little Eric DeGroot at my side. He was screaming and frightened. His parents were at the top of the cliff. Everyone around us was suddenly shouting, crying out, stumbling through the blinding cloud and running for cover. But there was no cover, only open shore filled with huge boulders and bushes. I grabbed Eric and pushed him toward the river, plunging his little body in and out in a constant blur of bees, dumping water over his little blond head which was covered with the frenzied creatures. We were too shallow and I was afraid to take him out into the raging waters. I am not a strong swimmer. Would I lose hold of him in the swift current? What if Eric bashed his head on the submerged boulders? Art and Andrew had gone that way and they were no where in sight.

My heart sank with the realization that I had to go back to the shore, back into the path of the bees or I would never get Eric up the cliffs to safety. If we went back would we even see the cliffs through the piercing yellow fog? Staying close to the snaking river we jumped into the water when the bees got into our eyes and mouths and threatened to overwhelm us. Massive boulders fenced us off from getting to the cliffs above and in our blindness we fell again and again. Parents and others watched on in horror from the top of the cliff. They too had to run for cover.

Amidst the pricks and stings and fighting I spotted Art's tee shirt lying on the ground. I grabbed it, soaked it, and put it over Eric's head. It would help cover his body since he was only in a swimsuit. I knew there were bees underneath but there were hundreds more on the outside. With Eric's tiny legs we could not move quickly. I picked him up but then I could not see the path ahead and Eric had to contend with the bees that were swarming all over me. Suddenly we lost our footing and fell straight forward into a wide mud hole. Black, oozy mud was all around us and I knew God put it there- an old wive's tale maybe, but looking back, God used it.

I smeared it all over Eric. "The bees don't like mud Eric, help me put it on you." I had told him earlier "The bees don't like water Eric" and he had let me plunge his head under over and over without a fight, trusting me. He was so brave. All the time I could hear myself praying," Jesus, Jesus, help us through this, take the bees away, and help us find the cliff." If we could just spot the edge of the cliff, we could dare to leave the river.

Then I remembered about the shepherd. "Eric, do you remember the story about the shepherd? The Lord is our shepherd, he will help us." Show us someone on that cliff Lord, someone to guide us." And so our shepherd led us. I saw Leo Degner first descending the cliff and beckoning us toward him. He didn't come near us at first, there were still so many bees, but he went ahead of us showing us the way up the cliff. As we climbed higher, Eric called out "Look Auntie Willie, the bees are going, they are going." Leo was now able to come nearer. He began to bat at the bees which were crawling all over us and he reached out and pulled us higher up the cliff.

Then Len MacKay was there. He picked Eric out of my arms and carried him to safety. Phil Schmidt reached out and helped me the rest of the way. An older man took over guiding me as Phil went back to help others. Pamela came next, covered me with her Kanga and comforted me, praying with me as I staggered up the cliff, and praying for all who were still suffering below.

Smart thinking Marti Plett was at the top of the cliff feeding antihistamines to all who came up. I thanked her for the drugs, "You've saved my life, Marti." I knew it then and I know it now. John Clifford drove me back to the ISM Mission compound where Art, Andrew, Eric and many others were being washed off and cared for.

My friends Jane Green and Janice Kornelson cared for me as the venom racked my body. I began to vomit and vomit almost continually hardly able to come up for air. My clothes were drenched with sweat. Lovingly they held my head, fed me sips of water, and began the process of pulling hundreds of stingers from my body. They used metal pinchers which unknowingly squeezed the venom back into my body until someone told us to gently remove the myriads of stingers with our finger nails. Marti was there for awhile too but I heard her say to the others, "I can't do this." I'm sure it was an awful sight.

Eventually a doctor came, who gave injectable Phenergan to Janice, to give to me. It controlled the retching. I stopped being cold and hot, but felt only half aware of what was happening. Eric was with his Mom and Dad somewhere nearby. I heard his little voice whimpering in my mental haze.

Through the night Art watched over me, giving me medication for the pain. Denying his own many stings, Art moved from Andrew who was also vomiting and suffering in the room next door and then back to me. All evening Len was there, keeping Andrew company, but as night fell only Art was there selflessly tending to Andrew and I through the night. Many times over he had to assure me that Andrew was going to be okay.

I needed to know what had happened to them. There I learned that Art and Andrew had stayed under the water for as long as they could hold their breath. Art told Andrew that the bees didn't like the water. They popped up over and over, splashing and splashing so as to get enough air to go under again. The current was forcing them down the river. Art was holding tightly to Andrew's wrist. If Art let go, Andrew would surely be dashed against the rocks. At one point, the force of the water pinned Art with his head down and feet up. He needed two hands to turn around but could not let go of Andrew. Suddenly, at the moment when he could no longer hold his breath, the current swirled Art right side up, flinging them both to the surface. They crawled out further down along the river.

In another building the missionaries gathered and prayed for us for many hours. There was so much to rejoice in. So far no one had died. There was so much to pray for: comfort, healing, peace.

The next day Don Winter, the pilot came to take us back to Dodoma. He took one look at me, closed his eyes and turned away. I guess I was swollen like a sausage. There were many passengers on the plane with swollen eyes and hands and feet. Conversation on the return trip home was subdued. We looked as if we were fresh from a battle zone. Andrew with his terrible facial swelling tossed about, then slept fitfully in my arms.

When we arrived home our yard men and Marietta our house helper gasped at the sight of us. We went right to bed. As we slept Marietta quietly, efficiently cleaned the house. We awoke the next morning to its spotlessness. How I thanked God for Marietta's quiet ministry.

January 9,1990 Wednesday

Early this morning Andrew had nightmares just before waking. He called out, "Daddy, I see them." He was remembering the bees and seemed frightened. "Remember the horses at the conference," I encouraged. "Remember how you brushed them and fed them from the buckets of oats." So he remembered, smiled, and fell immediately back to sleep.

Wednesday afternoon.

Andrew has been watching a video this morning but pulled at the buttons on his shirt and said, "What are these, Mom?" Three times he asked me who sent the packet of green Kool-Aid in the mail but he couldn't absorb the answer. It was in a letter from his cousin Laura. His face seems even more swollen today, if that be possible. I know the facial swellings drain this way so I comfort myself that this is normal even if it looks dreadful.

I am recovered enough to think about my other dear lambs. Hope is on interims by now. "Lord keep her safe and give her joy and health to enjoy." Amy is alone for a week at R.V.A. "Lord, don't let her be lonely without her sister there, please help her to be safe and happy. Thank goodness they did not go to the conference with us. And for Art who is so tired and sore, let him feel you close to him today."

Wednesday Evening

Eric has been better today. He had about thirty stings. I have seventeen in one arm, ten in the other, maybe fifty on my face, and about a hundred on my head and hair. I know because when I washed my hair, there were hundreds of stingers swirling around in the water. I am so glad the pain has decreased so I can finally wash my scalp.

After thoughts

I feel as if the attack was deliberate. I am so thankful for a good shepherd who goes through trials with us. I have been fearful for Andrew, that in his sometimes muddled thought patterns he might have some long term fears.... But no, I must reject those fears and think about God's mercy because God has carried all of us this far. Andrew will be okay.

Several Months later

In the weeks following I developed an eye infection which was a painful result of the many stings around my eyelashes and lids. My cornea was lacerated but in the fall after we had returned to Canada for good, I saw an eye doctor who said there was no evidence of any remaining eye damage. That was God's goodness again. I was reminded of Romans 8:28 "And we know that in all things, (the good and the bad things) God works for the good of those who love him, who have been called according to his purpose."

TALES FROM THE BELLY OF LAZARUS

Preparations

Several weeks ago my husband, Art said he wanted to pick up an RV which had been sitting for some time in his brother's yard in Valleyview, Alberta. For the moment Tom had no immediate dreams for it, but Art on the other hand had dreams. When you are retired there is one thing that fuels a man and that is dreams. He was already trying to figure out where we could sleep the grandchildren in the RV including Isaac who at thirteen is already six foot two. Art is all about family.

Since we live in Ontario, we would need to fly to Edmonton and then Tom would pick us up and drive us to his home. That was no small feat since he lives at least four hours away. Personally I had some major rearranging to do in order to cancel life in Ontario and set off for the great Canadian prairies. I could not leave Art to make the journey by himself, though in retrospect, he may have occasionally wished he was doing it solo.

For several nights before the trip, I was waking up with that Guy Lombardo tune going through my head "Enjoy yourself, it's later than you think." I did have some fears concerning the journey but my husband has no time for fear. He was single minded about making the trip which is the gentlest way of explaining things. My 'irrational fears' were basically that winter was coming on and I was not sure I wanted to be caught in a snow drift along the road side somewhere between Ontario and Alberta. I was pretty sure I would not be learning to drive the thing at least not on this trip. It helps with these kinds of decisions in a marriage to be on the same page. I was saying to Art "Why do it now? Wait for Spring!" and he was saying "Why wait for Spring? Do it now!"

I was concerned most about my dear husband in case he should take sick or something. What would we do? The thing is 31 feet long and I can't parallel park my Toyota Echo. Maybe I was really thinking about myself. Tom really solved it for me and that was long after we got to Alberta. He said, gallantly, that if bad things happened he would come to our rescue. Brothers just have that wonderful way about them. Later on during the trip our two sons-in-law also offered to bail us out but that is getting ahead of the story. Suffice it to say, we have wonderful family.

So we flew to Edmonton on Friday, Sept.12. Tom owns a beautiful quarter section of land and is in the process of building a home on it. As we entered his yard, we saw the motor-home for the first time. We would not want to seem ungrateful, especially to Tom. He is one of the most generous human beings I have ever met, but he is also an optimist, a man of great faith, and Jack of all trades. He also has mounds of pioneering spirit coursing wildly through his veins.

My mechanical expertise begins and ends with turning the wing nut on my manual can opener. The RV had a lot of dust and mud on it but dusk was coming on; perhaps we were just not seeing it properly. There was a forlorn look about it, as if no one had paid much attention to it in some time. The back bumper had chrome curling off of it with large rust patches peering out from the inside. The outside showed blue patches, suspicious of mildew. Beyond that there was fading paint and a general appearance of intense deprivation. I was at a loss for words which is sometimes a very good thing.

We all left to go into town for dinner. As we sat down in the restaurant, Tom headed for the men's room. It was at that first moment of privacy when my husband turned to me and said with reference to the RV "Well what do you think?" It all came out of me at once with a hysterical fit of giggles which continued to erupt at inopportune times over the next few days and in fact weeks. "I'm... I'm horrified." I laughed again with more hysteria, and began to bite my cheeks in case Tom reappeared.

The next morning we had a closer view. I decided right then and there that Tom should be selling real estate or used cars. He showed us everything good about Lazarus. Yes it needs some resurrecting, so I have named it accordingly, but I quickly concluded that an entire make-over would have been a logical start. The roof had leaked badly so unfortunately there was some interior water damage but then it was a 1986 model. On the other hand it was a Triple E, Regency. Tom said it had been the top of the line in its day. The way he described it, he made us think it could be a 2014 land yacht. Well it was considerably younger than me so I should not be too critical.

I suppose Tom inspired me, in fact I'm sure of it, because from there on I wanted to take Lazarus under my wing and clean it. I found Art on a tall ladder where he had already begun cleaning off the exterior mildew. So I started on the inside and that began an ongoing process. In my imagination I was actually seeing Lazarus with new curtains and paint. Cleaning is one of my gifts. I soon found that the cleaning must be done carefully because many things were in danger of falling off into one's hand in the process of touching them. I was also highly suspicious when I found a screw, among other strange items, on the floor. The shaking and rattling of travel must have loosened many things which ought never to have been loosened.

I had told a friend back home that maybe God would use this trip to stretch me. That was said because I was trying to bring some meaning to this pre winter safari. I was hoping the Lord would give me a green light to move ahead; something from the Scriptures to validate this imminent adventure. All I got was a few phrases from Philippians 4:6 ' DO NOT BE ANXIOUS about anything, but in everything by prayer and petition, WITH THANKSGIVING, present your requests to God and the PEACE OF GOD which transcends all understanding will guard your hearts and minds in Christ Jesus. So, there would be something to cause anxiety. I must be thankful. And of course God's peace would come. I am not sure that I was immediately comforted, but God's grace comes in the midst of the trial so He wasn't wasting his comfort on my imagined worries.

Lazarus began to improve with some TLC. I found no signs of mildew and no sign of mice on the inside. Now that was enough to make me write up the adoption papers. However, when I first saw the toilet in Lazarus, it looked old and cracked and brown. It was the brown that worried me, so I said to Tom, "Maybe we should change out the toilet." He said "Oh! That isn't crap, that's just old glue." "Well, that was a relief!"

Tom and Art began to trouble shoot the systems many of which did not work. It took an hour or so of trying to track down a leak in the water system to discover that the valve in the toilet was broken. They could not repair it so ended up installing a nice, new, clean, no stain toilet. Now as I said, Tom and Art worked very hard to sort things out. In fact they spent long hours, turning into days, working things over. I made meals because that was all I really could think of to do to help the whole process and I did ' important' things like cleaning out cupboards.

One day Art came in and said that the watery pond pooling on top of the roof was "electric". He had gotten a good buzz off of it; almost as good as the buzz off the front bumper which Tom got the next day. Seems old Lazarus was not well grounded. Apparently that was okay since it only happened if the RV was plugged in... and it was probably a good idea to stay off the roof...

One day Art told me we would have to give up the wonderful, soft, comfortable, warm bed in Tom's guest room and begin to sleep in the belly of Lazarus to see how we would manage with it before we hit the road for real. I was happy to see that the bed was a Queen size. Making it up with sheets and bedding became my morning workout. The mattress is against the wall on three sides. Have you ever made a bed while sitting on top of it? It takes skill and I believe you can actually lose weight in the process since you have to perform many contortions to accomplish the feat. Whether I go home skinnier remains to be seen; first of all I have to live that long.

The first few nights I encountered cold fingers of air, but I eventually used three afghans and two pillows to stop up the holes to the outside of the RV. Art rarely feels the cold like I do so it is difficult to really convey my gut fears to him about freezing to death. The furnace was not responding. I could already see the newspaper headlines about the couple who froze to death in an RV while traversing Canada in the late Fall. They were written up as having been experienced RVers. No one understood how this could have happened to them.... Eventually, we progressed to being snuggly and warm beneath our quilts but for most of the trip we had no working furnace.

We had to learn all about connecting up water, sewage and electricity, as well as getting both the gasoline and propane tanks filled without blowing up any gas bars or RV parks. The engine was made to operate on gas but the original owner had installed a propane system that could be switched on and off. Propane is much cheaper in Alberta. We carried two propane tanks of about 150 litres each and a gas tank with over 200 litres.

Finally, we decided to get Lazarus fired up and off to Grand Prairie for a spin, about 125 Km. Art had to be comfortable driving it. I was feeling confident because he had driven bus when we were first married and that was only forty four years ago.

I could tell when Art started the engine, that something exciting was coming. Lazarus rumbled and snorted and sprang to life, stretching forth all of its 31 ft. I began to cheer nervously. I wanted to holler, "Lazarus Come Forth!" On the other hand the start up meant we would be committed to taking Lazarus home. Well, why not? This was an adventure!

I could tell we were going to be alright when Art backed Lazarus up in Tom's driveway and moved it onto the road missing the ditches on either side. I have always admired his prowess as a driver but at that moment he was truly my hero at the wheel. I watched and prayed seeing the many moods cross his brow in the ensuing trip, especially when we cut off another driver in traffic. Fortunately he was too busy at the wheel to see the other driver's response.

When we started back to Tom's from Grand Prairie, I knew my prayers had been answered because Art began to sing "Happy Trails to you ". I figured he had probably regressed to the old days when bus driving was like putting your pants on.

We left Valleyview on Oct.2. Goodbye to rest, peace and comfort zone....the elastic band was ready to stretch. Grocery prices in Valleyview were high, so we decided to buy later when we were further down the road at Whitecourt. We also needed a battery tester and a battery charger.

At Whitecourt we went into the Canadian Tire to pick up a battery charger and tester along with some duct tape to seal the driver's door which 'whistled' as we drove along. When we stopped in the parking lot we discovered that the exhaust had fallen off the onboard generator, that provides AC electricity. It had been dragging for some time and was warn smooth by the road. For some reason the generator, that had been working perfectly, now would not start. We returned to the RV only to find that the toilet tank had overflowed into the cabin. The flush handle was sticking and had to be pushed more forcefully otherwise the overflow would result. This happened twice on our journey, as if once was not lesson enough. By 11am we were mopped up and back on the road again.

Three Hills

After another 400 kilometres, we found a great RV park in Three Hills right across from the hospital. In the evening we had a great meal with Rick and Amy Willms, long time missionaries with Mission Aviation Fellowship. They were so accommodating, feeding us a wonderful meal, then lending us 'Bob', their truck. Three Hills, Alberta is the home of Prairie Bible Institute with the school of aviation, where many missionary pilots that Art has worked with, were trained.

When we returned to the RV, we turned something on and 'POP'...we blew a fuse or something. Thankfully we had 'Bob' who took us to the airport where we saw a friend, Nathan, and borrowed his electrical multimeter. Art searched and searched but could not find a problem with Lazarus. Finally he tested the campground output and found that it had failed. We moved to another site, plugged in and everything came to life.

When I recruit friends to pray for us, I always hope they will be sincere in their commitment. We needed that covering every step of the way.

Leaving Three Hills was both glorious in the first half of the day and treacherous for the rest. We had set out quite early in the morning from Three Hills for Castor to see our friends Clayton and Connie Richardson. We were eager for the reunion since it had been a number of years and they have always ministered to us by their faithful lives and model of prayerfulness. We needed to remind them of our gratitude for many past instances when they had held us up in prayer.

The sky was nearly cloudless and an exceptional blue. The sights along the way were wondrous: the white bull in the field, the many varieties of cattle, the waving fields of wheat, the diverse kinds of equipment which were harvesting and clouds of seagulls rising and soaring like some silent symphony. It was all very captivating when suddenly I looked at the compound mirror on my side and saw it dangling from one of its three mounts. God in His mercy put a bus sized pullout right in front of us. We stopped and Art used black duct tape to reaffix the mirror in place. Yes, our prayer partners were at work. There is a remoteness to the prairies which would have meant long travels without that mirror.

The Richardsons hosted us for a wonderful lunch and tour of the retirement home where they are still serving the Lord faithfully in spite of personal health issues. We introduced our friends to Lazarus. Then Connie served us farm sized pieces of lemon meringue pie and their tasty choke cherry syrup with lime soda. We enjoyed precious fellowship with them.

We left Clayton and Connie around 4:30 hoping to get to Rosetown, SK before dark. As we crossed into Saskatchewan, we were horrified to see the condition of some of the roads.

Along the way road construction caused us to alter our course again and again on to slippery gravel surfaces which had been patched time and again. Travel became ominous. Chunks of pavement mixed with stretches of gravel and glaring potholes were badly in need of repair. These were not the appropriate surfaces for traveling with a large RV. Lazarus rumbled and shook until it seemed every nut and bolt would be removed. I was praying against the arrival of darkness since navigating was already becoming a trial. The GPS was not updated for all the new roads we were encountering. Some of the roads were detours. Many had no center lines and no defined shoulders. Suddenly the bumping and thrashing of the RV loosened the bed over the cab and it began to fall on Art's head as he drove. He gave a mighty shove to push it back into place but one of the brackets which locked it in place was broken from then on. The GPS also flew off the panel in the confusion. Fortunately, Art was able to handle Lazarus. God's good hand was upon us.

We were also experiencing the smell of propane fumes along the way. We would open the windows to clear the cabin but then it got too cold to keep the windows open for any extended periods. We had conversations about how noxious the fumes might be. Darkness was continuing to come on fast but with it came a gift from the Lord, a full moon which shed light on our way.

Long after we had planned to arrive, we saw the lights of Rosetown from a road which the GPS simply referred to as "an unnamed road". We found the RV Park after only one wrong turn. We hooked up to water, sewage and electricity. When Art tried to turn off the headlights we discovered that the switch was not attached to the inside of the panel so he had to open the panel cover, reach in through the wires and hold the switch in place so it could be turned off. The park boasted hot showers but we opted for bed and slept well from exhaustion, especially Art who had done all the driving.

Well, this was about the time that we asked some of those rhetorical questions like: "I wonder what we are doing here wearing multi layers of clothes to bed to survive the cold?" Or, "When that person prayed for us why did they refer to this time as a holiday?" Or, "Does God intend for us to meet someone or help someone along the way?" Or, "Now that we are half way across Canada, are we doing the right thing?" Or, "The oil pressure and water temperature gauges on the panel are no longer working; I wonder if there is a loose wire under the panel?"

Our thoughts were often toward Winkler which had the factory where Lazarus was built. We hoped someone there would be able to help us with the propane problems and the electrical and the many challenges we had been facing.

Moose Jaw/Caronport

The next day we headed for an RV park in Moose Jaw. In the RV travel book it boasted a hot tub and pool and we were eager to try them out but when we checked in, these amenities were permanently closed. It did have a wonderful laundry! Once we had established our park site we headed to Caronport to see Stephanie Wright at Briarcrest Bible Institute. Stephanie is hard at work doing day and evening classes with the goal of teaching English as a second language and possibly returning to working abroad. She was our first dinner guest though we had entertained before in Lazarus, but just for tea. We had ribs as our oven was working well. Looking back we always had hot water in our taps and a working stove, what more could you want? We did not have to crawl out of a cold tent to go to the bathroom or fend off bears (which had demolished our last camping expedition). We could stand up our full height in Lazarus and even though we went along hundreds of kilometres of prairie roads where we rarely saw a car, we did know how to read a map and had a bed and food if we broke down. It always helps to count your blessings!

Regina

Art has long been an associate with Freedom in Christ ministries in Regina. Here was his chance to show me the headquarters and for us to meet with the current staff. While there, we spent time in prayer together. Later, Clay Bergen took us for a walk around the lake there, to the government building and to supper afterward. Rita the receptionist was a special blessing as she prayed Psalm 91 over us. The verses became especially meaningful. Almost from the beginning of the trip we could not get the door to lock on the RV. We had to claim the promise every day and night of vs.11 **"For he will command his angels concerning you to keep you in all your ways."** We had to leave the RV for periods when grocery shopping etc. and we always walked away from an unlocked RV.

Boissevain

We left the next day for Boissevain to see Howard and Kathy Weir who direct the Turtle Mountain Bible Camp. Art used a chain saw to cut down some of the camp ground trees. He was working in the area which will be the new building site for a dining hall/chapel. My job was to help clear out the Director's den, an old cabin which has to come down for the future facility. It was exciting to hear of stories of changed lives of young people over the years and many miracles the Lord has done to provide for this ongoing ministry.

Before leaving Art and I walked around Partridge Lake at the heart of the Turtle Mt. Camp. We followed the edge of the lake with its harvested fields. We crawled under several barbed wire fences and through some swamp lands and horse pastures along the way. We met some of the neighbors who say they love to hear the campfire music wafting across the lake and they can hear many of the words on a calm evening.

We experienced some beautiful sunsets from the windows of Lazarus as we sat ensconced on top of the camp hill. Off season the camp is very quiet. It was hard to leave the place. Kathy and Howard had been so hospitable and fun to be with. There had been time to just enjoy the peace and presence of God there; "to rest in the shadow of the Almighty." Ps.91:1. Howard and Kathy minister selflessly at this camp and depend upon the Lord to sustain them from year to year. It was such a blessing to hear the story about the little boy who came to summer camp. He had only been there for perhaps an hour or so when he said to a staff person, "When I have to leave here I sure am going to miss you guys." We left with similar feelings.

We refueled at Boissevain where the propane had jumped to 1.60 per litre. It was 85 cents in Alberta. Gas was only 1.20 and we wished we could access that tank. We had hardly left the town when we realized the propane gauges, after a complete fill were showing empty. It is hard for a pilot when you can't trust the instruments, so this was stressful. Finally we went back to Boissevain to get our tanks checked but it did not appear that we had lost much fuel. The gauges for propane rarely worked properly, in fact they showed empty a lot of the time. Trying to gauge our kilometers used and our distance traveled, required careful monitoring.

Steinbach

We arrived in Steinbach toward evening. According to the website, our RV Park was closing for the season in two days but when we got there the park had already closed. We headed for the 'Black Sands' of the Walmart parking lot. With no hook ups we sat in the darkness of the cabin, singing along to old gospel tunes on the radio and watching a delightful sunset. Our night was eventful when a couple of cars began screeching around and doing donuts in the parking lot just a few meters from where we were sleeping.

Later they sped up and down the nearby highway right in front of the police station but no one slowed them down. Since that continued for hours, we didn't get much sleep. The propane fumes were also still bothering us whenever the winds changed. That night I pulled out cloths from the holes I had stuffed against the cold so that we had fresh air to breathe.

We met our friends Marti and Jeff Plett for coffee the next morning and later shared a wonderful Thanksgiving meal with them and some of their family. We worked in Africa together with them and they are very special to us. I always embarrass Marti when I remind her how she saved my life in Africa. She did, and that makes her very special in my life.

Winkler

Finally on Thanksgiving Day, in the afternoon, we made our way to Winkler. We stayed with Willie and Sharon Enns, friends from our Mission Aviation Fellowship years. We stayed for four days as we tried to get the RV looked at. The Triple E maintenance yard, adjacent to the facilities where Lazarus was built, was full of beautiful RVs, all of them needing to be worked on so we had to be prepared to wait. Without the RV, since it was locked up in the yard, we were temporarily homeless, so Willie and Sharon cared for us in their beautiful home. They provided a car to help us monitor what was happening with the RV and treated us royally while we continued to wait. Willie also gave us a tour of the Lode King factory where he works. From then on we noticed Lode King trailers with hoppers all across the prairies. Willie also shared with us the amazing story of Triple E, the RV factory. His Dad founded the company with two of his brothers-in law. It is a story of their entrepreneurial spirit and hard work.

Before leaving Winkler we purchased a duck down duvet at the Walmart. As we crossed the country most of the RV parks began to close for the season, so we had to stay in parking lots and cold places with no electrical hook ups and the words in PS.91:4 came alive to us: 'he will cover you with his <u>feathers</u> (duck down?) and under his wings you will find refuge.' After four days, we did not have the time to continue to wait for help. The factory did provide a mechanic to give us some assistance but by now we really had to head for home.

We headed back to Steinbach, MB where we filled with propane but as soon as we left town, we began to encounter problems with the propane tanks which refused to switch at the panel. We tried to find a mechanic but nothing was open. After Steinbach only one tank was accessible making the need to refuel often. Propane became more scarce when we entered Ontario. On the prairies it was easy to find anywhere but some smart lawyers in Ontario have caused anyone selling auto propane to jump through so many hoops and pay so much for insurance that very few people will even try to sell it. We had the same 200 litres of gasoline in the gas tank as when we left Valleyview but the switches would still not allow us to access it. As we encountered difficulties we would consult with Tom and tried everything he had ever done with the switches. For Tom and Art the dilemma continued. We had no recourse except to move on down the road. We were told there was fuel in Dryden.

Dryden, ON

We found a Superior dealer in town who was the first of many to tell us how rare auto propane was in Ontario. In case you are wondering, all propane is the same. The stuff for your BBQ comes in bottles but the stuff needed to run an automobile is dispensed from a special pump by a specially licensed person, directly into the vehicle tank. The dealer in Dryden told us that he thought there was some in Kakabeka Falls. So we continued.

Upsala, ON

As evening approached we would always begin to watch for a picnic site or some acceptable pull out. Sitting on the edge of a highway would not be a safe place to be. Just as we came to Upsala we found a campsite by a river. We backed in and had a great spot where we sensed real peace. We had been singing songs like "Praise the name of Jesus" as we rode down the highway and so we sang again at this site and experienced a peaceful night's sleep. After breakfast, we headed for Kakabeka Falls. The gauge on the one functioning tank was reading below zero when we arrived, only to find that there was none in the town. Thunder Bay is nearby but after some missed turns, Art was fairly sure that we could not make it. When we finally did get there and found what was likely the only station with auto propane, the tank took a little over 144 litres. Up until now, we believed that the tanks only held 120. We were told that the next place would be Nipigon but after that, no one knew. We noticed after a fill that Lazarus hummed down the highway as if having no cares in the world. However, unlike the flat prairies, the steep hills of Ontario consumed about twice the fuel per kilometer. We reached the red rock area at the top of Lake Superior and viewed this majestic lake with its ocean like waves and stunning views.

Nipigon, ON

Never order food in a truck stop! The portions were so huge we both had to walk away from our plates. We really went there for the WIFI and searched for ages all the websites of possible propane stops along the route. We even phoned ahead and received promises of propane which ended up being a big disappointment. No propane was pumped on Sundays. Serves us right, we should have been in church. Propane leaks continued. We concluded that we were paying over fifty cents per kilometre.

In our discouragement we approached dusk again, when we suddenly came upon a camp ground at Rossport.

Rossport, ON

Rossport is on the shore, or coast as they call it of Lake Superior. We parked Lazarus right near the shore. The beach was long and in summer would have looked like a tropical beach in Florida. The rocks on the beach were pink giving the whole beach a pink glow. We found we had no cell service in this area. We couldn't tell our kids or anyone where we were but we found comfort again that we were in the 'shelter of the Almighty'. We wore toques to bed and hid beneath two quilts and a duvet. In the morning the cabin was 5.5 degrees and our breath vaporized before us. We had Art's amazing porridge and green tea, took pictures of this gorgeous place and comforted by the website we had seen, we sang some more on our way to Marathon where propane should be available.

Marathon, ON

The Canadian Tire at Marathon had big propane tanks but only pumped into bottles not RV tanks. We had passed Terrace bay where they had propane but they refused to pump on weekends. Marathon had the promise of Superior propane being open if we waited until the next day so we found a parking lot for the night. I bought a fat, thicker, silly looking toque since our furnace was not working now that we no longer had places to hook up. We had experienced that day, the heaviest rain in our whole trip. We had an enormous number of days with dry roads and sunshine, so rain was not really something we should complain about.

As we sat in that parking lot, Art felt we should go back to the Canadian tire parking lot where we parked under a street lamp. However the light went out and we were plunged into darkness.

There was a club across the street with raucous clientele and we began to feel uneasy. Well what could we do but go to bed and commit our unlocked door to the Lord one more time. As we checked our bed we found that the roof had leaked and our pillows, sheets and duvet were sopping wet from the rain.

Art said, "We are going to a motel." and so we went to the Zero Motel; had hot baths and a continental breakfast following a good night's sleep. No one at the motel asked why we brought along a 31 ft. motor home.

In the morning we headed over to an out of the way, gravel road in the direction of the Superior propane yard. Just as Art turned onto the road, Lazarus coughed and the engine died. Art immediately lost the power steering and power brakes. We ended up in the oncoming lane. He had to manually force the motor home into the correct lane. We prayed, the engine started again and we rode to the yard only to find there was no auto propane there. Art showed them the website and told them he had phoned ahead but nothing mattered since there was no way to pump auto propane. We could find no help from anyone and simply had to leave the yard and proceed down the road. For awhile Lazarus just hummed along like nothing had happened. We were told to go to the White Lake Lodge about 50 km down the road. We sang as we went down the highway again using praise as a weapon against despair and because God is always worthy of our praise.

We were overjoyed to see propane tanks in the White Lake Lodge parking lot but wondered why they were wrapped in a green tarpaulin. The lady in the hunting lodge said her gas handler had gone for the season. The lodge looked barren except for a stuffed owl, a fox and a racoon. She had propane but no one certified to pump it for us. She was waiting for the last of the hunters to return so she could close the doors for the winter. She believed the next propane was over 300 km away in Sault Ste. Marie.

What could we do except drive down the road on whatever was left in the tanks? We drove on past White River where the little bear named Winnie the Poo was found. This area had no cell phone service and no propane. We were at the bottom of our physical resources. To go very far would be impossible but God loves the impossible and we needed a miracle.

Depew River, ON

It was now about 10:00am when Lazarus began to act strangely. The engine slowed to about 30 km and chugged slowly along. We were facing a long hill when Art said that he didn't think we would make it. Suddenly a picnic site came into view and we drove off the road and down into the area below the highway.

The area had no cell phone coverage, so we flagged down a car and a man named Sean took our CAA number and information back to the police in White Lake. A cruiser came by telling us someone would come in about an hour. A tow truck operator came by in his pickup to assess the situation. He grumbled something about his heavy tow truck being gone and left. After some time a couple stopped to use the facilities on the picnic site and they took our concerns to the police in Wawa. Then we waited and waited. We walked along the bank of the river and Art dug up a Charlie Brown Christmas tree for me (the conifer which turns yellow in the fall.) It was only a tiny sapling. Again the police arrived to say that everything was in order and we should be hearing from the tow truck guy right away. He never returned.

By 7:30 it was totally dark so finally we went to bed with all of our layers on. It was damp and getting very cold. Under the duvet was the place to be. We slept for about an hour when a giant truck from the CAA arrived. It had lights and strobes and more lights. It was not from the company in White River, who we had originally seen but from Sault Ste Marie. About an hour later the driver had Lazarus hooked up. The man had a horrible job, lying in the mud under the bus disconnecting the drive shaft and putting the front tires into heavy steel braces.

We couldn't really help him. He clearly knew exactly what he was doing. We both stood back though and had a long look at Lazarus. At that point we were ready to let go of Lazarus. Any attraction had vanished and Lazarus was likely going to be orphaned but where do you begin to get rid of a very big, old motor home? Maybe there was a big cliff in Sault Ste. Marie? We pulled out after 9 PM, 10 ½ hours after we had pulled in.

Climbing into the cab of the big truck and hurtling down the highway into the darkness was really quite exhilarating. I felt as if we had left a great weight behind but of course Lazarus was still with us. Maybe the chains would break? I couldn't wait to get home and tell my grandkids about the tow truck. We drove for about four hours and about 2 AM the driver dropped us in the parking lot of a propane depot. We climbed back under the duvet until it opened at 8am.

Art decided that this part of the trip was the most economical. God had prompted Art, before the trip to buy the CAA RV premium package which provides for a free tow of 320km. Our overnight excursion was 320km long.

Sault Ste.Marie, ON

By now our sons-in-law were preparing to launch rescue missions but next morning we met a jovial store owner at the depot who pumped about $200.00 into our tank and gave us the name of the 'best mechanic in the Sault'. Indeed this man turned out to be an angel. We had to wait for most of the day for the work to be accomplished. Lui Cundari who is 6'9" is the tallest man I have ever known. He also has a huge heart. He is the father of a caring friend, Becky Stanley, who heard about our plight. Lui lent us his truck for the best part of the day. He also directed us to Judi and Ernie's cafe where we had the best breakfast ever. This man was such an angel in our time of need.

The waitress at the cafe was one of the best. She seemed to fly around the place taking care of everyone at once. She told us that she had renovated two RVs over the years and just went on and on about all the fun she had with them. One of hers was much older than Lazarus. By the time we left I could see the new curtains again floating in Lazarus' windows. I was mentally choosing the paint for the interior renovation. I floated out of the restaurant. I'm not sure how Art was feeling. I think he just wanted to get back to reality. We spent the rest of the day touring Sault Ste. Marie and then stayed in a mall to keep warm. Sure enough the angelic mechanic was able to connect our two propane tanks and gave us twice the range of traveling distance. We headed for the night to Espanola where we stayed in a Tim Horton's parking lot surrounded by huge trucks where other drivers were catching some sleep. There was fuel at Espanola. From Espanola we headed homeward through a magnificent tour of fall colours. The landscape was brilliant with the Lord's paintings. We came to our home with thankfulness, weariness and blessing and Lazarus is sitting in our driveway... Neither Tom nor Art nor I ever anticipated this unusual journey. Through it all we were never abandoned by the Lord. Praising Him, trusting Him, we were led along. He is our refuge. Thank you friends for your faithful prayers. The ending of this story could have been very different.

In keeping with the Biblical story of Lazarus, the old grave clothes had to be taken from him when he was raised from the dead. We are moth balling Lazarus for the winter, filling his tanks with antifreeze, draining water lines etc. and in the Spring, we are looking forward to getting him out of his grave clothes....perhaps he will live again for a little while longer.

Willie Mitchell

APPENDIX

LOOSE ROOTS:

<u>Grandfather</u>, John Cameron Mitchell

<u>Grandmother</u>, Florance Catherine Lewis
(originally Loos)

<u>Father</u>, Thomas Charles Mitchell "Charlie"

<u>Father's birth order:</u> Myrtle (Sandell, Majors) Florance (Tolmie), Phyllis (Sims), Charlie, George, John "Jack", Arthur, Katherine (Bailey).

<u>Mother</u>, born Doris Audrey McGuire—
Edna May Homeniuk; Thompson; Colisneck; Mitchell; Kolinski; Mitchell

First Born: Arthur Peter Mitchell, July 2, 1942. First lived in upstairs apartment at Pape Ave. and Queen St., Toronto. Moved to 6 Blong Ave. as a baby.

<u>Brother</u>: Thomas Charles Mitchell, October 20 1943.

<u>Sister</u>: Florance Mary Edna (Marshall) September 28, 1946.

PLACES WHERE I HAVE LIVED:
Toronto - Blong Ave 1942 -1949.
  kindergarten, grade 1x2   [2]

Rouge Hill - Woodview Rd (2 houses)
1949-1952. grades 2&3 [2]
Hagersville - SS No.19 Wallpole School,
 1952-1953. grade 4 [1]
Toronto Aunt Phyllis for a few months, polio. [1]
Rouge Hill, Woodview Rd (3rd house) 1953.
 grade 5 [1]
Cherrywood, 1954 grade 6 [1]
Fairport Beach, Dunbarton Pub. School
1954-1956 grade 7&8 [2]
Fairport Beach, Ajax HS 1957-1960
 grade 9x2 & 10x1.5 [1]
Navy 1960-63 N.S. B.C. N.S. [3]
NBTC 1963-67. Burnaby (1), Ft. McMurray
 (x2), Ft. Chipewyan, Fairport Beach, [2]
Vancouver City College 1967-68 [2]
Langley 1970-71 [1]
Surrey 1971-72 [1]
AIM 1972-80 Toronto, NY, deputation,
 [2] Langley (the Fosters-Hope born) [1]
Switzerland March 1973- July74 [1]
Zaire 1974-1976 [2]
Powell River, Ramona, Ca. Campbell River [x2], L.A. x2, Ft Langley, 1976-1980 =[7]
Zaire, Kinshasa, Nyankunde, Bukavu [x2], Kinshasa, Bukavu [x2] 1980-88 =[8]
Tanzania 1988-90 [2]
Esperanza 1990-92 [1]
Guelph MAF-Flypass March 1992-2002 [1]
Breslau, Flypass, March 2002-2004 [1]
Kitchener MAF March 2004-2008 [1]
Keswick MHBC-MAF March 2008-2013 [1]
Sutton-By-The-Lake September, 2013—

[1] = NUMBER OF ADDRESSES AT THAT LOCATION, WHERE I LIVED.

ABOUT THE AUTHOR

Art Mitchell was born in Toronto on July 2, 1942. He has lived more 'lives' in his 70 plus years than most have in twice the time. God called him to ministry fresh out of the navy and his passion has always been to reach the lost. As a Bible school teacher for Africa Inland Mission, then a pilot for The Shantymen and Mission Aviation Fellowship, he did just that up until he returned to Canada in 1990. There he continued to minister to others through counseling missionaries back from the mission field or those being sent out. While owner of Flypass, he also developed the first prototype experimental aircraft (the CH 801) to be used in the Amazon. Many Christians and non-Christians have been touched by God as a result of Art's obedience in following the great commission in his community. Father of three, grandfather of four, husband of one, Art embodies Christ to the world around him. His story is one of struggles, redemption and above all, gives glory to God.

Made in the USA
Charleston, SC
27 November 2016